D0998727

Hibernia

Literature and Nation in
Victorian Ireland

A series of facsimile reprints chosen and introduced by
JOHN KELLY

Thomas Davis

———

Literary and Historical Essays
1846

Woodstock Books
Poole · Washington D.C.
1998

This edition first published 1998 by
Woodstock Books
c/o Cassell plc, 3 Fleets Lane
Poole, England BH15 3AJ
and
Cassell Academic
PO Box 605, Herndon
VA. 20172
U.S.A.

ISBN 1 85477 222 8
Reproduced by permission from a copy in the
London Library, St James's Square, London SW1
New matter copyright © John Kelly 1998
Type size has been enlarged by ten per cent.

British Library Cataloguing-in-Publication Data
A catalogue record for this book is
available from the British Library

Library of Congress Cataloging-in-Publication Data
Davis, Thomas Osborne, 1814-1845.
    Literary and historical essays / Thomas Davis.
        p. cm. – (Hibernia)
    ISBN 1-85477-222-8 (hardback : alk. paper)
    1. Ireland – Civilization.   I. Title   II. Series.
PR4525.D58E8   1998
824'.8—DC21

97-6475
CIP

Printed and bound in Great Britain by
Smith Settle
Otley, West Yorkshire LS21 3JP

Introduction

It is almost impossible to exaggerate the importance of
Thomas Osborne Davis and the Young Irelanders to
Irish politics and culture in the latter half of the
nineteenth century. Writing in 1877 the historian and
politician A. M. Sullivan credited the Movement with
bringing about the enormous 'changes in Irish political
life – in its modes of thought and action – within the
past forty years'. John O'Leary, the Fenian and early
mentor of Yeats, discloses in his memoirs that Davis
was 'the fountain and the origin' for 'all that is Irish in
me, and above all, for the inspiration that made me
Irish', and men as different in outlook as T. W.
Rolleston, Arthur Griffith and Patrick Pearse were
united in their admiration for him. Yeats, too, was at
first an enthusiast, and although he later came to think
the influence of Young Ireland on Irish literature
pernicious, he freely acknowledged that Davis's
magnanimity and honesty had stimulated 'generations
of our young men [to] turn over the pages of an old
newspaper as though it were some classic of literature'.
And when in 1892, in the shock after the fall and death
of Parnell, the Dublin weekly *United Ireland* began to set
about creating an Irish cultural revival and a racy
public opinion, it opened its campaign by publishing a
biography of Davis and reprinting passages from his
work, explaining in a preamble why it was doing so:
'for three generations now, this brave young Irishman
who was true to himself and to Ireland, has remained
an inspiration, a model, and a guide for his young
countrymen. He sowed the seed, and it grew and bore
fruit a hundredfold.' A couple of years later William
O'Brien, one of the most active Irish politicians of the
period, drew attention in his *Irish Ideas* to 'that peculiar

glow and charm which have enabled Thomas Davis to acquire an empire over the Irish youth of the present generation even more powerful than over his own', and to a large extent Davis's untimely death in 1845 does mark the beginning of his reputation. In his lifetime he published only one short and anonymous pamphlet, and his articles and poems, mostly unsigned or pseudonymous, remained uncollected. It was with the appearance of the present volume of essays in 1846 that the cultural empire of which O'Brien speaks began to establish itself – but, as a brief account of the man and his ideas reveals, his ascendancy over future generations rested on more substantial qualities than mere 'glow and charm'.

Three men, Thomas Davis, Charles Gavan Duffy and John Blake Dillon, began the Young Ireland Movement when they agreed in 1842 to found a weekly nationalist newspaper. This journal, the *Nation*, became the rallying point for a group of gifted and educated young writers who associated themselves with O'Connell's Repeal Movement, but who prized the literary and cultural roots of Irish nationalism above its institutional manifestations. They also believed that a nationalist movement should be as inclusive as possible, especially in so divided an island as Ireland, and their own collaboration embodied just such an ecumenical aspiration: Davis was the son of an English Protestant from Munster, Duffy, an upwardly mobile northern Catholic journalist, and Dillon was a Connaught Catholic whose father had been dispossessed for supporting the 1798 Rebellion. They were soon joined by others – John Pigot, John O'Hagan, Denis Florence MacCarthy, Thomas MacNevin, Michael Barry, and Denny Lane – mostly educated at Trinity College, Dublin, and nearly all of them (even Duffy, who had not attended a university) barristers. They represented a new, middle-class professional generation, an intelligentsia, drawn from both the Catholic and Protestant traditions, who were open to the influences of new ideas on nationality. The name 'Young Ireland' was first used in scorn by an English journalist who suspected the group of trying to imitate Mazzini's 'Young Italy', but was subsequently accepted as a term of honour by MacNevin, although the others remained ambivalent about it. In fact, the adjective 'young' was appropriate, not only because they were all under thirty when they started the *Nation*, but also in that it distinguished them from the 'old Ireland' of Daniel O'Connell – for, although they recognized him as national leader, their agenda did not precisely coincide with his, and they prized independence of thought too much to defer to his sometimes autocratic manner.

At this time O'Connell's political fortunes were at a turning point. His triumph in bringing about Catholic Emancipation in 1829 had not been matched by his subsequent performance as leader of the Irish party at Westminster, where his alliance with the Whigs had failed to produce the results he had hoped for. After the victory of the Tories in the general election of 1841, and the concomitant breakdown of his understanding with the Whigs, he had turned from London to Ireland, realising that in the circumstances 'Repeal and Repeal alone is and must be the grand basis of all future operations'. He had already set up a Repeal Association in Dublin in April 1840, and almost exactly a year later Davis and Dillon enrolled in the organization. It was a courageous act for Davis, whose staunchly Unionist friends and relations looked upon O'Connell as a dangerous demagogue. Duffy, with characteristic hyperbole, later claimed that in becoming a Repealer

Davis had 'separated in action from his family and from many of his familiar friends, and had relinquished the chances of success in his profession. He employed his splendid abilities in the public cause without reward and almost without recognition'. O'Connell, however, recognized him: delighted to have attracted an intellectual young Protestant to an Association which was in danger of being too uniformly identified as a Catholic cause, he made a florid speech of welcome, and immediately placed him on the general committee. Dillon was registered with rather less fuss.

In fact Davis was willingly recognised as paramount by his fellows, although he never insisted upon his pre-eminence. Born in Mallow, Cork, in 1814, he was the son of a surgeon in the British Army, who came from Essex and who had been posted to Ireland after serving in the Peninsula War. Here he married a local Protestant woman, Mary Atkins, who bore him four children, the last, Thomas, born a month after his father's death. The widowed mother remained in Mallow until 1818, when the family moved to Dublin, where Thomas was sent to one of the best Protestant schools. He seems to have had an unremarkable upbringing (one of his relatives described him as 'a dull child') and even after entering Trinity College at the age of sixteen he was regarded by his more lively contemporaries as a colourless swot. The credit for transforming him into an enthusiastic nationalist was subsequently claimed by Thomas Clarke Wallis, an impoverished tutor, who styled himself 'Professor of Things in General and Patriotism in Particular', and who boasted that he had 'loosed the tenacious phlegm that clogged Davis's nature and hid his powers from himself and the world'. Hitherto Davis had been a Benthamite liberal, under which influence he published an anonymous pamphlet urging the reform of the House of Lords, but after his conversion to nationalism he vehemently opposed the 'mechanical' and 'English' systems advocated by Utilitarianism. After leaving university in 1835 he read for the Irish Bar and was called in 1838. As well as studying law during this period, he may also have travelled on the Continent; certainly he came into contact with the Romantic nationalism then flourishing in Europe, and he was particularly impressed with the lessons, both ideological and practical, that contemporary Germany held out for Ireland.

Davis's abrupt rejection of Utilitarianism – apparently an almost Pauline conversion – can be matched by other examples at this period (the critic Malcolm Brown astutely compares it with that of John Stuart Mill's). It was part of a more widespread anxiety about modernity, and particularly about its thrust to value reason over feeling, the general over the particular, and the mechanical over the organic. In this Davis fits into a familiar pattern of cultural nationalism that had first been articulated by the German philosophers, particularly Kant and Herder. How far Davis knew their work at first hand is difficult to ascertain, but he read widely, and his thought is an amalgam of confluent influences. His views on the importance of history and culture to the national consciousness derive from Herder and Fichte; his conviction that 'a nation is a spiritual essence' follows Edmund Burke; and his belief in the importance of great men in shaping national identity he owes to Thomas Carlyle. Many of his anti-Utilitarian arguments also come from Carlyle, as well as from the Swiss historian and economist, Jean de Sismondi – particularly from his *Nouveaux Principes de l'Economie*

Politique (1819). His Romantic historiography Davis imbibed from the French historians Jules Michelet and Augustin Thierry, and his insistence on the necessity of independent thought and self-help in education from the German thinkers Lessing and Fichte.

Although disparate, these sources provided him with a coherent core of ideas, and the essays in the present collection are informed by a consistent system of thought. This consistency is tacitly divulged by Gavan Duffy's arrangement of the pieces he chose to include. The book opens and closes with four essays on education, the first two treating self-improvement, the final two on institutionalised instruction and the importance of trained minds to the modern nation. If these framing essays deal with methods of education, the articles within are clustered not chronologically but sequentially around the six topics – history, economics, art, language, sociology, and literature – that Davis thought should constitute the substance of the national curriculum. And each topic and every essay is inspired and informed by his theory of nationalism.

Following his mentors, Davis regarded the nation as a natural, organic community, the product of a unique tradition, culture and geography, whose legitimacy was not based merely on rights but, more importantly, on passions inculcated by nature and history. Since the nation can only be articulated as an organic whole, he came to believe that its most important representatives and interpreters were not politicians and constitutional lawyers but historians and artists. The assertion of German cultural and linguistic individuality had been in large part a reaction against the dominance of French civilization and the universalist Enlightenment values it assumed. For Davis and the Young Irelanders the reaction was not against France and the Enlightenment but against England and Utilitarianism, which, he warned his friend Maddyn, was more insidious and dangerous than Papal supremacy:

Modern Anglicism, i.e. Utilitarianism … this thing, call it Yankeeism or Englishism, which measures prosperity by exchangeable value, measures duty by gain and limits desire to clothes, food, and respectability; this damned thing has come into Ireland under the Whigs, and is equally the favourite of the *Peel* Tories. … To use every literary and political engine against this seems to me the first duty of an Irish patriot who can foresee consequences.

Only through self-determination could the Irish genius, expressing itself in an Irish culture, develop along its natural lines, for the British connection was likely to stifle it in an alien and uncongenial philosophy.

Davis conceived of his six major topics as performing multiple tasks in the national struggle. Irish literature, history, art and language expressed and defined the national soul; by their very existence they proved the people's claim to separate nationality both to themselves and to foreigners, and they acted as bulwarks against un-Irish modes of thought, especially against Anglicization and cosmopolitanism. Romantic nationalism appeals especially to those, like Davis, who feel a need to recover a sense of community in the face of an external and universalizing industrial culture, and who seek a return to the cohesive world of the 'Folk' through cultural and linguistic refabrication. These feelings are often intensified in those who (like Davis, Pearse, and de Valera) are of mixed nationality, and who are obliged to choose their homeland consciously. Nevertheless, as his views on economics and sociology indicate, it would be an error to regard Davis's position as one of dreamy nostalgia for a factitious golden age.

Certainly the brutal aspects of modernity and industrialization appalled him, and in an early article, written before the founding of the *Nation*, he had proposed that Ireland should adopt 'udalism', the land-tenure system of Norway, and so establish a society based upon a sturdy yeomanry rather than on 'the poor, broken-bodied, brokenhearted denizens of a manufacturing town'. This ideal lingered: it is just such a 'yeomanry' that he extols in his idealising essay on 'Memorials of Wexford', while in his optimistic article on 'The Resources of Ireland' he laments the replacement of cottage industries, with their 'home-bred, and home-taught, and home-faithful' workers, by factories 'full of creatures who live amid the eternal roll, and clash, and glimmer of spindles and rollers': 'We abhor that state; we prefer the life of the old times, or of modern Norway'.

But by the time he came to write this essay, in June 1844, he realised that such a preference could not be sustained, and after a half-hearted suggestion that the Prussian Tenure Code might turn the people into viable small proprietors, concedes that Ireland will probably have to industrialize. This was an ideological dilemma he never successfully solved: caught between a Jeffersonian belief in a society of yeomen and small-town merchants, and yet eager that Ireland should stand on some sort of parity with England's accelerating commercial might, Davis's economics oscillate uneasily between a desire for rural self-sufficiency and wildly optimistic estimations of Ireland's industrial potentiality. In 'A Commercial History of Ireland' he proposes that an 'absentee tax and a resident government, and the progress of public industry and education, would enable an Irish Parliament to create vast manufactures here by protecting duties in the first instance', although the precise mechanisms by which these 'vast manufactures' are to come into being are left tantalizingly vague. A little later (in an article Duffy did not reprint), intoxicated by Sir Robert Kane's over-sanguine account of Irish mineral resources, he proclaims that 'Arigna must be pierced with shafts and Bonmahon flaming with smelting houses. … Our coal must move a thousand engines, our rivers ten thousand wheels'. As modern economists have shown, such splendidly round figures were unattainable, and even a more modest industrialization could have been bought only at the cost of underpaying Irish workmen (a price Davis was happy to entertain), and stiff protectionist tariffs that would almost certainly have crippled other parts of the Irish economy.

If Davis's enthusiasm led him to underestimate the problems faced by the Irish economy, his approach to Irish social and sectarian divisions, while no less ardent, were more focused. The German thinkers had appealed to a shared racial and religious identity, as well as to culture and language as defining a national community, but in the Irish situation race and religion were problematic categories, since they were agents of division not, as elsewhere, homogeneity. As a Protestant and of settler stock, Davis was acutely aware of this, and so history rather than creed and ethnicity heads his nationalist agenda. Indeed, his version of Irish history stresses the plurality of Irish origins, and, partly influenced by the ideas of Thierry, insists that it is a shared culture and geography that has fused different invaders into a single nation. Invaded by Danes and Normans, and conquered by the English, Ireland was, Davis insisted, racially and religiously mixed; even the Milesians, as he artfully pointed out, were themselves interlopers, who had overrun the indigenous, pre-Celtic aborigines, and in his article on the contribution of the men of Wexford to the '98 rebellion he went out of his way to recall that 'their blood is for the most part English and Welsh, though mixed with the Danish and Gaelic, yet they are Irish in thought and feeling'. He also warned that the 'greatest vice' in a projected History of Ireland would be 'bigotry of race or creed', and many of the ballads published in the *Nation* echoed his ecumenicalism.

The German nationalists had discredited the notion of a 'universal' history, which argued that all histories conform to a general paradigm, and that any deviations from this blueprint should be disregarded as aberrant. Herder, in particular, insisted on the contrary position: that God had made all nations different and each individual national history therefore had its own validity. Davis similarly saw history as crucial to national identity, and even his writings on art and literature have a pronounced historical leaning – the subjects he recommends to Irish painters are signal incidents from the Irish past, he values ballads chiefly for their power to intensify the historical imagination, and he acclaims William Carleton as the historian of the Irish peasantry, as well as a novelist *per se*. In 1844 he even contemplated giving up the *Nation* to devote himself to writing a History of Ireland. Such a work would evidently have modelled itself on the style of Augustin Thierry, who emphasized the importance of local colour and creating the 'atmosphere of the period', and whom Davis praises for his imaginative passion: 'there is more deep dramatic skill, more picturesque and coloured scenery, more distinct and characteristic grouping, and more lively faith to the look and spirit of men and times and feelings of which he writes … than in any other historian that ever lived.'

It is this kind of imaginative and empathetic historiography that he urged from the beginning of his public career. History does not merely record facts but studies these facts 'as manifestations of human nature on great occasions'. Thus history teaches both head and heart by providing 'example that gives impulse and vitality to principles', and in this respect is more valuable than the abstractions of philosophy. Indeed, 'without knowing the history of a time', Davis claims, 'we cannot accurately comprehend its philosophy'. In other words, there is no universal philosophy which can transcend the historical process: history's central value is to provide a series of tableaux, which, imaginatively rendered and apprehended, sustain and strengthen national self-awareness: 'History well read is a series of pictures of great men and great scenes and great acts. It impresses the principles and despair, the hopes and powers of the Titans of our race.' For Davis, then, history is not an account of institutions or constitutions: it is, and here his reading of Carlyle is evident, a drama of personalities, of national heroes, whose deeds become exemplary to later generations: 'to set up in our souls the memory of great men, who shall then be as models and judges of our actions – these are the highest duties of history'.

Solid historical research, especially into periods of pre-history, is also important, not in this case because it dramatizes national heroes, but because it preserves and enlarges the memory of the *'Volk'*, the People, who have no written memorials and in whom ancient chroniclers took little interest. For while great men may articulate the People they are incapable of creating a civilization, which, being popular and spontaneous, can only be resuscitated from its communal foundations. Such an excavation is made possible through what were in the 1840s newly emerging disciplines such as archaeology, folklore, and philology, studies which Davis championed as protecting Irish traditions from a modernism intent on erasing them. Thus he insists that the Archaeological Society should be supported by all those 'who do not wish to lose the heritage of centuries, nor to feel ourselves living among nameless ruins, when we might have an ancestral home'. The Society's work, that of John O'Donovan, George Petrie, and even the amateur antiquarians of the eighteenth century have done great good by giving 'a pedigree to nationhood and created a faith that Ireland could and should be great again by magnifying what she had been'. And, as Davis points out in 'Irish Antiquities', pre-history is even more important to Ireland since her recorded history is almost entirely a record of colonization and defeat.

Literature, like history, is crucial to Davis's concept of nationalism since it is one of the most vibrant and affecting expressions of individuality. It is through poetry, in particular, that the essential sprit of the nation is known, for it 'is the very flowering of the soul – the greatest evidence of its health the greatest excellence of its beauty'. Just as in Davis's Romantic conception history should present exalted and heroic examples of patriotic conduct, so national literature 'shows us magnified and ennobles our hearts, our intellects, our country and our countrymen – binds us to the land by its condensed and gem-like history, to the future by examples and by aspirations'. In achieving this, in acting as 'the recognised envoy of our minds among all mankind and to all time', literature is a far more potent force than any mere political agitation, and, in the final analysis more potent even than history: 'Great as Herodotus and Thierry are, Homer and

Béranger **are greater**. The ideal has resources beyond the actual. It is infinite, and Art is indefinitely powerful.'

'Ballad Poetry of Ireland', an essay written a few weeks before his death, is one of Davis's most powerful defences of the superiority of cultural over political nationalism. Here he observes that the Irish have been a long time in coming to understand true Nationality. He dismisses the Celticists' dream of restoring a pre-Invasion Gaelic state as a nostalgic and racially divisive fantasy; the Anglo-Irish of the eighteenth century 'mistook Ireland for a colony wronged', and the ideal of an Irish Parliament in College Green which they introduced (and for which, essentially, O'Connell's movement was agitating) he repudiates as a 'lower form of nationhood', since it did not take into account 'the moral elements and tendencies of the country'. By allowing themselves to become 'narrow bigots to the omnipotency of an institution' such parliamentarians were indistinguishable from 'any Cockney Radical'. But cultural and literary nationalism is of a far healthier and far broader kind, and anyone working for Irish literature and art has in fact fostered Irish independence, even those who, paradoxically, regarded independence as a dangerous dream. Cultural nationalism has at last enabled the Irish 'to see what we are, and what is our destiny', and this destiny is ecumenical, pluralist, and yet communitarian, for it 'must contain and represent the races of Ireland. It must not be Celtic, it must not be Saxon – it must be Irish. ... a literature which shall exhibit in combination the passions and idioms of all, and which shall equally express our mind in its romantic, its religious, its forensic, and its practical tendencies'.

Davis's ideas on Irish art are at one with his views of history and literature; in fact, he regards a national art as directly analogous to a national literature and a national history, since to create 'great pictures, statues, and buildings, is of the same sort of ennoblement to a people as to create great poems or histories'. Like literature and history, high art is art 'used to instruct and ennoble men; to teach them great deeds, whether historical, religious, or romantic', and a national art 'is essential to our civilization and renown' since 'a school of eminent Irish artists' would 'illustrate their country's history and character' and so enhance both their fame and that of their country.

In one respect Davis's cultural nationalism went further than that of his contemporaries and this was in his efforts to re-establish Irish as the spoken national tongue. At the time he was writing the National Schools, the Gaelic-speaking parents, the Catholic clergy, and Daniel O'Connell were all doing their best to eradicate the language, and even his own friends, Duffy and MacNevin, found his concern for Gaelic amusingly wrong-headed. O'Connell, although (unlike Davis) a fluent Irish-speaker, had argued that the language should be allowed to die on materialistic grounds: it was a barrier to trade and education. Davis maintained that it should be kept precisely because it was a barrier – not necessarily to trade and education but certainly to external and especially Anglicising influences which might undermine national integrity. He asserted that a 'nation should guard its language more than its territories – 'tis a surer barrier, and more important frontier, than fortress or river.'

But the importance of the language is not merely negative and defensive; far more valuably, the language knits together the national soul and gives it vitality. Davis pointed to the example of Germany whose genius 'sprung up fresh and triumphant' as soon as she had halted the progress of French. Above all, he argued, the Irish should speak Irish because it expressed the Irish mind and imagination in a unique way: 'The language which grows up with a people is conformed to their organs, descriptive of their climate, constitution, and manners, mingled inseparably with their history and their soil, fitted beyond any other language to express their prevalent thoughts in the most natural and efficient way.'

As always Davis refused to leave his discussion at a theoretical level. In a later article he put forward detailed plans for popularising Irish, suggesting a bilingual paper, the introduction of scientific terms into the vocabulary, and raising the status of the language by encouraging its use among the upper classes. The hope that English speakers would become fluent in the language through exposure to a few newspaper articles in Irish was hopelessly optimistic, and within a few years the Famine was to reduce the number of Gaelic speakers in Ireland beneath anything he could imagine, but, as in so many other cases, his ideas were taken up again at the end of the century by the Gaelic League. Indeed, Griffith's *United Irishman* was to claim in 1900 that 'if there is a field for the Gaelic League or the slightest hope for the future of the country, to the Young Irelanders and their teachings we owe it all'.

In his espousal of cultural nationalism, Davis insisted upon the pre-eminence of imagination and feeling but these were always to be put at the service of education. In this he was as Utilitarian as any Benthamite. There is hardly one of his essays in which he does not match theory with detailed suggestions as to how his ideas might be put into practice, whether it be writing national poems, painting national pictures, or writing national history. He, Duffy, and Dillon acknowledged their educational mission from the beginning; during their very first discussion about setting up the *Nation* they soon found, as Duffy recalled, 'that our purpose was the same – to raise up Ireland morally, socially, and politically, and put the sceptre of self-government into her hands'. Their goal was national independence for Ireland through repeal if possible or force if necessary, but they realised, as Old Ireland could not, that education was in the process of opening up new possibilities for Irish nationalism. They saw it as their mission to encourage this educational process not merely as it touched upon politics but in all its aspects. As Davis exhorted William Smith O'Brien, who was later to lead the Young Irelanders: 'We must do more to educate this people. This is the only moral force in which I have any faith. Mere agitation is either bullying or preparation for war. I condemn the former, the others of the party condemn the latter. But we all agree in the policy of education …'. The objects of this policy were two-fold. First and foremost the People had to be taught self-reliance and self-respect, but it was also important to appeal to the upper and middle classes to take up patriotic duties. Davis grounded his appeal to both constituencies upon the urgent need to liberate their intellects from prejudice and ignorance by thinking for themselves. This insistence upon self-education and self-sufficiency, leading to an increased self-awareness and self-confidence, is the central theme of the essays in this collection.

It was certainly the theme of Davis's first public exposition of his nationalist views, the Address to 'The Young Irishmen of the Middle Classes', which antedated the *Nation* by two years. This lecture, given to the Historical Society, the influential – but overwhelmingly Protestant and Unionist – Trinity College debating club, took as its text Lessing's maxim, 'Think wrongly if you will, but think for yourself', and Davis assured his audience that he cared 'little for the fate of any opinions, but much for the fate of free discussions'. In an Ireland riven by sectarianism and political animus, this was not only bold and refreshing advice, but also advice based on a shrewd appreciation of the shifting power-structures in Irish life. The Address was directed to a privileged élite who attended an institution whose Fellowships were still barred to Catholics, and from whose doors many Catholic undergraduates were deterred by its Ascendancy ethos and high fees. But the Ascendancy hegemony was weakening, and the purpose of Davis's Address was to persuade the young men of the privileged class to rethink their patriotic responsibilities by alerting them to the fact that their time for such rethinking was running out. He warned them that the proposed provincial colleges would soon put higher education within the reach of the Catholic middle class, further consolidating its position after Emancipation, while the National Schools, 'the first bold attempt to regenerate Ireland are working, aye, and with all their faults, working well'. These schools, he prophesied, would initiate a social revolution by raising literacy and national consciousness among the lower orders to a point where they would no longer tolerate the neglect of an anti-national ruling class. He entreated his listeners to educate themselves in patriotism by augmenting the unimaginative and inflexible syllabuses at Trinity College with the study of modern literature and Irish history, and, that done, to go out and educate the country: 'Education, the apostle of progress hath gone forth. ... Seek to make your country forward in her progress to that goal, where she, in common with the other nations may hear that annunciation of virtue, and share that advent of happiness, holiness, and peace.'

The Young Irelanders' attitude to the Irish upper classes was ambivalent; they hoped for the best but feared the worst. Both they and O'Connell saw that their major contribution to the cause might lie in their capacity to attract young professionals to Repeal, and in rendering Repeal less repugnant to the Ascendancy in general. The addition of the distinguished Protestant landowner and politician William Smith O'Brien to the Repeal Association in October 1843 strengthened these hopes, and early in 1845 Davis was instrumental in founding the Eighty-Two Club, which, taking its name from the date of Grattan's declaration of independence for the Protestant Irish parliament in 1782, was intended to be a sort of officer cadre within the Repeal Association. But despite a snappy semi-military uniform (designed by Davis) it was hardly the success in attracting intelligent upper-class recruits that might have been hoped, and Davis's essays indicate his ambivalent attitude to the Protestant Ascendancy. In 'Ireland's People' he attacks the Irish aristocracy and gentry, but the real purpose of the article is to shame them into playing a larger part in patriotic endeavours. He uses a similar tactic in 'The State of the Irish Peasantry', where an appeal to pity and love is given a darker edge by references to possible land wars; and many other uncollected articles in the *Nation* berated the landlords for their various impositions and derelictions, hinted at popular retribution, and exhorted them to take up their national duties and the cause of Repeal before it was too late.

If the upper classes were uncertain in their allegiances,

there was no doubt about the People, and Davis contrasted 'the strength, the fortitude, the patience, the bravery of those the enrichers of the country, with the meanness in mind and courage of those who are opposed to them'. It was this class that he wanted to reach so that it could be taught to articulate its patriotism, and by 1842 such a mission was more feasible than it had ever been before. With the decline of the Penal Laws towards the end of the eighteenth century indigenous Catholic schools began to appear. The first Christian Brothers School opened in Waterford in 1802, the Jesuits established Clongowes College in 1814, and by 1825 several orders of nuns were training some six thousand girls. The State, too, began to concern itself with the problem of education, in the first instance through the Kildare Place Society which was founded in 1811. This Society promoted a system of undenominational religious teaching, the first time that such a policy had been adopted in Ireland, and from 1815 the government paid it an annual grant, rising from £6,980 to £30,000 in 1831. At first the mixed teaching seemed to work, but in 1820 the Catholic members, led by O'Connell, resigned from the undertaking and a Royal Commission of 1825 reported that the religious compromise had never really succeeded. In 1831, therefore, the government decided to play a direct role in Irish education, and established a Board to run a network of national schools. Although it was intended that the schools should be mixed, this condition aroused such hostility among both Presbyterians and Catholics that the schools were soon organized *de facto* on an exclusive religious basis.

A persistent criticism levelled at the scheme, particularly by the Young Irelanders, was its a-national policy. All specifically Irish books were banned and the children were taught to think of themselves as English. A verse to this effect was hung in every classroom:

> I thank the goodness and the grace
> That on my birth have smiled,
> And made me in these Christian days
> A happy English child.

and the second edition of the schools' reading books omitted a number of poems which might provoke nationalist emotions, including Scott's 'Breathes there a Man with Soul so Dead?'. The Irish language, too, was actively discouraged, but this was with the active support of most parents since Gaelic was considered not only useless but vulgar, even by those who spoke it. The standard of education in the new schools was not high, and as Davis complained in the *Nation* in 1844 the rates of Irish illiteracy were slow to decline. Nevertheless there was for the first-time in Ireland a form of education available to the common people and it was upon this rudimentary system that Davis and the *Nation* built their policies. In particular they set out to compensate for the lack of Irish history and literature in the National Schools through three institutions: the *Nation* newspaper, the Repeal Reading-Rooms, and the Library of Ireland Series – institutions whose influence was long to outlive their founders. So energetically did Davis apply himself to this work of supplementing the efforts of the schools that he could confidently write in 1844 that there were 'three great schoolmasters in Ireland – the National Board, the Press and the Repeal Association.'

The *Nation* was the first institution established by the Young Irelanders, and it was in this weekly newspaper that the following essays first appeared. Davis had contributed articles to the *Citizen*, a small-circulation periodical produced by members of the Historical Society, and when this began to falter he and Dillon attempted to transform the staid *Morning Register* into a more aggressively nationalist paper. This initiative failed but a meeting in 1842 with the more experienced Duffy, who was editor of the Belfast *Vindicator,* resulted in a completely new weekly, which was to be called the *Nation*. Duffy describes the launching of the new paper in enthusiastic but accurate terms:

The first issue of the *Nation* was published on the 15th October, 1842. The prospectus and the list of contributors, had excited unusual interest, and it was eagerly waited for. In shape, size, distribution of materials and typography, it departed from the ordinary practice of Irish journals, which were immethodical and slovenly in that day. And the new form was designed to typify a new spirit. It took a motto which expressed its exact purpose ... 'To create and foster public opinion in Ireland, and make it racy of the soil'.

The new paper was an immediate triumph; the first issue was sold out within a day and copies were soon changing hands for two or three times the published price. And its popularity continued. Duffy estimated its circulation at over 10,000 copies by the end of 1843, well above its nearest rival, and pointed out that this meant it was being read by over a quarter of a million people.

There were a number of reasons for its success. In the first place, although more expensive than most of its rivals, it was good value; the first issue invited subscribers to use their tape-measures to 'convince themselves it is, as we promised it should be, THE LARGEST PAPER EVER PUBLISHED IN IRELAND'. It also contained wide and lively coverage of national and international news, including accounts of duels and bankruptcies, rumours of seductions and abductions, and sports reports and racing intelligence. But the chief reason for its popularity was that it gave a new direction to the nationalistic fervour that O'Connell had roused with his campaign for Repeal but which he soon found impossible to satisfy. From its first number the paper took an aggressively nationalist line. Apart from editorials on English iniquities, its comprehensive accounts of activities in the Repeal Association, and the regular patriotic ballads, it also published various series on Continental literature and politics to emphasize that Ireland was a European nation in its own right and not merely an English dependency. The pedigree of this sovereignty it persistently emphasized in articles on Irish history and literature, which insist upon or assume the cultural and social equality of the Irish with the English.

O'Connell's Repeal campaign came to a climax in 1843 – announced as 'Repeal Year – with a series of 'Monster Meetings' which attracted audiences numbered in hundreds of thousands at carefully selected historic sites. But when in October Peel banned a proposed meeting in the Dublin suburb of Clontarf, O'Connell at once acquiesced and called it off. The government followed up its victory by arresting nine leading Repealers (including O'Connell) for sedition, and the Repeal movement appeared to have lost its way. Although in public they supported O'Connell's submission, the Young Irelanders were devastated by what had happened and Davis even thought of quitting the Association. Instead, they decided to re-emphasize their long-term cultural goals, goals which Duffy was later to describe as 'projects of education and discipline … projects fostering a lofty but not impracticable nationality'. Such a redeployment of nationalist energies was timely, not only educationally but also psychologically. As Duffy recalled, Irish intellectual life was at a low ebb; the 'class who lived by letters was not numerous, but it was in a decisive degree English in spirit and sympathy'. The dynamism of the *Nation* galvanised this lethargic society into new life, and Duffy with a customary rhetorical flourish speaks of 'the amazement, the consternation swelling almost to panic, and the final enthusiasm and intoxication of joy with which the new teaching was received, especially by the young of all classes. Every number of the *Nation* contained new trains of thought, new projects and suggestions, new poems and essays, which thrilled the national mind like electric shocks.'

A high proportion of these 'new projects and suggestions' were the product of Davis's unceasing efforts. In article after article he hammered home his insistence on education; besides the detailed instructions on how to paint national pictures and write national ballads we have already noticed, he also wrote long and sometimes tedious pieces on the valuation and the topography of Ireland, crammed with technical information on different types of maps and their scales, uses and prices. Even Irish holiday-makers on visits to the Continent were instructed to 'study other lands wisely, and to bring back all knowledge for the sustenance and decoration of their dear home'. Driving all these essays, even those most weighed down by detailed facts, was the conviction that knowledge and organisation must set Ireland free and make her prosperous, for Davis believed that 'if the people be not wise and manageable, they cannot gain liberty but by accident, nor use it to their service', and that 'if we are too idle, too dull, or too capricious to learn the arts of strength, wealth, and liberty, let us not murmur at being slaves.' This emphasis on self-reliance and self-confidence was to be taken as a central policy by

Arthur Griffith and Sinn Fein at the turn of the twentieth century.

Benedict Anderson has drawn attention to the importance of newspapers as agents of national consciousness, and the *Nation* was one of the earliest and most effective examples of this process at work. It did much to compensate for the lack of instruction on Irish topics in the National Schools, and Davis proposed that its work would be greatly advanced by setting up Repeal Reading-Rooms throughout the country. The Repeal Association had established a nation-wide organization to collect money and distribute propaganda through local wardens, and the Young Irelanders urged that these local clubs should be increased in number and that they should extend their remit to cover educational well as political matters. As he first conceived them, these Reading Rooms were to cater principally for the generation that was too old to benefit from National Education, but in his appeal for money and organisers he makes more sweeping claims: 'The Repeal Association has now constituted itself Schoolmaster of the People of Ireland, and must be prepared to carry out its pretension. The People, knowing the attempt, must sustain it with increased funds and zeal.' He proposed that every parish should set up a Reading-Room and that each should have its own committee to deal with its special needs. It was hoped, too, to persuade Protestant and Catholic clergymen to act as patrons of the rooms and to appoint inspectors to tour the country, checking that the rooms were being run effectively. O'Connell remained lukewarm about these ideas, but he was prevailed upon to make funds available, and the new institutions flourished, so that by 1845 the *Nation* was selling 1100 copies to Reading Rooms.

But the sale of the paper was not the primary function that Davis envisaged for the Rooms; he also wanted them to become local libraries. One of the most formidable stumbling-blocks in the way of Irish popular education throughout the nineteenth century was purely practical: there were, according to Davis, *'ten counties in Ireland without a single bookseller in them'*, and even where booksellers did exist they were 'generally unfit' to advise their customers on what to read. This situation could be remedied, he advised, through the building up Repeal Reading Rooms. At first a Room would be supplied with Association Reports and newspapers, but if it 'continue and give proof of being in earnest, the Repeal Association will aid it by gifts of books, maps etc., and thus a Library, the centre of knowledge and nursery of useful and strong minds, will be made in that district.'

Once such libraries had been established, there yet remained the question of where to find appropriate Irish books at popular prices to stock them. The solution came about almost by accident. From the beginning, Duffy had been eager to include nationalistic ballads in the *Nation*, and in a short time a sizeable school of balladeers had grown up around the paper. Since, in Duffy's estimation, their work 'was the agent which produced the most signal and immediate results', he decided to issue an anthology of ballads from the paper in book form, under the title *The Spirit of the Nation.* Initially the book was published from the *Nation* office but it proved so popular that other arrangements had to be made and it was subsequently handled by James Duffy, a Dublin publisher. Then in 1845 the Repeal Association offered a prize for an up-to-date and accurate history of Ireland and, since no one writer could be found to undertake it, it was finally decided to split the work up into parts and entrust it to 'as many competent writers as could be procured'. Gavan Duffy then suggested that the project should be augmented and published by James Duffy (who was no relation) as 'a series of shilling volumes of biography, poetry, and criticism to be called the "Library of Ireland," in which the historical design might be carried out.'

The first book to be published in the Library of Ireland was MacNevin's *Irish Volunteers* and thereafter James Duffy issued a fresh volume every month for two years. The influence of these books during the rest of a century of growing literacy was seminal. Looking back in 1880, Duffy wrote that the 'little books had an immediate success, and after the lapse of a generation, when the writers for the most part are dead, new editions constantly issue from the press of Ireland and America'. The influence they exerted was two-fold. On the one hand they shaped the ideas of countless Irish people on history and on what a good Irish poem should be, and, on the other, they stood as a model for later publishing ventures of the same kind. Although they were never mere propaganda, they were definitely didactic and meant to be so. Writing to Smith O'Brien about the second volume of the Library, Davis made this abundantly clear: 'The Ballad Poetry has reached a real third edition, and cannot be printed fast enough for the sale. It is every way good. Not an Irish Conservative of education but will read it, and be brought nearer to Ireland by it. That is a propagandism worth a thousand harangues such as you ask me to make.'

Davis's Romantic nationalism had a lasting effect on Irish politics, but, more immediately, it also distanced him at an intellectual level from O'Connell. O'Connell was the product of that Enlightenment thought which German Romanticism and Idealist philosophy did most to undermine: he was concerned with constitutional rather than cultural politics, put his faith in political institutions rather than communal sympathies and antipathies, and supported individual rather than collective rights. At first these differences did not show because O'Connell seemed close to winning a measure of political independence, but after Clontarf the rifts between him and the Young Irelanders became more public.

There had been a little sniping from the beginning, but this had come mainly from O'Connell's lieutenants, and particularly Richard Barrett, proprietor and editor of the Repealist newspaper, the *Pilot*. While some of this may be put down to commercial jealousy on Barrett's part, there were more substantial grounds of difference. Barrett thought that the *Nation* was merely climbing on the Repeal band-wagon, found the Young Irelanders uncongenial and cliquish, and dismissed Davis's enthusiastic idealism as politically naive. Moreover, the *Pilot* equated Irishness with Catholicism, and propounded the notion of 'two nations on one soil', rather than the inclusive and religiously all-embracing nationalism of the *Nation*. Davis, with his espousal of mixed education, undetermined religious beliefs and delight in independent thought, was particularly suspect. O'Connell had little interest in Young Ireland's concern with popular education, opposed their support for the Poor Law, and disparaged their backing for the English Chartists. He was also baffled by their praise of writers like Charles Lever and William Carleton, whom he considered anti-national. More serious political differences emerged over the Young Irelanders' refusal to condemn the use of physical force in all circumstances, and O'Connell felt that the warlike tone of some of their articles had compromised him while in prison, complaining on his release in 1844 that 'The *Nation* was read against me – passages I disapproved of and condemned were read against me'. (O'Connell's protests did little to dampen Davis's interest in armed struggle, as his essays on Grattan, Wexford and the Irish Brigade indicate.) There were further disagreements over O'Connell's apparent sympathy for a Federal solution to the Irish question, but the real break came, almost inevitably, over the question of education and the government's proposal to set up an undenominational system of university colleges. Influential sections of the Catholic hierarchy denounced such 'godless colleges', and O'Connell took that side: not merely out of political expediency, but because his form of liberalism, shaped by the eighteenth century, regarded religious education as the concern of the individual conscience rather than a means of bringing about the social and nationalist engineering that Davis favoured.

The debate on mixed education was at its most intense from February 1845, when the Colleges Bill was announced, to the following May. O'Connell postponed discussion as long as he could, but it was too important an issue to be quietly passed over, and as time went by Davis became alarmed by what he regarded as the growing sectarianism in the Repeal Association. It was all bound to end in tears, and this it did spectacularly on 26 May when a lightweight young journalist, M. G. Conway, who had been rejected as a member of the Eighty-Two Club, ridiculed the contribution to the debate of the Young Irelander Michael Barry, remarking condescendingly that 'there was an imbecility in his speech characteristic of his party and his principles; a

party which the strong hand of O'Connell must, not exterminate, but warn.' O'Connell apparently added to this insult by 'waving his cap repeatedly over his head during its delivery and cheering vociferously', and, as a report of the proceedings shows, Davis's attempt to diffuse the situation with an ironic rebuke backfired disastrously:

I have not … more than a few words to say, in reply to the useful judicious and spirited speech of my old college friend, my Catholic friend, my very Catholic friend, Mr Conway.

Mr O'Connell: It is no crime to be a Catholic I hope?
Mr Davis: No, surely no, for –
Mr O'Connell: The sneer with which you used the word would lead to the inference.
Mr Davis: No! sir, no! My best friends, my nearest friends, my truest friends are Catholics. I was brought up in a mixed seminary, where I learned to know and knowing to love my Catholic countrymen, a love that shall not be disturbed by these casual and unhappy dissensions. Disunion, alas, has destroyed our country for centuries. Men of Ireland, shall it destroy it again?

He went on to try to show that his view of the Bill coincided with that of the Catholic bishops, and that, in an amended form, the measure should be welcomed. But by now O'Connell's blood was up and the frustrated irritations and jealousies of years burst out in his reply:

The principle of the bill has been lauded by Mr Davis, and was advocated in a newspaper professing to be the organ of the Roman Catholic people of this country, but which I emphatically pronounce to be no such thing. The section of politicians styling themselves the Young Ireland party, anxious to rule the destinies of this country, start up and support this measure. There is no such party as that styled Young Ireland. There may be a few individuals who take that denomination on themselves. I am for Old Ireland. 'Tis time that this delusion should be put an end to. Young Ireland may play what pranks they please. I do not envy them the name they rejoice in, I shall stand by Old Ireland. And I have some slight notion that Old Ireland will stand by me.

O'Connell sat down to universal consternation, but the afternoon was saved by a lachrymose *schwamerie*. On advice, O'Connell rose again to withdraw the term 'Young Ireland' as he understood that it was 'disclaimed by those to whom it was applied'. Davis immediately grasped this opportunity to deny that there was factionalism in the Association, and insisted that 'they were bound to work together for Irish nationality. They were bound among other motives by a strong affection towards Daniel O'Connell; a feeling which he himself had habitually expressed'. At which point, as Duffy put it, 'the strong self-restrained man paused from emotion, and broke into irrepressible tears'. O'Connell responded at once, declaring that he had 'never felt more gratified than by this evidence of regard. If Mr. Davis were overcome, it overcame him also', whereupon he threw his arms round him and cried out 'Davis I love you'. The Association applauded enthusiastically: but the question of mixed education remained.

Not that this was to concern Davis for much longer. In July 1845 he at last obtained permission from her parents to become engaged to Annie Hutton, the daughter of a prosperous Dublin businessman whom he had known since December 1843. No date was settled for the marriage, and Annie planned to visit Rome for the winter, where Davis was to join her. But early in September he fell ill with what he described as 'slight scarlatina'; neither he nor his friends took this seriously and Duffy even joshed him by reporting that a fellow contributor to the *Nation*, John O'Hagan, 'says you have an opportunity of rivalling Mirabeau, by dying at this minute; but he begs you won't be tempted by the inviting opportunity'. However, on 16 September Duffy was summoned to the Davis family house in Baggot Street 'to see the most tragic sight my eyes had ever looked upon', the lifeless body of his friend.

Davis's other friends were as thunderstruck as Duffy, and the *Nation* went into black-bordered mourning. Among the fulsome tributes from Duffy, Smith O'Brien and Thomas Meagher, was one penned by O'Connell from his home in Derrynane:

My mind is bewildered and my heart afflicted. The loss of my beloved friend, my noble-minded friend, is a source of the deepest sorrow to my mind. What a blow – what a cruel blow to the cause of Irish nationality! He was a creature of transcendent quality of mind and heart; his learning was universal, his knowledge was as minute as it was general. And then he was a being of such incessant energy and continuous exertion. I … cannot expect to look upon his like again, or to see the place he has left vacant adequately filled up; and I solemnly declare that I never knew any man who could be so useful to Ireland in the present stage of her struggles. His loss is indeed irreparable. … I can write no more – my tears blind me … '

Not the least astonishing thing about the Young Ireland Movement was how much it managed to achieve in a comparatively short time, for, within three years of Davis's death the party was broken. Although the quarrel with O'Connell over the Colleges Bill was patched up, the breach was never fully healed and John O'Connell, the Liberator's son, began a whispering campaign with other of O'Connell's supporters against a group they increasingly regarded as subversive and dangerous. The final split came at a repeal meeting in

July 1846 when the Young Irelanders refused to give a categorical undertaking not to use force for political ends, and marched out of the Repeal Association's headquarters. Thereafter they formed themselves into the Irish Confederation, but both this and the Repeal Association were overtaken by the Famine. John Mitchel, who had come to prominence after Davis's death, grew militant in the face of the national disaster and in December 1847 he and Devin Reilly left the *Nation* to start their own more radical newspaper, the *United Irishman*. This ran for only sixteen weeks before it was suppressed, and Mitchel arrested, tried, and transported. But by then he had won over many of the Young Irelanders to the necessity of physical force, an idea that was strengthened by the French Revolution of 1848 and an increasing sense of helplessness over the Famine. The insurrection organised by the Confederation broke out on 29 July in Ballingarry and took the form of a small affray which was soon quelled. With the imprisonment and transportation of many of the rebels the Young Ireland Movement came to an end.

But its spirit and its teaching lived on. And for good reason. The Young Irelanders set about their task of national education 'not with the zeal of a schoolmaster', as Duffy put it, 'but with the fervour of a lover'. It is sometimes easy to smile at the way in which this fervour can excite Davis into extravagant hyperbole – Grattan's speeches 'are the finest specimens of imaginative eloquence in the English, or in any language', no other writer in the language 'except Shakespeare, has so sublime and suggestive a diction', William Carleton's characters are 'not surpassed by even Shakespeare for originality, grandeur, and distinctness', the 'overbearing grandeur' of the artist James Barry throws 'the whole of the English painters into insignificance', while Forde and Maclise 'learned to draw better than any moderns, except Cornelius and his living brethren'. Incorrigible economic problems are to be magically solved by 'some invention, which should bring the might of machinery in a wholesome and cheap form to the cabin'. Reviewing O'Donovan's *Irish Grammar,* he optimistically but improbably notes that in 'the chapter on Prepositions alone (running to thirty-eight close pages) there are pleasant materials for long study to any student of Ireland, be he ever so ignorant of Irish.' Elsewhere he seems more sensitive to his readers' limitations ('The reader has probably now had enough of Vallancey's etymology', 'The reader is, probably, wearied enough of this catalogue'), and sometimes, as in his suggestions about Art Institutions, he is aware that his plans will be laughed at as 'fanciful and improbable' but, yet, 'we think it easy and we think it will be done'. It is this mixture of idealism, enthusiasm, and can-do practicality that marks Davis's theme and his style, as he cajoles, exhorts, upbraids and entreats his readers to educate themselves and to work for the nation's good. It is no wonder that one of the Young Irelanders' most enthusiastic supporters was Samuel Smiles, author of that quintessentially Victorian vade-mecum, *Self-Help.*

And it was to the Young Irelanders that young writers and thinkers looked back with pride and emulation in the 1890s. Although Yeats was to react against his didactic purpose, for many Irishmen Davis remained the true Irish poet and essayist, and in 1889 a kinsman of Arthur Griffith's wrote that Davis, Duffy and Dillon had attracted to the *Nation* 'a galaxy of Geniuses unparalleled in the History of any country'. The seed of Davis's teaching fell in an evil time, as the potatoes rotted in the damp Irish fields, but that seed was destined to quicken and to fructify in a later generation.

J.K.

Dates of publication in the *Nation*

8 Feb 1845	Study
18 Feb 1843	Means and Aids to Self-Education
5 April 1845	The History of Ireland
10 Aug 1844	Ancient Ireland
28 Oct 1843	Historical Monuments of Ireland
6 July 1844	Irish Antiquities
11 May 1844	The Sea Kings
10 May 1845	The Round Towers of Ireland
5 Oct 1844	Ethnology of the Irish Race
7 June 1845	The Irish Brigade
22 Feb 1845	The Speeches of Grattan
26 July 1845	Memorials of Wexford [Wexford]
28 Dec 1844	History of To-day
15 June 1844	The Resources of Ireland
20 April 1844	Irish Topography
13, 20 July 1844	The Valuation of Ireland (two parts)
9, 23 Dec 1843	National Art (two parts)
27 April 1844	Art Unions
19 April 1845	Illustrations of Ireland [Irish Pictures]
29 July 1843	Hints for Irish Historical Paintings
1 April, 30 Dec 1843	Our National Language
23 Aug 1845	O'Donovan's Irish Grammar
17 May, 5 July 1845	Institutions of Dublin (two parts)

LITERARY AND HISTORICAL

ESSAYS.

BY THOMAS DAVIS.

" Táinig anam a n-Éirinn."

" A Soul came into Ireland."

DUBLIN:

PUBLISHED BY JAMES DUFFY,

23, ANGLESEA-STREET.

1846.

Stereotyped and Printed by
T. COLDWELL, 50, CAPEL-STREET.

I DEDICATE

THIS VOLUME OF THE WORKS OF

THOMAS DAVIS

TO

JOHN B. DILLON,

HIS DEAR AND TRUSTED FRIEND

AND

MINE.

THE EDITOR.

Dec. 1845.

PREFACE.

In this Volume I have endeavoured to do for THOMAS DAVIS what I once hoped to see him do for himself—to gather together such of his historical and literary Miscellanies as were mainly devoted to the illustration of Ireland. I have done so with care and reverence, and I believe they will be found to make a rich and suggestive book, and one with a true soul in it.

In selecting them I kept in view—as I know he would have desired—not fame for the dead, but usefulness to the living.

I chose such as were most likely to awaken and instruct the People, and contribute to the purpose for which DAVIS lived. He has written nothing wanting vitality and power; but those who have still to become familiar with his writings, must not think they have materials for an estimate of him here. He has done greater and more striking things. This is but the reflection of one phasis of his mind.

I meditated, originally, accompanying these Essays with some account of his intellectual character and his influence upon his time and his contemporaries. But, neither his life nor writings need any defence, and the period for interpreting between him and the people has not yet come.

It is not Death alone, but Time and Death that canonize the Patriot.

We are still too near to see his proportions truly. The friends to whom his singularly noble and loveable character was familiar, and who knew all the great designs he was bringing to maturity, are in no fit condition to measure his intellectual force with a calm judgment. The people who knew him imperfectly, or not at all— for it was one of the practical lessons he taught the young men of his generation, to be chary of notoriety—have still to gather from his works whatever faint image of a true Great Man, can ever be collected from books. Till they have done this, they will not be prepared to hear the whole truth of him.

All he was, and might have become, they can never fully know ; as it is, their unconsciousness of what they have lost, impresses those who knew him, and them, with that pitying pain we

feel for the indifference of a child to the death of
his father

Students who will be eager to estimate him
for themselves, must take in connexion with his
works the fact, that over the grave of this man,
living only to manhood, and occupying only a
private station, there gathered a union of parties,
and a combination of intellect that would have
met round the tomb of no other man living, or
who has lived in our time. No life—not that of
Guttenberg, or Franklin, or Tone, illustrates
more strikingly than his, how often it is necessary to turn aside from the *dais* on which stand
the great and titled, for the real moving power
of the time—the men who are stirring like a soul
in the bosom of society. Such a one they will
speedily discover Davis to have been.

It is perhaps unnecessary to announce that his
friends will give his entire works in succession
to the public. All that is left of him, his reputation and his labours, will be their dear and
special care.

His poetry, carefully edited and noted by
one of his friends, will form an early volume in
this series—his political writings (which cannot
be included in the "Library of Ireland,") will

be selected and classified by another friend, and appear in a distinct shape. When these have had time to sink into the people's mind, his "Life and Correspondence" will be published—and some attempt made to convey an impression of what he was in life and action.

All the Essays in the present collection are taken from *The Nation ;* selections from his Pamphlets, and contributions to *The Irish Monthly Magazine* will make another volume of the same character.

C. G. D.

Christmas Eve, 1845.

CONTENTS.

LITERARY AND HISTORICAL

ESSAYS.

STUDY.

Beside a library, how poor are all the other greatest deeds of man—his constitution, brigade, factory, man of war, cathedral—how poor are all miracles in comparison! Look at that wall of motley calf-skin, open those slips of inked rags—who would fancy them as valuable as the rows of stamped cloth in a warehouse? Yet Aladdin's lamp was a child's kaliedoscope in comparison. There the thoughts and deeds of the most efficient men during three thousand years are accumulated, and every one who will learn a few conventional signs—24 (magic) letters—can pass at pleasure from Plato to Napoleon, from the Argonauts to the Affghans, from the woven mathematics of La Place to the mythology of Egypt, and the lyrics of Burns. Young reader! pause steadily, and look at this fact till it blaze before you; look till your imagination summon up even the few acts and thoughts named in that last sentence; and when these visions—from the Greek pirate to the fiery-eyed Scotchman—have begun to dim, solemnly resolve to use these glorious opportunities, as one whose breast has been sobbing at the far sight of a mountain, resolves to climb it, and already strains and exults in his purposed toil.

Throughout the country, at this moment, thousands are consulting how to obtain and use books. We feel painfully anxious that this noble purpose should be well directed. It is possible that these sanguine young men, who are wildly pressing for knowledge, may grow weary or be misled—to their own and Ireland's injury. We intend, therefore, to put down a few hints and warnings for them. Unless they, themselves, ponder and discuss these hints and warnings they will be useless, nay, worse than useless.

On the selection and purchase of books it is hard to say what is useful without going into detail. Carlyle says that a library is the true University of our days, where every sort of knowledge is brought together to be studied; but the student needs guides in the library as much as in the University. He does not need rules nor rulers; but light and classification. Let a boy loose in a library, and if he have years of leisure and a creative spirit he will come out a master-mind. If he have the leisure without the original spring he will become a book-worm—a useful help, perhaps, to his neighbours, but himself a very feeble and poor creature. For one man who gains weapons from idle reading, we know twenty who lose their simplicity without getting strength, and purchase cold recollections of other men's thoughts by the sacrifice of nature.

Just as men are bewildered and lost from want of guides in a large library, so are others from an equal want of direction in the purchase of a small one. We know from bitter experience how much money it costs a young man to get a sufficient library. Still more hard we should think it for a club of young men to do so. But worse than the loss of money, are the weariness from reading dull and shallow books, the corruption from reading vicious, extravagant, and confused books, and the waste of time and patience from reading idle and impertinent books. The remedy is not by saying "this book you shall read, and this other you shall not read under penalty;" but by inducing students to regard their self-education solemnly, by giving them information on the classification of books, and by setting them to judge authors vigorously and for themselves.

Booksellers, especially in small towns, exercise no small influence in the choice of books—yet they are generally unfit to do so. They are like agents for the sale of patent medicines—knowing the prices but not the ingredients, nor the comparative worth of their goods, yet puffing them for the commission sake.

If some competent person would write a book on books, he would do the world a great favour; but he had need be a man of caution, above political bias or personal motive, and indifferent to the outcries of party. Todd's Students' Manual,

Vericour's Modern French Literature, and the like, are rather childish affairs, though better than nothing. M'Cullagh's " Rise and Study of History" is, on its peculiar subject, a book of much value. Men will differ in judging the style; but it honestly, learnedly, and in a suggestive, candid way examines the great histories from Horodotus down. We wish to see it more generally in the people's hands. Occasionally one meets in a Review a comprehensive and just estimate of the authorities on some subject; but most of these periodicals are written for some party or interested purpose, and are not trustworthy. Hallam's Literature of Europe, Sismondi and Schlegel are guides of the highest value in the formation of a large library, but we fear their use in Ireland is remote.

One of the first mistakes a young, ardent student falls into is, that he can master all knowledge. The desire for universal attainment is natural and glorious; but he, who feels it, is in danger of hurrying over a multitude of books, and confusing himself into the belief that he is about to know every thing because he has skimmed many things.

Another evil is apt to grow from this. A young man who gets a name for a great variety of knowledge often is ashamed to appear ignorant of what he does not know. He is appealed to as an authority, and, instead of manfully and wisely avowing his ignorance, he harangues from the title-page, or skilfully parades the opinions of other men as if they were his own observations.

Looking through books in order to talk of

them is one of the worst and commonest vices.
It is an acted lie, a device to conceal laziness
and ignorance, or to compensate for want of wit;
a stupid device, too, for it is soon found out, the
employer of it gets the character of being a
literary cheat, he is thought a pretender, even
when well-informed, and a plagiarist when most
original.

Reading to consume time is an honest but weak
employment. It is a positive disease with mul-
titudes of people. They crouch in corners, going
over novels and biographies at the rate of two
volumes a day, when they would have been far
better employed in digging or playing shuttle-
cock. Still it is hard to distinguish between this
long-looking through books and the voracity of
a curious and powerful mind gathering stores
which it will afterwards arrange and use. Indeed
the highest reading of all (what we may name
epic reading) is of this class. When we are
youngest and heartiest we read thus. The fate
and passions of men are all in all to us; for
we are then true-lovers, candidates for laurel
crowns, assured Liberators and conquerors of the
earth, rivals of archangels perchance in our
dreams. We never pause then upon the artistical excellence of a book—we never try to
look at and realise the scenery or sounds described (if the author make them clear, well and
good—if not, no matter)—we hurry on to the
end of the shipwreck, or the battle, the courtship,
or the journey—palpitating for our hero's fate.
This, we repeat, is the highest kind of reading.

This sort of reading is most common in human narrative.

Earnest readers of science read their books at first as ordinary people do their histories—for the plot.

Some of us can recollect the zealous rush through a fresh book on mathematics or chymistry to know the subtle scheme of reasoning, or understand the just unveiled secrets of nature, as we read " Sinbad the Sailor" or " Mungo Park's Travels."

But most readers of science read in order to use it. They try to acquire command over each part for convenience sake, and not from curiosity or love. All men who persevere in science do this latter mainly ; but all of them retain or acquire the epic spirit in reading, and we have seen a dry lawyer swallow a stiff treatise, not thinking of its use in his arguments, but its intrinsic beauty of system and accuracy of logic.

He who seeks to make much use, too, of narrative literature (be it novel, poem, drama, history, or travel), must learn scientific as well as epic reading.

He need not formally criticise and review every book, still less need he pause on every sentence and word till the full meaning of it stands before him.

But he must often do this. He must analyse as well as enjoy. He must consider the elements as well as the argument of a book just as, long dwelling on a landscape, he will begin to know the trees and rocks, the sun-flooded hollow, and the cloud-crowned top, which go to make the scene—or, to use a more illustrative thought—as one, long listening to the noise on a summer day, comes to separate and mark the bleat of the lamb, the hoarse caw of the crow, the song of the thrush, the buzz of the bee, and the tinkle of the brook.

Doing this *deliberately* is an evil to the mind whether the subject be nature or books. The evil is not because the act is one of analysis, though that has been said. It is proof of higher power to combine new ideas out of what is before you, or to notice combinations not at first obvious, than to distinguish and separate. The latter tends to logic, which is our humblest exercise of mind, the former to creation, which is our highest. Yet analysis is not an unhealthy act of mind, nor is the process we have described always analytical.

The evil of deliberate criticism is, that it generates scepticism. Of course we do not mean religious, but general scepticism. The process goes on till one sees only stratification in the slope, gases in the stream, cunning tissues in the face, associations in the mind, and an astronomical machine in the sky. A more miserable state of soul no mortal ever suffered than this. But an earnest man living and loving vigorously is in little danger of this condition, nor does it last long with any man of strong character.

Another evil, confined chiefly to men who write or talk for effect, is that they become spies (as Emerson calls them) on Nature. They do not wonder at love, or hate what they see. All

books and men are arsenals to be used, or, more
properly, stores to be plundered by them.   But
their punishment is sharp.   They love insight
into the godlier qualities, they love the sight of
sympathy, and become conscious actors of a poor
farce.

Happiest is he who judges and knows books,
and nature, and men (himself included), spon-
taneously or from early training—whose feelings
are assessors with his intellects, and who is thoroughly in earnest.   An actor or a spy is weak
as well as wretched; yet it may be needful for
him who was blinded by the low principles, the
tasteless rules, and the stupid habits of his family
and teachers, to face this danger, deliberately to
analyze his own and others' nature, deliberately to
study how faculties are acquired and results produced, and thus to cure himself of blindness,
and deafness, and dumbness, and become a man,
observant and skilful.   He will suffer much, and
run great danger, but if he go through this faith-
fully, and then fling himself into action and
undertake responsibility, he shall be great and
happy.

MEANS AND AIDS TO SELF-EDUCATION.

" What good were it for me to manufacture perfect iron, while my own breast is full of dross? What would it stead me to put properties of land in order, while I am at variance with myself? To speak it in a word; the cultivation of my individual self, here as I am, has from my youth upwards been constantly though dimly my wish and my purpose."

" Men are so inclined to content themselves with what is commonest; the spirit and the senses so easily grow dead to the impressions of the beautiful and perfect; that every one should study to nourish in his mind the faculty of feeling these things by every method in his power. For no man can bear to be entirely deprived of such enjoyments: it is only because they are not used to taste of what is excellent, that the generality of people take delight in silly and insipid things, provided they be new. For this reason, he would add, ' one ought every day at least to hear a little song, read a good poem, see a fine picture, and, if it were possible, to speak a few reasonable words.' "—
Goethe.

WE have been often asked by certain of the Temperance Societies to give them some advice on Self-Education. Lately we promised one of these bodies to write some hints, as to how the members of it could use their association for their mental improvement.

We said, and say again, that the Temperance Societies can be made use of by the people for their instruction as well as pleasure. Assemblies of any kind are not the *best* places either for study or invention. Home or solitude are better—home is the great teacher. In domestic business we learn mechanical skill, the nature of those material bodies with which we have most to deal in life—we learn labour by example and by kindly precepts—we learn (in a prudent home) decorum, cleanliness, order—in a virtuous home we learn more than these, we learn reverence for the old, affection without passion, truth, piety, and justice. These are the greatest things man can know. Having these he is well; without them attainments of wealth or talent are of little worth. Home is the great teacher; and its teaching passes down in honest homes from generation to generation, and neither the generation that gives, nor the generation that takes it, lays down plans for bringing it to pass.

Again, to come to designed learning. We learn arts and professions by apprenticeships, that is, much after the fashion we learned walking or stitching, or fire-making, or love-making at home—by example, precept, and practice combined. Apprentices at anything, from ditching, basket-work, or watch-making, to merchant-trading, legislation, or surgery, submit either to a nominal or an actual apprenticeship. They see other men do these things, they desire to do the same, and they learn to do so by watching *how*, and *when*, and asking, or guessing *why* each part of the business is done; and as fast as they know, or are supposed to know, any one part, whether it be sloping the ditch, or totting the accounts, or dressing the limb, they begin to do that, and, being directed when they fail, they

learn at last to do it well, and are thereby prepared to attempt some other or harder part of the
business.

Thus it is by experience—or trying to do, and
often doing a thing—combined with teaching, or
seeing, and being told how and why other people,
more experienced, do that thing, that most of the
practical business of life is learned.

In some trades, formal apprenticeship and
planned teaching exist as little as in ordinary
home-teaching. Few men are, of set purpose,
taught to dig; and just as few are taught to
legislate.

Where formal teaching is usual, as in what
are called learned professions, and in delicate
trades, fewer men know anything of these busi-
nesses. Those who learn them at all, do so exactly and fully, but commonly practise them in a
formal and technical way, and invent and improve them little. In those occupations which
most men take up casually—as book-writing,
digging, singing, and legislation, and the like—
there is much less exact knowledge, less form,
more originality and progress, and more of the
public know something about them in an unpro-
fessional way.

The Caste system of India, Egypt, and Ancient
Ireland, carried out the formal apprenticeship
plan to its full extent. The United States of
America have very little of it. Modern Europe
is between the two, as she has in most things
abolished caste or hereditary professions (kings
and nobles excepted), but has, in many things,
retained exact apprenticeships.

Marriage, and the bringing up of children, the employment of dependants, travel, and daily sights, and society, are our chief teachers of morals, sentiment, taste, prudence, and manners. Mechanical and literary skill of all sorts, and most accomplishments, are usually picked up in this same way.

We have said all this, lest our less-instructed readers should fall into a mistake common to all beginners in study, that books, and schooling, and lectures, are the chief teachers in life; whereas most of the things we learn here are learned from the experience of home, and of the practical parts of our trades and amusements.

We pray our humbler friends to think long and often on this.

But let them not suppose we undervalue, or wish them to neglect other kinds of teaching; on the contrary, they should mark how much the influences of home, and business, and society, are affected by the quantity and sort of their scholarship.

Home life is obviously enough affected by education. Where the parents read and write, the children learn to do so too, early in life, and with little trouble; where they know something of their religious creed, they give its rites a higher meaning than mere forms; where they know the history of the country well, every field, every old tower or arch is a subject of amusement, of fine old stories, and fine young hopes; where they know the nature of other people and countries, their own country and people become texts to be commented on, and likewise supply a living comment on those peculiarities of which they have read.

Again, where the members of a family can read aloud, or play, or sing, they have a well of pleasant thoughts and good feelings, which can hardly be dried or frozen up; and so of other things.

And in the trades and professions of life, to study in books the objects, customs, and rules of that trade or profession to which you are going saves time, enables you to improve your practice of it, and makes you less dependent on the teaching of other practitioners, who are often interested in delaying you.

In these, and a thousand ways besides, study and science produce the best effects upon the practical parts of life.

Besides, the *first* business of life is the improvement of one's own heart and mind. The study of the thoughts and deeds of great men, the laws of human, and animal, and vegetable, and lifeless nature, the principles of fine and mechanical arts, and of morals, society, and religion—all directly give us nobler and greater desires, more wide and generous judgments, and more refined pleasures.

Learning in this latter sense may be got either at home, or at school, by solitary study, or in associations. Home *learning* depends, of course, on the knowledge, good sense, and leisure of the parents. The German Jean Paul, the American Emerson, and others of an inferior sort, have written deep and fruitful truths on bringing up, and teaching at home. Yet, con-

sidering its importance, it has not been sufficiently studied. Upon schools much has been
written. Almost all the private schools in this
country are bad. They merely cram the memories of pupils with facts or words, without deve-
loping their judgment, taste, or invention, or
teaching them the *application* of any knowledge.
Besides, the things taught are commonly those
least worth learning. This is especially true of
the middle and richer classes. Instead of being
taught the nature, products, and history, first of
their own, and then of other countries, they are
buried in classical frivolities, languages which
they never master, and manners and races which
they cannot appreciate. Instead of being disciplined to think exactly, to speak and write
accurately, they are crammed with rules, and
taught to repeat forms by rote.

The National Schools are a vast improvement
on anything hitherto in this country, but still
they have great faults. From the miserably
small grant, the teachers are badly paid, and
therefore hastily and meagerly educated.

The maps, drawing, and musical instruments,
museums, and scientific apparatus, which should
be in every school, are mostly wanting altogether.
The books, also, are defective.

The information has the worst fault of the
French system ; it is too exclusively on physical
science and natural history. Fancy a *National*
School which teaches the children no more of
the state and history of Ireland than of Belgium
or Japan ! We have spoken to pupils, nay, to
masters of the *National* Schools, who were igno-

rant of the physical character of every part of
Ireland except their native villages—who knew
not how the people lived, or died, or sported, or
fought—who had never heard of Tara, Clontarf,
Limerick, or Dungannon—to whom the O'Neills
and Sarsfields, the Swifts and Sternes, the Grat-
tans and Barrys, our generals, statesmen, authors,
orators, and artists, were alike and utterly unknown! Even the hedge schools kept up something of the romance, history, and music of the
country.

Until the *National* Schools fall under national
control, the people must take *diligent care to procure books on the history, men, language, music,
and manners of Ireland for their children.* These
schools are very good so far as they go, and the
children should be sent to them; but they are
not *national*, they do not use the Irish language,
nor teach anything peculiarly Irish.

As to solitary study, lists of books, pictures,
and maps, can alone be given; and to do this usefully would exceed our space at present.

As it is, we find that we have no more room,
and have not said a word on what we proposed
to write—namely, Self-Education through the
Temperance Societies.

We do not regret having wandered from our
professed subject, as, if treated exclusively, it
might lead men into errors which no after-
thought could cure.

What we chiefly desire is, to set the people on
making out plans for their own and their children's education. Thinking cannot be done by
deputy—they must think for themselves.

THE HISTORY OF IRELAND.

SOMETHING has been done to rescue Ireland from the reproach that she was a wailing and ignorant slave.

Brag as we like, the reproach was not undeserved, nor is it quite removed.

She is still a serf-nation, but she is struggling wisely and patiently, and is ready to struggle with all the energy her advisers think politic, for liberty. She has ceased to wail—she is beginning to make up a record of English crime and Irish suffering, in order to explain the past, to justify the present, and caution the future. She begins to study the past—not to acquire a beggar's eloquence in petition, but a hero's wrath in strife. She no longer tears and parades her wounds, to win her smiter's mercy; and now she should look upon her breast and say—"That wound makes me distrust, and this makes me guard, and they all will make me steadier to resist, or, if all else fails, fiercer to avenge."

Thus will Ireland do naturally and honourably.

Our spirit has increased—our liberty is not far off.

But to make our spirit lasting and wise as it is bold—to make our liberty an inheritance for our children, and a charter for our prosperity, we must study as well as strive, and learn as well as feel.

If we attempt to govern ourselves without statesmanship—to be a nation without a knowledge of the country's history, and of the propensities to good and ill of the people—or to fight without generalship, we will fail in policy, society, and war. These—all these things—we, people of Ireland, must know if we would be a free, strong nation. A mockery of Irish independence is not what we want. The bauble of a powerless parliament does not lure us. We are not children. The office of supplying England with recruits, artizans, and corn, under the benign interpositions of an Irish Grand Jury, *shall* not be our destiny. By our deep conviction—by the power of mind over the people, we say, No!

We are true to our colour, "the green," and true to our watchword, "Ireland for the Irish." We want to win Ireland and keep it. If we win it, we will not lose it, nor give it away to a bribing, a bullying, or a flattering minister. But, to be able to keep it, and use it, and govern it, the men of Ireland must know what it is, what it was, and what it can be made. They must study her history, perfectly know her present state, physical and moral—and train themselves up by science, poetry, music, industry, skill, and by all the studies and accomplishments of peace and war.

If Ireland were in national health, her history would be familiar by books, pictures, statuary, and music to every cabin and shop in the land—her resources as an agricultural, manufacturing, and trading people, would be equally known—

and every young man would be trained, and
every grown man able to defend her coast, her
plains, her towns, and her hills —not with his
right arm merely, but by his disciplined habits
and military accomplishments. These are the
pillars of independence.

Academies of art, institutes of science, colleges of literature, schools and camps of war are
a nation's means for teaching itself strength, and
winning safety and honour; and when we are a
nation, please God, we shall have them all.   Till
then, we must work for ourselves.   So far as we
can study music in societies, art in schools, literature in institutes, science in our colleges, or
soldiership in theory, we are bound as good
citizens to learn.   Where these are denied by
power, or unattainable by clubbing the resources of neighbours, we must try and study
for ourselves.   We must visit museums and antiquities, and study, and buy, and assist books of
history to know what the country and people
were, how they fell, how they suffered, and how
they rose again.   We must read books of statistics—and let us pause to regret that there is no
work on the statistics of Ireland, except the
scarce lithograph of Moreau, the papers in the
second Report of the Railway Commission, and the
chapters in *M'Culloch's Statistics of the British
Empire*—the Repeal Association ought to have
a hand-book first, and then an elaborate and vast
account of Ireland's statistics brought out.

To resume, we must read such statistics as we
have, and try and get better; and we must get
the best maps of the country—the Ordnance and

County Index Maps, price 2s. 6d. each, and the Railway Map, price 1l.—into our Mechanics' Institutes, Temperance Reading-rooms, and schools. We must, in making our journeys of business and pleasure, observe and ask for the nature and amount of the agriculture, commerce, and manufactures of the place we are in, and its shape, population, scenery, antiquities, arts, music, dress, and capabilities for improvement. A large portion of our people travel a great deal within Ireland, and often return with no knowledge, save of the inns they slept in, and the traders they dealt with.

We must give our children in schools the best knowledge of science, art, and literary elements possible. And at home they should see and hear as much of national pictures, music, poetry, and military science as possible.

And, finally, we must keep our own souls, and try, by teaching and example, to lift up the souls of all our family and neighbours, to that pitch of industry, courage, information, and wisdom necessary to enable an enslaved, dark, and starving people to become free, and rich, and rational.

Well, as to this National History—L'Abbe MacGeoghegan published a history of Ireland, in French, in 3 vols. quarto, dedicated to the Irish Brigade. Writing in France, he was free from the English censorship; writing for "The Brigade," he avoided the impudence of Huguenot historians. The sneers of the Deist Voltaire, and the lies of the Catholic Cambrensis, receive a sharp chastisement in his preface, and a full

answer in his text. He was a man of the most
varied acquirements and an elegant writer.
More full references and the correction of a
few errors of detail, would render his book more
satisfactory to the professor of history, but for
the student it is the best in the world. He is
graphic, easy, and Irish. He is not a bigot,
but apparently a genuine Catholic. His information as to the numbers of troops, and other
facts of our Irish battles, is superior to any other
general historian's; and they who know it well
need not blush, as most Irishmen must now, at
their ignorance of Irish history.

But the Association for liberating Ireland has
offered a prize for a new history of the country,
and given ample time for preparation.

Let no man postpone the preparation who
hopes the prize. An original and highly-finished
work is what is demanded, and for the composition of such a work the time affords no
leisure.

Few persons, we suppose, hitherto quite ignorant of Irish history, will compete; but we would
not discourage even these. There is neither in
theory nor fact any limit to the possible achievements of genius and energy. Some of the greatest works in existence were written rapidly, and
many an old book-worm fails where a young
book-thrasher succeeds.

Let us now consider some of the qualities
which should belong to this history.

*It should, in the first place, be written from
the original authorities.* We have some notion
of giving a set of papers on these authorities, **but**.

there are reasons against such a course, and we counsel no man to rely on us—every one on himself; besides, such a historian should rather make himself able to teach us, than need to learn from us.

However, no one can now be at a loss to know what these authorities are. A list of the choicest of them is printed on the back of the Volunteer's card for this year, and was also printed in the *Nation*.* These authorities are not enough for a

The following is the list of books given as the present sources of history :—

SOME OF THE ORIGINAL SOURCES OF IRISH HISTORY.

ANCIENT IRISH TIMES.

Annals of Tigernach, abbot of Clonmacnoise, from A. D. 200, to his death, 1188, partly compiled from writers of the eighth, seventh, and sixth centuries.
Lives of St. Patrick, St. Columbanus, &c.
Annals of Four Masters, from the earliest times to 1616.
Other Annals, such as those of Innisfallen, Ulster, Boyle, &c. Publications of the Irish Archæological Society, Danish and Icelandic Annals.

ENGLISH INVASION AND THE PALE.

Gerald de Barri, surnamed Cambrensis " Topography " and " Conquest of Ireland." Four Masters, Tracts in Harris's Hibernica. Campion's, Hanmer's, Marlborough's, Camden's, Holingshed's, Stanihurst's, and Ware's Histories. Hardiman's Statutes of Kilkenny.
Henry VIII. and Elizabeth—Harris's Ware. O'Sullivan's Catholic ;History. Four Masters. Spencer's View. Sir G. Carew's Pacata Hibernia. State Papers, Temp. II. VIII. Fyne's Morrison's Itinerary.
James I.—Harris's Hibernica. Sir John Davies' Tracts.
Charles I.—Strafford's Letters. Carte's Life of Ormond. Lodge's Desiderata. Clarendon's Rebellion. Tichborne's Drogheda. State Trials. Rinuncini's

historian. The materials, since the Revolution especially, exist mainly in pamphlets, and even for the time previous only the leading authorities are in the list. The list is not faulty in this, as it was meant for learners, not teachers; but any one using these authorities will readily learn from them what the others are, and can so track out for himself.

There are, however, three tracts specially on the subject of Irish writers. First is Bishop

Letters. Pamphlets. Castlehaven's Memoirs. Clanrickarde's Memoirs. Peter Walsh. Sir J. Temple.

Charles II.—Lord Orrery's Letters. Essex's Letters.

James II. and William III.—King's State of Protestants, and Lesley's Answer. The Green Book. Statutes of James's Parliament, in Dublin Magazine, 1843. Clarendon's Letters. Rawdon Papers. Tracts. Molyneux's Case of Ireland.

George I. and II.—Swift's Life. Lucas's Tracts. Howard's Cases under Popery Laws. O'Leary's Tracts. Boulter's Letters. O'Connor's and Parnell's Irish Catholics. Foreman on "The Brigade."

George III.—Grattan's and Curran's Speeches and Lives —Memoirs of Charlemont. Wilson's Volunteers. Barrington's Rise and Fall. Wolfe Tone's Memoirs. Moore's Fitzgerald. Wyse's Catholic Association. Madden's United Irishmen. Hay, Teeling, &c., on '98. Tracts. Mac Nevin's State Trials. O'Connell's and Sheil's Speeches. Plowden's History.

Compilations—Moore. M'Geoghehan. Curry's Civil Wars. Carey's Vindiciæ. O'Connell's Ireland. Leland.

Current Authorities—The Acts of Parliament. Lords' and Commons' Journals and Debates. Lynch's Legal Institutions.

Antiquities, Dress, Arms — Royal Irish Academy's Transactions and Museum. Walker's Irish Bards. British Costume, in Library of Entertaining Knowledge.

Nicholson's " Irish Historical Library." It gives
accounts of numerous writers, but is wretchedly
meagre. In Harris's " Hibernica" is a short
tract on the same subject ; and in Harris's edition of Ware's works an ample treatise on *Irish
Writers.* This treatise is most valuable, but
must be read with caution, as Ware was slightly,
and Harris enormously, prejudiced against the
native Irish and against the later Catholic writers.
The criticisms of Harris, indeed, on all books
relative to the Religious Wars are partial and
deceptious ; but we repeat that the work is of
great value.

The only more recent work on the subject is a
volume written by Edward O'Reilly, for the
Iberno-Celtic Society, on the Native Irish Poets ;
an interesting work, and containing morsels invaluable to a picturesque historian.

By the way, we may hope, that the studies for
this prize history will be fruitful for historical
ballads.

Too many of the original works can only be
bought at an expense beyond the means of most
of those likely to compete. For instance, Harris's
"Ware," Fynes' "Morrison," and "The State Papers of Henry the Eighth," are very dear. The
works of the Archæological Society can only be
got by a member. The price of O'Connor's "Rerum Hibernicarum Scriptores Veteres," is eighteen
guineas ; and yet, in it alone, the annals of
Tigernach, Boyle, Innisfallen, and the early
part of the " Four Masters," are to be found.
The great majority of the books, however, are
tolerably cheap ; some of the dearer books might

be got by combination among several persons, and afterwards given to the Repeal Reading-rooms.

However, persons resident in, or able to visit Dublin, Cork, or Belfast, can study all, even the scarcest of these works, without any real difficulty.

As to the qualities of such a history, they have been concisely enough intimated by the Committee.

It is to be A HISTORY. One of the most absurd pieces of cant going is that against history, because it is full of wars, and kings, and usurpers, and mobs. History describes, and is meant to describe, *forces*, not proprieties—the mights, the acted realities of men, bad and good—their historical importance depending on their mightiness, not their holiness. Let us by all means have then a "graphic" narrative of what was, not a set of moral disquisitions on what ought to have been.

Yet the man who would keep chronicling the dry events would miss writing a history. He must fathom the social condition of the peasantry, the townsmen, the middle-classes, the nobles, and the clergy (Christian or Pagan,) in each period—how they fed, dressed, armed, and housed themselves. He must exhibit the nature of the government, the manners, the administration of law, the state of useful and fine arts, of commerce, of foreign relations. He must let us see the decay and rise of great principles and conditions—till we look on a tottering sovereignty, a rising creed, an incipient war, as distinctly as, by turning to the highway, we can see the old man, the vigorous youth, or the infant child. He must paint—the council robed in its hall—the priest in his temple—the conspirator—the outlaw—the judge—the general—the martyr. The arms must clash and shine with genuine, not romantic likeness; and the brigades or clans join battle, or divide in flight, before the reader's thought. Above all, a historian should be able to seize on character, not vaguely eulogising nor cursing; but feeling and expressing the pressure of a great mind on his time, and on after-times.

Such things may be done partly in disquisitions, as in Mitchelet's "France;" but they must now be done in narrative; and nowhere, not even in Livy, is there a finer specimen of how all these things may be done by narrative than in Augustine Thierry's "Norman Conquest and Merovingian Scenes." The only danger to be avoided in dealing with so long a period in Thierry's way is the continuing to attach importance to a once great influence, when it has sunk to be an exceptive power. He who thinks it possible to dash off a profoundly coloured and shaded narrative like this of Thierry's will find himself bitterly wrong. Even a great philosophical view may much more easily be extemporised than this lasting and finished image of past times.

The greatest vice in such a work would be bigotry—bigotry of race or creed. We know a descendant of a great Milesian family who supports the Union, because he thinks the descendants of the Anglo-Irish—his ancestors' foes—would mainly rule Ireland, were she independent. The opposite rage against the older races is still more usual. A religious bigot is altogether unfit,

incurably unfit, for such a task ; and the writer
of such an Irish history must feel a love for all
sects, a philosophical eye to the merits and de-
merits of all, and a solemn and haughty impar-
tiality in speaking of all.

Need we say that a history, wherein glowing
oratory appeared in place of historical painting,
bold assertion instead of justified portraiture,
flattery to the living instead of justice to the
dead, clever plunder of other compilers instead
of original research, or a cramped and scholastic
instead of an idiomatic, "clear, and graphic"
style, would deserve rejection, and would, we
cannot doubt, obtain it.

To give such a history to Ireland as is now
sought, will be a proud and illustrious deed.—
Such a work would have no passing influence,
though its first political effect would be enormous;
it would be read by every class and side ; for
there is no readable book on the subject ; it
would people our streets, and glens, and castles,
and abbeys, and coasts with a hundred generations besides our own ; it would clear up the
grounds of our quarrels, and prepare reconcilia-
tion ; it would *unconsciously* make us recognise
the causes of our weakness; it would give us
great examples of men and of events, and materially influence our destiny.

Shall we get such a history ?   Think, reader !
has God given you the soul and perseverance to
create this marvel ?

ANCIENT IRELAND.

THERE was once civilization in Ireland. We never were very eminent to be sure for manufactures in metal, our houses were simple, our very palaces rude, our furniture scanty, our saffron shirts not often changed, and our foreign trade small. Yet was Ireland civilized. Strange thing! says some one whose ideas of civilization are identical with carpets and cut glass, fine masonry, and the steam-engine; yet 'tis true. For there was a time when learning was endowed by the rich and honoured by the poor, and taught all over our country. Not only did thousands of natives frequent our schools and colleges, but men of every rank came here from the Continent to study under the professors and system of Ireland, and we need not go beyond the testimonies of English antiquaries, from Bede to Camden, that these schools were regarded as the first in Europe. Ireland was equally remarkable for piety. In the Pagan times it was regarded as a sanctuary of the Magian or Druid creed. From the fifth century it became equally illustrious in Christendom. Without going into the disputed question of whether the Irish church was or was not independent of Rome, it is certain that Italy did not send out more apostles from the fifth to the ninth centuries than Ireland, and we find their names and achievements remembered through the Continent.

Of two names which Hallam thinks worth res-
cuing from the darkness of the dark ages one is
the Irish metaphysician, John Erigna. In a
recent communication to the " Association," we
had Bavarians acknowledging the Irish St. Kilian
as the apostle of their country.

Yet what beyond a catalogue of names and a
few marked events, do even the educated Irish
know of the heroic Pagans or the holy Christians
of old Ireland.   These men have left libraries of
biography, religion, philosophy, natural history,
topography, history, and romance. They *cannot
all be worthless;* yet, except the few volumes
given us by the Archæological Society, which of
their works have any of us read?

It is also certain that we possessed written
laws with extensive and minute comments and
reported decisions. These Brehon laws have been
foully misrepresented by Sir John Davies. Their
tenures were the Gavelkind once prevalent over
most of the world.   The land belonged to the
clan, and, on the death of a clansman his share
was re-apportioned according to the number and
wants of his family. The system of erics or fines
for offences has existed amongst every people
from the Hebrews downwards, nor can any one
knowing the multitude of crimes now punishable
by fines or damages, think the people of this empire justified in calling the ancient Irish barbarous, because they extended the system.   There
is in these laws, so far as they are known, minuteness and equity; and, what is a better test of
their goodness, we learn from Sir John Davies
himself, and from the still abler Baron Finglass,

that the people reverenced, obeyed, and clung to these laws, though to decide by or obey them was a high crime by England's code. Moreover, the Norman and Saxon settlers hastened to adopt these Irish laws, and used them more resolutely, if possible, than the Irish themselves.

Orderliness and hospitality were peculiarly cultivated. Public caravansaries were built for travellers in every district, and we have what would almost be legal evidence of the grant of vast tracts of land* for the supply of provisions for these houses of hospitality. The private hospitality of the chiefs was equally marked, nor was it quite rude. Ceremony was united with great freedom of intercourse ; age, and learning, and rank, and virtue were respected, and these men whose cookery was probably as coarse as that of Homer's heroes, had around their board harpers and bards who sang poetry as gallant and fiery, though not so grand as the Homeric ballad-singers, and flung off a music which Greece never rivalled.

Shall a people, pious, hospitable, and brave, faithful observers of family ties, cultivators of learning, music, and poetry, be called less than civilized, because mechanical arts were rude, and "comfort" despised by them ?

Scattered through the country in MS., are hundreds of books wherein the laws and achievements, the genealogies and possessions, the creeds, and manners and poetry of these our predecessors in Ireland are set down. Their music lives in the traditional airs of every valley.

Yet *mechanical civilization*, more cruel than

time, is trying to exterminate them, and, therefore, it becomes us all who do not wish to lose the heritage of centuries, nor to feel ourselves living among nameless ruins, when we might have an ancestral home—it becomes all who love learning, poetry, or music, or are curious of human progress, to aid in or originate a series of efforts to save all that remains of the past.

It becomes them to lose no opportunity of instilling into the minds of their neighbours, whether they be corporators or peasants, that it is a brutal, mean, and sacrilegious thing, to turn a castle, a church, a tomb, or a mound, into a quarry or a gravel pit, or to break the least morsel of sculpture, or to take any old coin or ornament they may find to a jeweller, so long as there is an Irish Academy in Dublin to pay for it or accept it.

Before the year is out we hope to see A Society for the Preservation of Irish Music established in Dublin, under the joint patronage of the leading men of all politics, with branches in the provincial towns for the collection and diffusion of Irish airs.

An effort—a great and decided one—must be made to have the Irish Academy so endowed out of the revenues of Ireland, that it may be A National School of Irish History and Literature and a Museum of Irish Antiquities, on the largest scale. In fact, the Academy should be a secular Irish College with professors of our old language, literature, history, antiquities, and topography; with suitable schools, lecture-rooms, and museums.

HISTORICAL MONUMENTS OF IRELAND.

WE were a little struck the other day in taking up a new book by Merimée to see after his name the title of "Inspector-General of the Historical Monuments of France." So, then, France, with the feeding, clothing, protecting, and humouring, of 36 million People to attend to, has leisure to employ a Board and Inspector, and money to pay them for looking after the Historical Monuments of France, lest the Bayeux tapestry which chronicles the conquest of England, or the Amphitheatre of Nimes, which marks the sojourn of the Romans, suffer any detriment.

And has Ireland no monuments of her history to guard, has she no tables of stone, no pictures, no temples, no weapons? Are there no Brehon's chairs on her hills to tell more clearly than Vallancey or Davies how justice was administered here? Do not you meet the Druid's altar, and the Guebre's tower in every barony almost, and the Ogham stones in many a sequestered spot, and shall we spend time and money to see, to guard, or to decipher Indian topes, and Tuscan graves, and Egyptian hieroglyphics, and shall every nation in Europe shelter and study the remains of what it once was, even as one guards the tomb of a parent, and shall Ireland let all go to ruin?

We have seen pigs housed in the piled friezes

of a broken church, cows stabled in the palaces of the Desmonds, and corn threshed on the floor of abbeys, and the sheep and the tearing wind tenant the corridors of Aileach.

Daily are more and more of our crosses broken, of our tombs effaced, of our abbeys shattered, of our castles torn down, of our cairns sacrilegiously pierced, of our urns broken up, and of our coins melted down. All classes, creeds, and politics are to blame in this. The peasant lugs down a pillar for his sty, the farmer for his gate, the priest for his chapel, the minister for his glebe. A mill-stream runs through Lord Moore's Castle, and the Commissioners of Galway have shaken, and threatened to remove, the Warden's house— that fine stone chronicle of Galway heroism.

How our children will despise us for all this! Why shall we seek for histories, why make museums, why study the manners of the dead, when we foully neglect or barbarously spoil their homes, their castles, their temples, their colleges, their courts, their graves? He who tramples on the past does not create for the future. The same ignorant and vagabond spirit which made him a destructive, prohibits him from creating for posterity.

Does not a man, by examining a few castles and arms, know more of the peaceful and warrior life of the dead nobles and gentry of our island than from a library of books; and yet a man is stamped as unlettered and rude if he does not know and value such knowledge. Ware's Antiquities, and Archdall, speak not half so clearly the taste, the habits, the every-day customs of the monks, as Adare Abbey, for the fine preservation of which we owe so much to Lord Dunraven.

The state of civilization among our Scótic or Milesian, or Norman, or Danish sires, is better seen from the Museum of the Irish Academy, and from a few raths, keeps, and old coast towns, than from all the prints and historical novels we have. An old castle in Kilkenny, a house in Galway give us a peep at the arts, the intercourse, the creed, the indoor, and some of the out-door ways of the gentry of the one, and of the merchants of the other, clearer than Scott could, were he to write, or Cattermole were he to paint for forty years.

We cannot expect Government to do anything so honourable and liberal as to imitate the example of France, and pay men to describe and save these remains of dead ages. But we do ask it of the Clergy, Protestant, Catholic, and Dissenting, if they would secure the character of men of education and taste—we call upon the gentry, if they have any pride of blood, and on the people if they reverence Old Ireland, to spare and guard every remnant of antiquity. We ask them to find other quarries than churches, abbeys, castles, and cairns—to bring rusted arms to a collector, and coins to a museum, and not to iron or gold smiths, and to take care that others do the like. We talk much of Old Ireland, and plunder and ruin all that remains of it—we neglect its language, fiddle with its ruins, and spoil its monuments.

IRISH ANTIQUITIES.

THERE is on the north (the left) bank of the Boyne, between Drogheda and Slane, a pile compared to which, in age, the Oldbridge obelisk is a thing of yesterday, and compared to which, in lasting interest, the Cathedrals of Dublin would be trivial. It is the Temple of Grange. History is too young to have noted its origin—Archæology knows not its time. It is a legacy from a forgotten ancestor, to prove that he, too, had art and religion. It may have marked the tomb of a hero who freed, or an invader who subdued—a Brian or a Strongbow. But whether or not a hero's or a saint's bones consecrated it at first, this is plain, it is a temple of nigh two thousand years, perfect as when the last Pagan sacrificed within it.

It is a thing to be proud of, as a proof of Ireland's antiquity, to be guarded as an illustration of her early creed and arts. It is one of a thousand muniments of our old nationality, which a national government would keep safe.

What, then, will be the reader's surprise and anger to hear that some people, having legal power or corrupt influence in Meath, are getting or have got *a presentment for a road to run right through the Temple of Grange !*

We do not know their names, nor, if the design be at once given up, as in deference to

public opinion it must finally be, shall we take
the trouble to find them out. But if they persist
in this brutal outrage against so precious a land-
mark of Irish history and civilization, then we
frankly say if the law will not reach them public
opinion shall, and they shall bitterly repent the
desecration. These men who design, and those
who consent to the act, may be Liberals or Tories, Protestants or Catholics, but beyond a doubt
they are tasteless blockheads—poor devils without
reverence or education—men who as Wordsworth
says—

> " Would peep and botanize
> Upon their mothers' graves."

·All over Europe the governments, the aristo-
cracies, and the people have been combining to
discover, gain, and guard every monument of
what their dead countrymen had done or been.
France has a permanent commission charged to
watch over her antiquities. She annually spends
more in publishing books, maps, and models, in
filling her museums and shielding her monuments
from the iron clutch of time, than all the roads
in Leinster cost. It is only on time she needs to
keep watch. A French peasant would blush to
meet his neighbour had he levelled a Gaulish
tomb, crammed the fair moulding of an abbey
into his wall, or sold to a crucible the coins
which tell that a Julius, a Charlemagne, or a
Philip Augustus swayed his native land. And
so it is everywhere. Republican Switzerland,
despotic Austria, Prussia, and Norway, Bavaria
and Greece, are all equally precious of everything that exhibits the architecture, sculpture,

rites, dress, or manners of their ancestors—nay, each little commune would guard with arms these local proofs that they were not men of yesterday. And why should not Ireland be as precious of its ruins, its manuscripts, its antique vases, coins, and ornaments, as these French and German men—nay as the English, for they, too, do not grudge princely grants to their museums, and restoration funds.

This island has been for centuries either in part or altogether a province. Now and then above the mist we see the wheel of Sarsfield's sword, the red battle-hand of O'Neil, and the points of O'Connor's spears; but 'tis a view through eight hundred years to recognise the Sunburst on a field of liberating victory. Reckoning back from Clontarf, our history grows ennobled (like that of a decayed house), and we see Lismore and Armagh centres of European learning; we see our missionaries seizing and taming the conquerors of Europe, and, farther still, rises the wizard pomp of Eman, and Tara— the palace of the Irish Pentarchy. And are we, the people to whom the English (whose fathers were painted savages, when Tyre and Sidon traded with this land) can address reproaches for our rudeness and irreverence? So it seems. The *Athenæum* says :—

" It is much to be regretted that the society lately established in England, having for its object the preservation of British antiquities, did not extend its design over those of the sister island, which are daily becoming fewer and fewer in number. That the gold ornaments which are so frequently found in various parts of Ireland should be melted down for the sake of the very pure

gold of which they are composed, is scarcely surprising;
but that carved stones and even immense druidical remains should be destroyed is, indeed, greatly to be
lamented. At one of the late meetings of the Royal
Irish Academy a communication was made of the intention of the proprietor of the estate at New Grange,
to destroy that most gigantic relic of druidical times,
which has justly been termed the Irish pyramid, merely
because its vast size ' cumbereth the ground.' At Mellifont a modern corn-mill of large size has been built out
of the stones of the beautiful monastic buildings, some
of which still adorn that charming spot. At Monaster-
boice, the churchyard of which contains one of the
finest of the round towers, are the ruins of two of the
little ancient stone Irish churches, and three most ela-
borately carved stone crosses, eighteen or twenty feet
high. The churchyard itself is overrun with weeds, the
sanctity of the place being its only safeguard. At Clonmacnoise, where, some forty years ago, several hundred
inscriptions in the ancient Irish character were to be seen
upon the gravestones, scarcely a dozen (and they the
least interesting) are now to be found—the large flat
stones on which they were carved forming excellent
slabs for doorways, the copings of walls, &c. ! It was
the discovery of some of these carved stones in such a
situation which had the effect of directing the attention
of Mr. Petre (then an artist in search of the picturesque, but now one of the most enlightened and conscientious of the Irish antiquaries) to the study of antiquities; and it is upon the careful series of drawings
made by him that future antiquarians must rely for very
much of ancient architectural detail now destroyed. As
to Glendalough, it is so much a holiday place for the
Dubliners that it is no wonder everything portable has
disappeared. Two or three of the seven churches are
levelled to the ground—all the characteristic carvings
described by Ledwich, and which were ' *quite unique in
Ireland,*' are gone. Some were removed and used as
key-stones for the arches of Derrybawn-bridge. Part of the
churchyard has been cleared of its gravestones, and forms
a famous place, where the villagers play at ball against
the old walls of the church. The little church, called

' St. Kevin's Kitchen, is given up to the sheep, and the font lies in one corner, and is used for the vilest purposes. The abbey church is choked up with trees and brambles, and being a little out of the way a very few of the carved stones still remain there, two of the most interesting of which I found used as coping-stones to the wall which surrounds it. The connexion between the ancient churches of Ireland and the north of England renders the preservation of the Irish antiquities especially interesting to the English antiquarian; and it is with the hope of drawing attention to the destruction of those ancient Irish monuments that I have written these few lines. The Irish themselves are, unfortunately, so engrossed with political and religious controversies, that it can scarcely be hoped that singlehanded they will be roused to the rescue even of these evidences of their former national greatness. Besides, a great obstacle exists against any interference with the religious antiquities of the country, from the strong feelings entertained by the people on the subject, although *practically*, as we have seen, of so little weight. Let us hope that the public attention directed to these objects will have a beneficial result and insure a greater share of ' justice to Ireland;' for will it be believed that the only establishment in Ireland for the propagation and diffusion of scientific and antiquarian knowledge—the Royal Irish Academy—receives annually the munificent sum of £300 from the government! And yet, notwithstanding this pittance, the members of that society have made a step in the right direction by the purchase of the late Dean of St. Patrick's Irish Archæological Collection, of which a fine series of drawings is now being made at the expense of the academy, and of which they would, doubtless, allow copies to be made, so as to obtain a return of a portion of the expense to which they are now subjected. Small, moreover, as the collection is, it forms a striking contrast with our own *National* Museum, which, rich in foreign antiquities, is almost without a single object of native archæological interest, if we except the series of English and Anglo-Saxon coins and MSS."

The Catholic clergy were long and naturally

the guardians of our antiquities, and many of
their archæological works testify their prodigious
learning. Of late, too, the honourable and wise
reverence brought back to England has reached
the Irish Protestant clergy, and they no longer
make antiquity a reproach, or make the maxims
of the iconoclast part of their creed.

Is it extravagant to speculate on the possibility
of the Episcopalian, Catholic, and Presbyterian
clergy joining in an Antiquarian Society to preserve our ecclesiastical remains—our churches,
our abbeys, our crosses, and our fathers' tombs,
from fellows like the Meath road-makers. It
would be a politic and a noble emulation of the
sects, restoring the temples wherein their sires
worshipped for their children to pray in. There's
hardly a barony wherein we could not find an
old parish or abbey church, capable of being restored to its former beauty and convenience at
a less expense than some beastly barn is run up,
as if to prove and confirm the fact that we have
little art, learning, or imagination.

Nor do we see why some of these hundreds of
half-spoiled buildings might not be used for civil
purposes—as alms-houses, schools, lecture-rooms,
town-halls. It would always add another grace
to an institution to have its home venerable with
age and restored to beauty. We have seen men
of all creeds join the Archæological Society to
preserve and revive our ancient literature. Why
may we not see, even without waiting for the aid
of an Irish Parliament, an Antiquarian Society,
equally embracing the chief civilians and divines,
and charging itself with the duties performed in

France by the Commission of Antiquities and Monuments?

The Irish antiquarians of the last century did much good. They called attention to the history and manners of our predecessors which we had forgotten. They gave a pedigree to nationhood, and created a faith that Ireland could and should be great again by magnifying what she had been. They excited the noblest passions—veneration, love of glory, beauty, and virtue. They awoke men's fancy by their gorgeous pictures of the past, and imagination strove to surpass them by its creations. They believed what they wrote, and thus their wildest stories sank into men's minds. To the exertions of Walker, O'Halloran, Vallancey, and a few other Irish academicians in the last century, we owe almost all the Irish knowledge possessed by our upper classes till very lately. It was small, but it was enough to give a dreamy renown to ancient Ireland; and if it did nothing else it smoothed the reception of Bunting's music, and identified Moore's poetry with his native country.

While, therefore, we at once concede that Vallancey was a bad scholar, O'Halloran a credulous historian, and Walker a shallow antiquarian, we claim for them gratitude and attachment, and protest, once for all, against the indiscriminate abuse of them now going in our educated circles.

But no one should lie down under the belief that they were the deep and exact men their cotemporaries thought them. They were not patient nor laborious. They were very graceful,

very fanciful, and often very wrong in their
statements and their guesses. How often they
avoided painful research by gay guessing we are
only now learning. O'Halloran and Keatinge
have told us bardic romances with the same tone
as true chronicles. Vallancey twisted language,
towers, and traditions into his wicker-work
theory of Pagan Ireland; and Walker built great
facts and great blunders, granite blocks and
rotten wood, into his antiquarian edifices. One
of the commonest errors, attributing immense
antiquity, oriental origin, and everything noble
in Ireland, to the Milesians, originated with these
men; or, rather, was transferred from the adula-
tory songs of clan-bards to grave stories. Now,
it is quite certain that several races flourished
here before the Milesians, and that every thing
Oriental, and much that was famous in Ireland,
belonged to some of these elder races, and not to
the Scoti or Milesians.

Premising this much of warning and defence
as to the men who first made anything of ancient
Ireland known to the mixed nation of modern
Ireland, we turn with pure pleasure to their
successors, the antiquarians and historians of our
own time.

We liked for awhile bounding from tussach to
tussach, or resting on a green esker in the domain
of the old academicians of Grattan's time; but
'tis pleasanter, after all, to tread the firm ground
of our own archæologists.

THE SEA KINGS.[*]

THESE Sea Kings were old friends and old foes of Ireland. History does not reach back to the age in which ships passed not between Ireland and Scandinavia. It seems highly probable that the Milesians themselves—that Scotic (or Scythian) race who gave our isle the name of Scotia Major—reached our shore, having sailed from the Baltic. They were old Sea Kings.

So were the Jutes, or Getæ, who came under Hengist and Horsa to England in the fifth century, and received the isle of Thanet as a reward for repelling the Irish invaders; and, not content with this pay, used their saxes (or short swords,) from whence we name them Saxons, till all the east of England obeyed them. So, too, were the Danes, who conquered that same England over again in the tenth century. So were the Black and White Strangers, who held our coast and ravaged our inland till Brien of Thomond trampled their raven at Clontarf on the 23d of April, 1014. And the Normans themselves, too, were of that self-same blood.

Mr. Laing has given us fresh materials for judging the race so related to Ireland. He has

[*] The Hemskringla, or Chronicle of the Kings of Norway, translated from the Icelandic of Snorro Sturleson, with a preliminary dissertation by Samuel Laing, Esq. 3 vols.

translated the greatest of their histories, and prefaced it by an account of the creed, literature,
and social condition of the Scandinavians.

There are strong reasons for believing that
these people came from the east, through Mus-
covy, and preferring the fish-filled bays and
game-filled hills of Norway and Sweden to the
flat plains of Germany, settled far north. Such
is the tradition of the country and the expressed
opinion of all their writers. The analogy of their
language to the Sanscrit, their polygamy and
their use of horse-flesh, all tend to prove that
they were once an equestrian tribe in Upper
Asia.

However this may be, we find them, from
remote times, living in the great Peninsula of the
North. Their manners were simple and hardy,
and their creed natural. The Cimbri, or Kymry,
whom Marius encountered, and the Milesians,
both apparently from Scandia, showed equal
valour, though not with the same fortune.

Their paganism was grand, though dark.
Idolaters they were, but idolatry is but an out-
ward sign. The people who bow to a stone have
got a notion of a god beyond it. That this
northern paganism originated in the natural
custom of all people to express their belief in
some soul mightier and better than their soul—
some ruler of the storm and the sun—we may
agree with Mr. Laing. But surely he is wrong
in jumping from this to a denial of Hero-worship.
Nothing seems more likely, nothing in mythology
is better proved, than that this feeling took the
shape of reverence for the soul of some dead chief

who had manifested superior might. Time would
obscure his history and glorify his attributes till
he became a demi-god.

The pagan gods rarely seem to be absolute
deities. Behind the greatest in renown of these
hero-gods lurks some Fate or Wisdom whose
creature he is.

The materials for the mythology of the Scandians are, according to Mr. Laing, very small.
The principal work is the older Edda, composed
by Sœmund. Of this there are only three fragments :—

" The one is called the ' Voluspa,' or the Prophecy of
Vola. In the Scotch words ' spæ-wife,' and in the English word ' spy,' we retain words derived from the same
root, and with the same meaning, as the word ' spa' of
the Voluspa. The second fragment is called ' Havamal,'
or the High Discourse ; the third is the Magic, or Song
of Odin. The Voluspa gives an account by the pro-
phetess of the actions and operations of the gods ; a description of chaos ; of the formation of the world ; of
giants, men, dwarfs ; of a final conflagration and disso-
lution of all things ; and of the future happiness of the
good, and punishment of the wicked. The Havamal is
a collection of moral and economical precepts. The
song of Odin is a collection of stanzas in celebration of
his magic powers. The younger Edda, composed 120
years after the older, by Snorro Sturleson, is a commentary upon the Voluspa ; illustrating it in a dialogue between Gylfe, the supposed contemporary of Odin, under
the assumed name of Gangir, and three divinities—Har
(the High), Jafnhar (equal to the High), and Triddi
(the Third)—at Asgard (the abode of the gods, or the
original Asiatic seat of Odin) to which Gylfe had gone
to ascertain the cause of the superiority of the Asiatics.
Both the Eddas appear to have been composed as hand-
books to assist in understanding the names of the gods,
and the allusions to them in the poetry of the Scalds ;

not to illustrate the doctrine of the religion of Odin. The absurd and the rational are consequently mingled. Many sublime conceptions, and many apparently borrowed by Sæmund and Snorro from Christianity—as for instance the Trinity with which Gangir converses—are mixed with fictions almost as puerile as those of the classical mythology. The genius of Snorro Sturleson shines even in these fables. In the grave humour with which the most extravagantly gigantic feats of Thor and Utgaard are related and explained, Swift himself is not more happy; and one would almost believe that Swift had the adventures of Thor and the giant Utgaard Loke before him when he wrote of Brobdignac. The practical forms or modes of worship in the religion of Odin are not to be discovered from the Eddas, nor from the sagas which the two Eddas were intended to illustrate. It is probable that much has been altered to suit the ideas of the age in which they were committed to writing, and of the scribes who compiled them. Christianity in Scandinavia seems, in the 11th century, to have consisted merely in the ceremony of baptism, without any instruction in its doctrines."

The priesthood consisted of the descendants of the twelve diars or goddars, who accompanied Odin from Asia; but they were judges as well as priests. Their temples were few, small, and rude. Their chief religious festivals were three in number. The first possesses a peculiar interest for us. It was called Yule from one of Odin's names, though held in honour of Thor, the supreme god of the Scandians. Occurring in mid-winter it became mixed with the Christmas festival, and gave its name thereto. The other festivals were in honour of the goddess Friggia (pronounced Freya,) and of Odin or Woden, the demigod or prophet. From these deities our Wednesday, Thursday, and Friday take their names. The Valhalla, or heaven of these Pagans, reserved for warriors, free from women, and abounding in beer and metheglin, is sufficiently known.

Centuries after Christianity had been received by their neighbours these Pagans held to Odinism, and Pagans they were when, in the 9th century, their great colonies went out.

The spread of the Northmen at that time came to pass in this way. Along the broken coast of the Northern peninsula reigned a crowd of independant chiefs, who lived partly on fishing and hunting, but much more by piracy.

In the beginning of the 9th century their expeditions became formidable. The north, and finally the whole of England, was overrun, and it took the genius of Alfred, Edmund, and Athelstane to deliver it even for a time. Ireland suffered hardly less. Some of these rovers even penetrated the Mediterranean, and Charlemagne is said to have wept at the sight of those galleys laden with wrath. The achievements of one of them, Regner Lodbrog, have been as nobly described in an Icelandic poem as anything Homer wrote of the Sea Kings of Greece who warred against Troy.

So powerful abroad, they paid slight allegiance to the King of Norway. At length, about 870, King Harald Haarfager (or the Fair Haired) resolved to stop their iniquities, or at least to free his own dominions from them. In a series of wars he subdued these sea kings, and forbade piracy on his coast or isles. Thus debarred from their old life at home they went out in still greater colonies than before.

One of these colonies was led by Rolf, who was surnamed Gan'gr, or the Walker, as from his great stature he could get no horse to carry him, and walked with his followers. Sailing south they entered the Seine, took Rouen, besieged Paris, and finally extorted from Charles the Bald that tract to which they gave the name of Normandy. But these events took many years.

Other bands came to the aid of their friends in England, Ireland, and the Scotch Isles, while a large and illustrious colony went to Iceland.

In that land of snow they found fish and game. They abandoned piracy and became merchants, trading through the whole west of Europe. Nor did they remain at this side of the Atlantic. Sailing north-west, they occupied Greenland, and visited some more southerly part of America, which they called Vinland.

But still a higher honor belongs to the Icelanders. They were the most famous Scalds or Bards who spoke the Norse tongue. Amongst the earliest institutions of the North were the laws of Gravelkind, and a strict entail of lands. Lands could not be sold or devised, the next of blood took them in equal shares. It was, therefore, of great value to preserve a knowledge of relationship, and this office fell to the literary class or Scalds. There was no law limiting the bardic office to natives of Iceland, yet, in fact, their superior skill won such an eminence for them that an Icelandic scald was as needed in every Norse settlement, from Rouen to Drontheim, as an Irish saint was in every part of Christian Europe.

Mr. Laing prints a list of about 200 Norse histories, romances, &c. Originally, it seems their sagas were oral, and it was not till the 12th century that any progress was made in transferring them to writing. The reader of Mr. Laing's details will be struck by many facts like those used in the controversy as to whether the Iliad was a collection of ballads, or an originally single work.

It seems that there is no manuscript saga older than the end of the 14th century in existence.

With his usual heartiness, Mr. Laing defends the Norsemen through thick and thin. In his opinion the best parts of the English constitution are due to them. He describes the Saxons as cowardly and slavish devotees when these gallant and free Pagans came in and renewed their vigour. The elective judges, and officers, and juries he traces to the Danes; and in the *Things* or popular assemblies of these Northmen he finds the origin of English parliaments. Nor would he have us judge them by the report of trembling monks who wrote Latin invectives and invocations against them, while through the window of their transcribing room they could see the homestead blaze and the Raven soar.

In this part of his case he seems rather successful. The writings of the Anglo-Saxons were a few dry chronicles in Latin; while the Northmen had an endless mass of histories and popular ballads. But even here he is in excess. He seems forgetful of the Saxon ballads of Brunanburgh, of Beowulf, and many others. If we can trust our recollections, or Thierry's quotations, there are many touching and lofty passages even in those old Latin Chronicles.

His proof of the knowledge of the useful arts possessed by the Northmen is very ingenious. It rests on the account of their shipping. One ship is described as being as large as a 40-gun frigate. To make vessels so large and efficient as even their smaller ships required skill in working timber, in raising, smelting, and preparing iron, masts, sails, ropes, and anchors for *such* ships; and the necessity of coopering water vessels, and salting meat for long voyages, imply the existence of several arts.

The amount of knowledge of countries and men, sure to be acquired in their giant piracies, should also be remembered.

He is very exclusive in his advocacy. So far from sanctioning the claim of the Teutonic race to *general* superiority over the Celts, he treats it as "the echo of the bray" first heard in the Ossianic controversy.

"The black hair, dark eye, and dusky skin of the small-sized Celt, were considered by those philosophers to indicate an habitation for souls less gifted than those which usually dwell under the yellow hair, blue eye, and fair skin of the bulky Goth. This conceit has been revived of late in Germany, and in America; and people talk of the superiority of the Gothic, Germanic, or Anglo-Saxon race, as if no such people had ever existed as the Romans, the Spaniards, the French—no such men as Cæsar, Buonaparte, Cicero, Montesquieu, Cervantes, Ariosto, Raphael, Michael Angelo. If the superiority they claim were true, it would be found not to belong at all to that branch of the one great northern race which is called Teutonic, Gothic, Germanic, or Anglo-Saxon— for that branch in England was, previous to the settle-

ments of the Danes or Northmen in the 10th or 11th
centuries, and is at this day throughout all Germany,
morally and socially degenerate, and all distinct and dis-
tinguishing spirit or nationality in it dead ; but to the
small cognate branch of the Northmen or Danes, who,
between the 9th and 12th centuries brought their Paganism, energy, and social institutions, to bear against, con-
quer, mingle with, and invigorate the priest-ridden, in-
ert, descendants of the old Anglo-Saxon race."

Mr. Laing's translation comes fresh and racy.
He seems to like the ship-building, and roving,
and fighting. Cast a few centuries earlier, he
had made a famous Viking. Notwithstanding
his Benthamite notions, his heart is strong and
natural, and he relishes vigorous humanity wherever it is found.

THE ROUND TOWERS OF IRELAND.

Accustomed from boyhood to regard these towers
as revelations of a gorgeous, but otherwise un-
defined antiquity—dazzled by oriental analogies—
finding a refuge in their primeval greatness from
the meanness or the misfortunes of our middle
ages, we clung to the belief of their Pagan origin.

In fancy, we had seen the white-robed Druid
tend the holy fire in their lower chambers—had
measured with the Tyrian-taught astronomer the
length of their shadows—and had almost knelt
to the elemental worship with nobles whose robes
had the dye of the Levant, and sailors whose

* The Transactions of the Royal Irish Academy. Vol.
XX. Dublin : Hodges and Smith, Grafton-street.

cheeks were brown with an Egyptian sun, and
soldiers whose bronze arms clashed as the trum-
pets from the tower-top said, that the sun had
risen. What wonder that we resented the attempt
to cure us of so sweet a frenzy ?

We plead guilty to having opened Mr. Petrie's
work strongly bigoted against his conclusion.

On the other hand, we could not forget the
authority of the book. Its author, we knew,
was familiar beyond almost any other with the
country—had not left one glen unsearched, not
one island untrod; had brought with him the
information of a life of antiquarian study, a
graceful and exact pencil, and feelings equally
national and lofty. We knew, also, that he had
the aid of the best Celtic scholars alive in the
progress of his work. The long time taken in
its preparation ensured maturity ; and the honest
men who had criticised it, and the adventurers
who had stolen from it enough to make false re-
putations, equally testified to its merits.

Yet, we repeat, we jealously watched for flaws
in Mr. Petrie's reasoning ; exulted, as he set
down the extracts from his opponents, in the
hope that he would fail in answering them, and
at last surrendered with a sullen despair.

Looking now more calmly at the discussion,
we are grateful to Mr. Petrie for having driven
away an idle fancy. In its stead he has given us
new and unlooked-for trophies, and more solid
information on Irish antiquities than any of his
predecessors. We may be well content to hand
over the Round Towers to Christians of the sixth
or the tenth century when we find that these

Christians were really eminent in knowledge as well as piety, had arched churches by the side of these *campanilia*, gave an alphabet to the Saxons, and hospitality and learning to the students of all western Europe—and the more readily, as we get in exchange *proofs* of a Pagan race having a Pelasgic architecture, and the arms and ornaments of a powerful and cultivated people.

The volume before us contains two parts of Mr. Petrie's essay. The first part is an examination of the false theories of the origin of these towers. The second is an account not only of what he thinks their real origin, but of every kind of early ecclesiastical structure in Ireland. The third part will contain a historical and descriptive account of every ecclesiastical building in Ireland of a date prior to the Anglo-Norman invasion of which remains now exist. The work is crowded with illustrations drawn with wonderful accuracy, and engraved in a style which proves that Mr. O'Hanlon, the engraver, has become so proficient as hardly to have a superior in wood-cutting.

We shall for the present limit ourselves to the first part of the work on the

" ERRONEOUS THEORIES WITH RESPECT TO THE ORIGIN AND USES OF THE ROUND TOWERS.

The first refutation is of the

" THEORY OF THE DANISH ORIGIN OF THE TOWERS."

John Lynch, in his *Cambrensis Eversus*, says

that the Danes are reported (*dicuntur*) to have
first erected the Round Towers as *watch*-towers,
but that the Christian Irish changed them into
clock or bell-towers. Peter Walsh repeated and
exaggerated the statement; and Ledwich, the
West British antiquary of last century, combined it with lies enough to settle his character,
though not that of the Towers. The only person, at once explicit and honest, who supported
this Danish theory was Dr. Molyneux. His arguments are, that all stone buildings, and indeed
all evidences of mechanical civilization, in Ireland were Danish; that some traditions attributed the Round Towers to them; that they had
fit models in the monuments of their own country; and that the word by which he says, the
native Irish call them, viz., "Clogachd," comes
from the Teutonic root, clugga, a bell. These
arguments are easily answered.

The Danes, so far from introducing stone
architecture, found it flourishing in Ireland, and
burned and ruined our finest buildings, and destroyed mechanical and every kind of civilization
wherever their ravages extended—doing thus in
Ireland precisely as they did in France and
England, as all annals (their own included)
testify. Tradition does not describe the towers
as Danish watch-towers, but as Christian belfries. The upright stones and the little barrows,
not twelve feet high, of Denmark, could neither
give models nor skill to the Danes. They had
much ampler possession of England and Scotland, and permanent possession of Normandy,
but never a Round Tower did they erect there;

and, finally, the native Irish name for a Round Tower is *cloic-theach*, from *teach*, a house, and *cloc*, the Irish word used for a bell in Irish works before " the Germans or Saxons had churches or bells," and before the Danes had ever sent a war-ship into our seas.

We pass readily from this ridiculous hypothesis with the remark, that the gossip which attributes to the Danes our lofty monumental pyramids and cairns, our Druid altars, our dry stone caisils or keeps, and our raths or fortified enclosures for the homes or cattle of our chiefs, is equally and utterly unfounded ; and is partly to be accounted for from the name of power and terror which these barbarians left behind, and partly from ignorant persons confounding them with the most illustrious and civilized of the Irish races—the Danaans.

THEORY OF THE EASTERN ORIGIN OF THE ROUND TOWERS.

Among the middle and upper classes in Ireland the Round Towers are regarded as one of the results of an intimate connexion between Ireland and the East, and are spoken of as either 1, Fire-Temples ; 2, Stations from whence Druid festivals were announced ; 3, Sun dials (gnomons) and astronomical observatories ; 4, Buddhist or Phallic temples, or two or more of these uses are attributed to them at the same time.

Mr. Petrie states that the theory of the Phœnician or Indo-Scythic origin of these towers was stated for the first time so recently as 1772 by General Vallancey, in his "Essay on the Antiquity

of the Irish Language," and was re-asserted by
him in many different and contradictory forms
in his " Collectanea de Rebus Hibernicis," published at intervals in the following years.

It may be well to premise who

GENERAL CHARLES VALLANCEY

was. His family were from Berry in France;
their name Le Brun, called de Valencia, from
their estate of that name. General Vallancey was
born in Flanders, but was educated at Eton College. When a Captain in the 12th Royal In-
fantry he was attached to the engineer department in Ireland, published a book on Field Engineering in 1756, and commenced a survey of
Ireland. During this he picked up something of
the Irish language, and is said to have studied
it under Morris O'Gorman, clerk of Mary's-lane
chapel. He died in his house, Lower Mount-
street, 18th August, 1812, aged 82 years.

His " Collectanea" and his discourses in the
Royal Irish Academy, of which he was an original member, spread far and wide his oriental
theories. He was an amiable and plausible man,
but of little learning, little industry, great bold-
ness, and no scruples; and while he certainly
stimulated men's feelings towards Irish antiquities, he has left us a re-producing swarm of falsehood, of which Mr. Petrie has happily begun
the destruction. Perhaps nothing gave Vallancey's follies more popularity than the opposition
of the Rev. Edward Ledwich, whose " Antiquities of Ireland" is a mass of falsehoods, disparaging to the people and the country.

FIRE TEMPLES.

Vallancey's first analogy is plausible. The Irish Druids honoured the elements and kept up sacred fires, and at a particular day in the year all the fires in the kingdom were put out, and had to be re-lighted from the Arch-Druid's fire. A similar creed and custom existed among the Parsees or Guebres of Persia, and he takes the resemblance to prove connexion and identity of creed and civilization. From this he immediately concludes the Round Towers to be Fire Temples. Now, there is no evidence that the Irish Pagans had sacred fires, except in open spaces (on the hill tops), and, therefore, none of course that they had them in towers round or square ; but Vallancey falls back on the *alleged existence of Round Towers in the East similar to ours, and on etymology.*

Here is a specimen of his etymologies. The Hebrew word *gadul* signifies *great,* and thence a tower ; the Irish name for a round tower, *cloghad,* is from this *gadul* or *gad* and *clogh,* a *stone :* and the Druids called every place of worship *cloghad.* To which it is answered—*gadul* is not *gad*—*clogh,* a *stone,* is not *cloch,* a *bell*— the Irish word for a Round Tower is *cloch-thach,* or bell-house, and there is no proof that the Druids called *any* place of worship cloghad.

Vallancey's guesses are numerous, and nearly all childish, and we shall quote some finishing specimens, with Mr. Petrie's answers :—

" This is another characteristic example of Vallancey's mode of quoting authorities ; he first makes O'Brien say,

that *Cuilceach* becomes corruptly *Claiceach*, and then that
the word *seems* to be corrupted *Clog-theach*. But O'Brien
does not say that *Cuilceach* is corruptly *Claiceach*, nor
has he the word *Culkak* or *Claiceach* in his book; neither does he say that *Cuilceach seems* to be a corruption
of *Clog-theach*, but states positively that it is so. The
following are the passages which Vallancey has so mis-
quoted and garbled :—

'CUILCEACH, a steeple, cuilceach, Cluan-umba,
Cloyne steeple—This word *is* a corruption of Clog-
theach.

'CLOIG-THEACH, a steeple, a belfry; *corruptè* Cuilg-
theach.'

" Our author next tells us that another name for the
Round Towers is *Sibheit, Sithbheit*, and *Sithbhein*, and
for this he refers us to O'Brien's and Shaw's Lexicons ;
but this quotation is equally false with those I have already exposed, for the words *Sibheit* and *Sithbheit* are
not to be found in either of the works referred to. The
word *Sithbhe* is, indeed, given in both Lexicons, but
explained, a city, not a round tower. The word *Sithbhein* is also given in both, but explained a fort, a tur-
ret, and the real meaning of the word as still understood
in many parts of Ireland, is a fairy hill, or hill of the
fairies, and is applied to a green round hill crowned by
a small sepulchral mound.

" He next tells us that *Caiceach*, the last name he finds
for the Round Towers, is supposed by the Glossarists to
be compounded of *cai*, a house, and *teach* a house, an
explanation, which, he playfully adds, is tautology with
a witness. But where did he find authority for the word
Caiceach ? I answer, nowhere ; and the tautology he
speaks of was either a creation or a blunder of his own.
It is evident to me that the Glossarist to whom he refers
is no other than his favourite Cormac ; but the latter
makes no such blunder, as will appear from the passage
which our author obviously refers to :—

'*Cai i. teach unde dicitur ceard cha i. teach cearda ;
creas cha i. teach cumang.*'

'Cai, *i. e.* a house; *unde dicitur ceard-cha, i. e.* the
house of the artificer ; *creas-cha, i. e.* a narrow
house.'"

The reader has probably now had enough of
Vallancey's etymology, but it is right to add
that Mr. Petrie goes through every hint of such
proof given by the General, and disposes of them
with greater facility.

The next person disposed of is Mr. Beauford,
who derives the name of our Round Towers from
Tlacht, earth—asserts that the foundations of
temples for Vestal fire exist in Rath-na-Emhain,
and other places (poor devil!)—that the Persian
Magi overran the world in the time of the great
Constantine, introducing Round Towers in place
of the Vestal mounds into Ireland, combining
their fire-worship with our Druidism—and that
the present Towers were built in imitation of
these Magian Towers. This is all, as Mr. Petrie
says, pure fallacy, without a particle of authority; but we should think "*twelfth*" is a mis-
print for "*seventh*" in the early part of Beauford's passage, and, therefore, that the last clause
of Mr. Petrie's censure is undeserved.

This Beauford is not to be confounded with
Miss Beaufort. She, too, paganizes the Towers
by aggravating some mis-statements of Mason's
Parochial Survey; but her errors are not worth
notice, except the assertion that the Psalters of
Tara and Cashel allege that the Towers were for
keeping the sacred fire. These Psalters are believed to have perished, and any mention of
sacred fires in the glossary of Cormac M'Culle-
nan, the supposed compiler of the Psalter of
Cashel, is adverse to their being in Towers. He
says—

"*Belltane*, i. e. *bil tene*, i. e. *tene bil*, i. e. the goodly-fire, *i. e.* two goodly fires, which the Druids were used to make, with great incantations on them, and they used to bring the cattle between them against the diseases of each year."

Another MS. says—

"*Beltaine*, i. e. *Bel-dine : Bel* was the name of an idol; it was on it (*i. e.* the festival) that a couple of the young of every cattle were exhibited as in the possession of *Bèl; unde Beltine.* Or, *Beltine*, i. e. *Bil-tine*, *i. e.* the goodly fire, *i. e.* two goodly fires, which the Druids were used to make with great incantations, and they were used to drive the cattle between them against the diseases of each year."

Mr. Petrie continues—

"It may be remarked, that remnants of this ancient custom, in perhaps a modified form, still exist in the May fires lighted in the streets and suburbs of Dublin, and also in the fires lighted on St. John's Eve, in all other parts of Ireland. The *Tinne Eigen* of the Highlands, of which Dr. Martin gives the following account, is probably a remnant of it also, but there is no instance of such fires being lighted in towers or houses of any description :—

'The Inhabitants here (Isle of Skye) did also make use of a Fire call'd *Tin-Egin* (*i. e.*) a forced Fire, or Fire of necessity, which they used as an Antidote against the *Plague* or *Murrain* in Cattle ; and it was performed thus :—All the Fires in the Parish were extinguish'd, and eighty one marry'd Men, being thought the necessary number for effecting this Design, took two great Planks of Wood, and nine of 'em were employ'd by turns, who by their repeated Efforts rubb'd one of the Planks against the other until the Heat thereof produced Fire ; and from this forc'd Fire each Family is supplied with new Fire, which is no sooner kindled, than a Pot full of water is quickly set on it, and afterwards sprinkled upon the People infected with the Plague, or upon cattle that have the Murrain. And this, they all say, they find successful by Experience.'—*Description of the Western Islands of Scotland*—(second edition,) p. 113.

"As authority for Miss Beaufort's second assertion, relative to the Tower of Thlachtga, &c., we are referred
to the *Psalter of Tara*, by Comerford, (p. 41,) cited in
the *Parochial Survey* (vol. iii. p. 320) ; and certainly in
the latter work we do find a passage in nearly the same
words which Miss Beaufort uses. But if the lady had
herself referred to Comerford's little work, she would
have discovered that the author of the article in the *Parochial Survey* had in reality no authority for his assertions, and had attempted a gross imposition on the credulity of his readers."

Mr. D'Alton relies much on a passage in
Cambrensis, wherein he says that the fishermen
on Lough Neagh (a lake certainly formed by an
inundation in the first century—A. D. 62) point
to such towers under the lake ; but this only
shows they were considered old in Cambrensis'
time (King John's) for Chambrensis calls them
turres ecclesiasticas (a Christian appellation) ; and
the fishermen of every lake have such idle traditions from the tall objects they are familiar
with ; and the steeples of Antrim, &c., were
handy to the Loch N-Eathach men.

One of the authorities quoted by all the Pa-
ganists is from the "Ulster Annals" at the year
448 ; it is, "Ingenti terremotu per loca varia
imminente plurime urbes auguste muri recenti
adhuc re-edificatione constructi, cum LVII. tur-
ribus corruerant." This was made to mean that
part of the wall of Armagh, with fifty-seven
Round Towers, fell in an earthquake in 448,
whereas the passage turns out to be a quotation
from "Marcellinus" of the fall of part of the defences of Constantinople—" Urbis Augustæ !"

References to Towers in Irish annals are quoted

by Mr. D'Alton ; but they turn out to be written
about the Cyclopean Forts, or low stone raths,
such as we find at Aileach, &c.

CELESTIAL INDEXES.

Dr. Charles O'Connor, of Stowe, is the chief
supporter of the astronomical theory. One of his
arguments is founded on the mistaken reading of
the word "*turaghun*" (which he derives from *tur*
a tower, and *aghan*, or *adhan*, the kindling of
flame), instead of "*truaghan*," an ascetic. The
only other authority of his which we have not
noticed is the passage in the "Ulster Annals,"
at the year 995, in which it is said that certain
Fidhnemead were burnt by lightning at Armagh.
He translates the word celestial indexes, and
paraphrases it Round Towers, and all because
fiadh means witness, and *neimhedh* heavenly or
sacred, the real meaning being holy wood, or
wood of the sanctuary, from *fidh* a wood, and
neimhedh holy, as is proved by a pile of *exact*
authorities.

Dr. Lanigan, in his ecclesiastical history, and
Moore, in his general history, repeat the arguments which we have mentioned. They also
bring objections against the alleged Christian
origin, which we hold over ; but it is plain that
nothing prevailed more with them than the
alleged resemblance of these towers to certain
oriental buildings. Assuredly, if there were a
close likeness between the Irish Round Towers
and oriental fire temples of proved antiquity, it
would be an argument for identity of use ; and
though direct testimony from our annals would

E

come in and show that the present Towers were
built as Christian belfries from the sixth to the
tenth centuries, the resemblance would at least
indicate that the belfries had been built after
the model of Pagan fire towers previously existing here. But "rotundos of above thirty feet in
diameter" in Persia, Turkish minarets of the
tenth or fourteenth centuries, and undated tur-
rets in India, which Lord Valentia thought like
our Round Towers, give no *such* resemblance.
We shall look anxiously for exact measurements
and dates of oriental buildings resembling Round
Towers, and weigh the evidence which may be
offered to show that there were any Pagan models
for the latter in Ireland or in Asia.

Mr. Windele, of Cork, besides using all the
previously-mentioned arguments for the Paganism of these Towers, finds another in the supposed resemblance to

THE NURAGGIS OF SARDINIA,

which are tombs or temples formed in that island,
and attributed to the Phœnicians. But, alas!
for the theory—they have turned out to be "as
broad as they're long." A square building, 57
feet in each side, with bee-hive towers at each
angle, and a centre bee-hive tower reaching to
45 or 65 feet high, with stone stairs, is sadly unlike a round tower!

The most recent theory is, that the Round
Towers are

HERO-MONUMENTS.

Mr. Windele and the South Munster Antiquarian Society started this, Sir William Betham sanctioned it, and several rash gentlemen dug under Towers to prove it. At Cashel, Kinsale, &c., they satisfied themselves that there were no sepulchres or bones ever under the Towers, but in some other places they took the rubbish bones casually thrown into the Towers, and in two cases the chance underlying of ancient burying-grounds, as proofs of this notion. But Mr. Petrie settles for this idea by showing that there is no such use of the Round Towers mentioned in our annals, and also by the following most interesting account of the cemeteries and monuments of all the races of Pagan Irish:—

HISTORY OF THE CEMETERIES.

" A great king of great judgments assumed the sovereignty of Erin, *i. e.* Cormac, son of Art, son of Conn of the Hundred Battles. Erin was prosperous in his time, because just judgments were distributed throughout it by him; so that no one durst attempt to wound a man in Erin during the short jubilee of seven years; for Cormac had the faith of the one true God, according to the law; for he said that he would not adore stones, or trees, but that he would adore 'Him who had made them, and who had power over all the elements, *i. e.* the one powerful God who created the elements; in Him he would believe. And he was the third person who had believed, in Erin, before the arrival of St. Patrick. Conchobor Mac Nessa, to whom Altus had told concerning the crucifixion of Christ *was the first;* Morann, the son of Cairbre Cinncait (who was surnamed Mac Main) was the second person; and Cormac was the third; and it is probable that others followed on their track in this belief.

" Where Cormac held his court was at Tara, in imitation of the kings who preceded him, until his eye was destroyed by Engus Gaibhuaiphnech, the son of Eoch-

aidh Finn Fuathairt : but afterwards he resided at Acaill
(the hill on which Scrin Colaim Cille is at this day,) and
at Cenannas (Kells,) and at the house of Cletech ; for it
was not lawful that a king with a *personal* blemish should
reside at Tara.   In the second year after the injuring of
his eye he came by his death at the house of Cletech,
the bone of a salmon having stuck in his throat.   And
he (Cormac) told his people not to bury him at Brugh
(because it was a cemetery of Idolaters,) for he did not
worship the same God as any of those interred at Brugh ;
but to bury him at Ros na righ, with his face to the east.
He afterwards died, and his servants of trust held a
council, and came to the resolution of burying him at
Brugh, the place where the kings of Tara, his predecessors, were *buried*.   The body of the king was afterwards thrice raised to be carried to Brugh, but the Boyne
swelled up thrice, so as that they could not come ; so that
they observed that it was ' violating the judgment of a
prince' to break through this Testament of the king,
and they afterwards dug his grave at Ros na righ, as he
himself had ordered.

"These were the chief cemeteries of Erin before the
Faith (*i. e.* before the introduction of Christianity,) viz.
Cruachu, Brugh, Tailltin, Luachair, Ailbe, Oenach
Ailbe, Oenach Culi, Oenach Colmain, Temhair Erann.

"Oenach Cruachan, in the first place, it was there the
race of Heremon, *i. e.* the kings of Tara, were used to
bury until the time of Cremhthann, the son of Lughaidh
Riabh-n-derg, (who was the first king of them that was
interred at Brugh), viz., Cobhlhach Coelbregh, and
Labhraidh Loingsech, and Eocho Fedhlech with his
three sons (*i. e.* the three Fidhemhna, *i. e.* Bres, Nar,
and Lothor), and Eocho Airemh, Lughaidh Riabh-n-
derg, the six daughters of Eocho Fedhlech (*i. e.* Medhbh,
and Clothru, Muresc, and Drebriu, Mugain, and Ele),
and Adill Mac Mada with his seven brothers (*i. e.* Cet,
Anlon, Doche, '*et ceteri*), and all the kings *down* to
Cremhthann (these were all buried at Cruachan).   Why
was it not at Brugh that the kings (of the race of Cobhthach down to Crimhthann) were interred?   Not difficult ; because the two provinces, which the race of
Heremon possessed were the province of Gailian (*i. e.*

the province of Leinster), and the province of Olnec-
macht (*i. e.* the province of Connaught). In the first
place the province of Gailian was occupied by the race
of Labhraidh Loingsech, and the province of Connaught
was the peculiar inheritance of the race of Cobhtach
Coelbregh; wherefore it (*i. e.* the province of Connaught) was given to Medhbh before every other province. (The reason that the government of this land
was given to Medhbh is, because there was none of the
race of Eochaidh fit to receive it but herself, for Lughaidh was not fit for action at the time.) And whenever, therefore, the monarchy of Erin was enjoyed by
any of the descendants of Cobhthach Coelbregh, the
province of Connaught was his *ruidles* (*i. e.* his native
principality). And for this reason they were interred at
Oenach na Cruachna. But they were interred at Brugh
from the time of Crimhthann (Niadh-nar) to the time of
Loeghaire, 'the son of Niall, except three persons,
namely, Art, the son of Conn, and Cormac, the son of
Art, and Niall of the Nine Hostages.

"We have already mentioned the cause for which Cormac was not interred there. The reason why Art was
not interred there is, because he 'believed,' the day
before the battle of Muccramma was fought, and he
predicted the Faith, (*i. e.*, that Christianity would prevail in Erin,) and he said that his own grave would be
at Dumha Dergluachra, where Treoit [Trevet] is at this
day, as he mentioned in a poem which he composed—
viz., *Cain do denna den*, (*i. e.*, a poem which Art composed, the beginning of which is *Cain do denna den*,
&c.) When his (Art's) body was afterwards carried
eastwards to Dumha Dergluachra, if all the men of
Erin were drawing it thence, they could not, so that he
was interred in that place, because there was a Catholic church to be afterwards at the place where he was
interred (*i. e.*, Treoit *hodie*) because the truth and the
Faith had been revealed to him through his regal
righteousness.

"Where Niall was interred was at Ochain, whence the
hill was called Ochain, *i. e. Och Caine*, *i. e.* from the
sighing and lamentation which the men of Erin made in
lamenting Niall.

"Conaire More was interred at Magh Feci in Bregia (*i..e.* at Fert Conaire); however some say that it was Conaire Carpraige was interred there, and not Conaire Mor, and that Conaire Mor was the third king who was interred at Tara, viz. Conaire, Loeghaira, and • •

"At Tailltin the kings of Ulster were used to bury, viz. Ollamh Fodhla, with his descendants down to Conchobhar, who wished that he should be carried to a place between Slea and the sea, with his face to the east, on account of the Faith which he had embraced.

"The nobles of the Tua ha De Danann were used to bury at Brugh (*i. e.* the Dagda with his three sons; also Lughaidh and Oe, and Ollam, and Ogma, and Etan, the Poetess, and Corpre, the son of Etan), and Cremhthann followed them because his wife Nar was of the Tuatha Dea, and it was she solicited him that he should adopt Brugh as a burial-place for himself and his descendants, and this was the cause that they did not bury at Cruachan.

"The Lagenians (*i. e.* Cathair with his race and the kings who were before them) were buried at Oenach Ailbhe. The Clann Dedad (*i. e.* the race of Conaire and Erna) at Temhair Erann; the men of Munster (*i. e.* the Dergthene) at Oenach Culi, and Oenach Colmain; and the Connacians at Cruachan."

ANCHORITE TOWERS.

Because Simon Stylites lived in a domicile, sized "scarce two cubits," *on* a pillar sixty feet high, and because other anchorites lived on pillars and in cells, Dean Richardson suggested that the Irish Round Towers were for hermits; and was supported by Walter Harris, Dr. Milner, Dr. King, &c.—The cloch angeoire, or hermit's stone, quoted in aid of this fancy, turns out to be a narrow cell; and so much for the hermits!!

The confusion of

TOURS AND TOWERS

is a stupid pun or a vulgar pronunciation in

English ; but in Irish gave rise to the antiquarian theory of Dr. Smith, who, in his " History
of Cork," concludes that the Round Towers were
penitential prisons, because the Irish word for a
penitential round or journey is *turas!*

THE PHALLIC THEORY

never had any support but poor Henry O'Brien's
enthusiastic ignorance, and the caricaturing pen
of his illustrator.

We have now done with the theories of these
Towers, which Mr. Petrie has shown, past doubt,
to be either positively false or quite unproved.
His own opinion is that they were used—1, as
belfries ; 2, as keeps, or houses of shelter for the
clergy and their treasures; and 3, as watch
towers and beacons; and into his evidence for
this opinion we shall go at a future day, thanking
him at present for having displaced a heap of in-
congruous, though agreeable fancies, and given
us the most learned, the most exact, and the most
important work ever published on the antiquities
of the Ancient Irish Nation.

ETHNOLOGY OF THE IRISH RACE.

DR. WILDE, the traveller, read a paper to the Dublin College of Physicians on the skulls of the races that had died in Ireland, and this paper he has printed, under the title of " A Lecture on the Ethnology of the Ancient Irish."

He introduces the subject by a summary of the means by which ancient races are commonly investigated. First, and rightly, he ranks architectural and implimental remains. The palaces, pyramids, and picture-filled tombs of Egypt tell us now the state of their arts, their appearance, government, and manners. How much we would learn of Greece had her writings perished, and her statuary and temples reached us ; and how much of the Romans if Pompeii alone remained, and remained without a clue to its manuscripts. So, in Ireland, we have the monuments of different races. We have the Ogham pillar-stone, the rested rock altar, the supported cromleach, the arched stone fort, the trenched rath, with or without stone facings, the clay or rubble pyramid, with a passage and chamber, the flag-made tomb. We have the round tower, the stone circle, the Brehon's or Druid's chair, and the stone-roofed crypt—to say nothing of our country castles, our town residences, our churches and monasteries, which one must see if he would know how men lived here in the middle ages.

Monumental and other sculptures tell us dress and arms better than any description in words. We are amply supplied with these to illustrate the middle ages in Ireland. Our old churches are full of such tombs—but grievously they are abused and neglected. Who can look upon the shattered monuments of Jerpoint and Mellifont, and not think that a double barbarism (that of the people and that of their oppressors) has been upon Ireland. Nay, within a few miles of Dublin, in the church of Lusk, we, the other day, found a noble monument broken in two, and it and another fine tomb left to the mercies of untaught and irreverent children, for want of a five shilling door to the roofless, but otherwise perfect church. Who is to blame for this, the Rector or the Commissioners? *Both*, we say. How fine a use may be made of these mediœval tombs, without wantonly stirring them, is shown, as we remarked before, in St. Canice's, Kilkenny, disgraced as that cathedral is by whitewash. Curse it for whitewash! 'tis the dirtiest, ugliest thing that ever was put outside a cottage wall or inside a large building—for the inside of small rooms 'tis well enough.

Then, again, there are weapons, and ornamental and economical implements to tell us the domestic and military habits, and the state of mechanical arts among a people. We shall have more to say on this head some other time. We pass to the other modes of investigating races.

The second means of Ethnology is language. Having a number of words in common proves

communication between races. If these words
are of a very simple and radical kind the communication must have been long and ancient.
If, in addition, the structure and character of the
languages be the same—if their use of articles
and tenses, of inflections in the ends of words, as
in Greek, Latin, and German, or in the beginning of them, as in Irish or Welsh, be alike, this
is evidence that their first language was one,
and, therefore, the races *probably* identical.

We say, probably identical, because identity
of language does not quite prove identity of
race. The negroes of the West Indies will most
likely speak English when their islands are in a
federal republic. The red men of Brazils will
most likely speak Portuguese. But the change
of language is wonderfully slow in an independent country. The people of Gascony and Pro-
vençe do not speak French. They speak Gascon
and Provençal. The different English counties
have their dialects, showing what branch of
Saxons or Danes they descend from. The Welsh
language is now as flourishing as it was when
Edward outlawed it ; and now, after centuries
of wrong, when Anglicism has made us serfs,
not a people, we have colleges founded for the
support of the Irish language.

Identity in the structure of language is, then,
a very strong proof of identity, and, as a study,
of the highest interest.

The third means classified by Mr. Wilde for
Ethnologic research, is by the written history
and oral traditions of a country. In this section

he indulges in some sneers, which had been better omitted. We doubt the taste and correctness of much of what he says on the topic.

There are other sorts of analogies, worth following out, not noticed by Mr. Wilde. Such is that so ingeniously thought of, and ably illustrated by Mr. Forde, of Cork. He *disproves* the European origin of our music, and reduces it to either an original construction here, or to an Eastern source. If Eastern, we could have got it from the Oriental Christians, or Pagans. The last seems Mr. Forde's opinion. We trust he will have further means of following out this subject.

Identity in form and substance of scientific knowledge proves little, as one man, or one book could well produce it ; but musical characteristics are, perhaps, the most spiritual and safe from confusion of any that can be imagined, and the surest to last in a country, if it be independent, or if it be rude. A country long refined, or enslaved, may lose every thing.

We now come to Mr. Wilde's peculiar subject, and that to which he (faultily) restricts the term, Ethnography—namely, the *natural* history of man. The study of man's animal form shows that each simple race has peculiarities in size, in shape of bones and limbs, in play of features, and carriage of body, and in colour.

Many of these peculiarities can be studied from the bones of a race. Of course, the bones, or *any* of them, show the size of the race. The skull shows not only the shape of the head, but of the features. The skull of a man with an aquiline nose, and open orbits, and massy jaws, is as distinguishable from one with the nose or eyes of a Hun or the jaw of a Bengalee, as from that of a rabbit.

The marks left by the muscles in the bones wherein their extremities worked, show, too, the "play of features" or expression of countenance to some extent.

Taking these principles with him, Mr. Wilde examined a number of skulls in old churchyards, and in barrows and cairns, both here and abroad, and tries from thence to classify the races of the Irish.

His conclusions are not very clearly made out, and his proofs are frequently loose, but his tract is suggestive and serviceable.

His opinion is that the first inhabitants of this country were what are called Firbolgs—men of Teutonic or German blood—small, lively, with aquiline noses, dark complexions, and heads of great length from front to back. This race used the stone and flint hatchets, shell ornaments, bone needles, stone mills, and clay urns. The second race, who came and subdued the Firbolgs, were (he conceives) those called Tuatha da Danaan— men of "fair hair and large size," as Mac Firbis says. They were, thinks Mr. Wilde, Celts, and used bronze in their weapons and implements. He asserts, too, that Norway and Sweden were colonised from Ireland by Firbolgs after they had learned the use of metals from the Tuatha da Danaan. The proof given is that skulls, such as he supposes peculiar to the Firbolgs, are found in Scandinavia associated with metal weapons.

There is evidence, too, that these Tuatha da Danaan were either Phœnicians, or from a Phœnician colony and so of the next invaders— the Milesians. Mr. Wilde *seems* to attribute a fine globular head to these Danaans ; but he seems elsewhere to say that no metal remains have been found with any heathen skulls, which would contradict his own hypothesis.

We shall conclude with a couple of extracts— the first, showing the uncertainty of the observations likely to be made, and the imprudence of all generalities (Mr. Wilde's included) now, and the other for illustration sake :—

" This leads me to the last locality in which bones of the ancient Irish people are said to have been found—I allude to the round towers, particularly to that lately excavated at Drumbo, in the county Down. Much interest has, as you are aware, been lately excited by this discovery, from the supposition that these human remains would offer some clue as to the origin and uses of these strange monuments, or to assist in determining the probable era of their erection. The enchanted palace of the Irish round tower will shortly be opened for our inspection, and, therefore, any, even a passing opinion as to anything connected with it would be out of place. Here, however, is a very beautiful cast of the skull found within the round tower of Drumbo ; and the moment it was presented to me, I felt convinced, that if it is of a contemporaneous age with the structure beneath which it was found, then the Irish round tower is not the ancient building we suppose it to be ; for this, compared with the other heads which I have laid before you, is of comparatively modern date. Now, nearly all round towers are in connexion with ancient burial places, and this one, in particular, was so ; and I need only dig around and without it to find many similar remains. We read that the skeleton was found at full length, embedded in the clay, within the ancient structure. Now,

I respectfully submit it to the antiquarian world that, if the round tower was erected as a monument over the person whose skeleton was found within it, it certainly would not have been buried thus in the simple earth without a vault or stone chamber, such as the enlightened architect who built the tower would be thoroughly acquainted with. Moreover, I do not believe that a skull thus placed loosely in the earth, without any surrounding chamber, would have remained thus perfect for the length of time, which even the most modernising antiquaries assign as the date of the round tower. At Larne, in the county of Antrim, a skeleton was lately discovered, which, from the iron sword and other weapons in connexion with it, appeared to have been that of a templar; and similar remains were, not long since, discovered at Kilmainham. This templar's skull, found at Larne, (which Mr. Wilde here produced) although it has an Irish physiognomy, and a Fir-Bolg form of head, cannot be traced back farther than the eleventh or twelfth century for its date.

"N.B.—Since this lecture was delivered, I had the gratification of receiving several communications from different parts of the country, on the subject of tumuli and human remains; so that one of the objects for which it was undertaken—that of calling attention to the matter—has been attained. Among these communications, I had the honour of receiving one of special interest, from A. N. Nugent, Esq., who lately opened a sepulchral mound in the neighbourhood of Portaferry.— 'There was,' he writes to me, 'a circle of large stones, containing an area of about a rood. Between each of these stones, there was a facing of flat ones, similar to the building of our modern fences. The outer coating was covered with white pebbles averaging the size of a goose-egg, of which there were several cart loads— although it would be difficult to collect even a small quantity at present along the beach.

" 'After this was taken away we came to a confused heap of rubbish, stone, and clay, and then some large flag stones on their ends—the tumulus still preserving a cone shape. In the centre we came to a chamber about six feet long, formed by eight very large upright stones, with a large flag stone at the bottom, on which lay, in one heap, of a foot in thickness, a mixture of black mould and bones.' These bones, some of which were kindly forwarded to me, are all human, and consist of portions of the ribs, vertebræ, and the ends of the long bones, together with pieces of the skull and some joints of the fingers of a full-grown person, and also several bones of a very young child ; none of these have been subject to the action of fire ; but among the parcel forwarded to me are several fragments of incinerated or calcined bones, also human. Either these latter were portions of the same bodies burned, or they belonged to an individual sacrificed to the manes of the person whose grave this was ; and I am inclined to think the latter is the more probable, from the circumstances under which similar remains have been discovered in other localities. Evidently this tumulus is of very ancient date—long prior to the authentic historic period—and was, I should say, erected over some person or family of note in that day. There were no urns, weapons, or ornaments discovered in connexion with it ; but my informant states, that in the field in which this barrow was opened, there have been at various times, small stone chambers, or kistvaens, discovered ; and in one of these a skull of the long, flat, and narrow character, was some time ago dug up. A farmer in the vicinity, likewise, told Mr. Nugent that many years ago, while ploughing in that same field, he turned up a stone chamber of the same kind, and that it contained a skull with a portion of hair of a deep red colour attached to it."

The subject is worthy of close study ; but *careless dabbling with it were worse than neglect.* There are some people—very curious, but neither reverent nor scientific—who, on reading this, will long to plunge into every cairn or grave that looks a few centuries old, to see whether Wilde is right or Wilde is wrong. We deprecate this. We entreat them to spare, nay, to guard, these as if they were precious caskets

entrusted to them. The Irish tombs must not
be Grahamed. It is not right for any man, who
has not spent years in studying comparative anatomy, to open the meanest tomb. Even had we
a scientific commission of the ablest men we
should insist upon a sparing and considerate use
of such violation of the dead man's home for the
sake of the live man's curiosity. He who does
not respect the remains of his fellow-creature,
and their last shelter, is without one of the finest
feelings of humanity. Even the hired soldier,
who slays for pay, is more human. Some of
these mounds can, and will be, opened hereafter
by the Irish Academy, when it is made, as it
must be, an Irish Antiquarian Institute. In the
meantime the subject had best be *practically*
left to Dr. Wilde and the few competent people
who are engaged on it. Let these tombs, whether on the mountain, or in the tilled field, or
the ruined churchyard, be religiously preserved;
and, above all, let the children be brought up
with tender reverence for these sanctuaries of
the departed. We have room enough without
trespassing on the grave.

THE IRISH BRIGADE.

WHEN valour becomes a reproach, when patriotism is thought a prejudice, and when a soldier's sword is a sign of shame, the Irish Brigade will be forgotten or despised.

The Irish are a military people—strong, nimble, and hardy, fond of adventure, irascible, brotherly, and generous—they have all the qualities that tempt men to war and make them good soldiers. Dazzled by their great fame on the Continent, and hearing of their insular wars chiefly through the interested lies of England, Voltaire expressed his wonder, that a nation which had behaved so gallantly abroad had " always fought badly at home." It would have been most wonderful.

It may be conceded that the Irish performed more illustrious actions on the Continent. They fought with the advantages of French discipline and equipment ; they fought as soldiers, with the rights of war, not " rebels, with halters round their necks ;" they fought by the side of great rivals and amid the gaze of Europe.

In the most of their domestic wars they appeared as divided clans or abrupt insurgents ; they were exposed to the treachery of a more instructed, of an unscrupulous and a compact enemy ; they had neither discipline, nor generalship, nor arms ; their victories were those of a mob, their defeats were followed by extermination.

We speak of their ordinary contests with England from the time of Roderick O'Connor to that of '98. Occasionally they had more opportunities, and their great qualities for war appeared. In Hugh (or rather Aodh) O'Neill they found a leader who only wanted material resources to have made them an independent nation. Cautious, as became the heir of so long a strife, he spent years in acquiring military knowledge and nursing up his clan into the kernel for a nation—crafty as Bacon and Cecil, and every other man of his time, he learned war in Elizabeth's armies, and got help from her store-houses. When the discontent of the Pale, religious tyranny, and the intrigues and hostility of Spain and Rome against England gave him an opening, he put his ordered clan into action, stormed the neighbouring garrisons, struck terror into his hereditary foes, and gave hope to all patriots; but finding that his ranks were too few for battle, he negotiated successfully for peace, but unavailingly for freedom; his grievances and designs remained, and he retired to repeat the same policy, till, after repeated guerillas and truces, he was strong enough to proclaim alliance with Spain and war with England, and to defeat and slay every deputy that assailed him, till at last he marched from the triumph of Beal-an-ath-Buidhe (where Marshal Bagenal and his army perished) to hold an almost royal court in Munster, and to reduce the Pale to the limits it had formed in the wars of the Roses; and even when the neglect of Spain, the genius of Mountjoy, the resources and intrigues of England, and the exhaustion and divisions of Ireland had rendered success hopeless, the Irish under O'Ruarc, O'Sullivan, and O'Doherty vindicated their military character.

From that period they, whose foreign services, since Dathi's time, had been limited to supplying feudatories to the English kings, began to fight under the flags of England's enemies in every corner of Europe. The artifices of the Stuarts regained them, and in the reign of Charles the First they were extensively enlisted for the English allies and for the crown; but it was under the guidance of another O'Neill, and for Ireland, they again exhibited the qualities which had sustained Tyrone. The battle of Benburb affords as great a proof of Irish soldiership as Fontenoy.

But it was when with a formal government and in a regular war they encountered the Dutch invader, they showed the full prowess of the Irish; and at the Boyne, Limerick, Athlone, and Aughrim, in victory or defeat, and always against *immensely superior numbers and armament*, proved that they fought well at home.

Since the day when Sarsfield sailed, the Irish have never had an opportunity of refuting the calumny of England which Voltaire accepted. In '98 they met enormous forces resting on all the magazines of England; they had no officers, their leaders, however brave, neither knew how to organize, provision, station or manœuvre troops —their arms were casual—their ignorance profound—their intemperance unrestrainable. If they put English supremacy in peril (and had

Arklow or Ballinahinch been attacked with skill, that supremacy was gone,) they did so by mere valour.

It is therefore on the Continent that one must chiefly look for Irish trophies. It is a pious and noble search ; but he who pursues it had need to guard against the error we have noticed in Voltaire, of disparaging Irish soldiership at home.

The materials for the history of the Irish Brigade are fast accumulating. We have before us the " Military History of the Irish Nation," by the late Matthew O'Conor. He was a barrister, but studied military subjects (as became a gentleman and a citizen,) peculiarly interested himself in the achievements of his countrymen, and prepared materials for a history of them. He died, leaving his work unfinished, yet happily sufficiently advanced to offer a continuous narrative of Irish internal wars, from Hugh O'Neill to Sarsfield, and of their foreign services up to the peace of Utrecht, in 1711. The style of the work is earnest and glowing, full of patriotism and liberality ; but Mr. O'Conor was no blind partisan, and he neither hides the occasional excesses of the Irish, nor disparages their opponents. His descriptions of battles are very superior to what one ordinarily meets in the works of civilians, and any one reading them with a military atlas will be gratified and instructed.

The value of the work is vastly augmented by the appendix, which is a memoir of the Brigade, written in French, in 1749, and including the war-office orders, and all the changes in organisation, numbers, and pay of the Brigade to that date. This memoir is authenticated thus :—

"His Excellency, the Duke of Feltré, Minister of War, was so kind as to communicate to me the original memoir above cited, of which this is a perfect copy, which I attest.

"DE MONTMORENCY MORRES (Hervé,) Adjutant-Commandant, Colonel.

"Paris, 1st September, 1813."

To give any account of the details of Mr. O'Conor's book we should abridge it, and an abridgment of a military history is a catalogue of names. It contains accounts of Hugh O'Neill's campaigns, and of the wars of William and James in Ireland. It describes (certainly a new chapter in our knowledge) the services of the Irish in the Low Countries and France during the religious wars in Henri Quatre's time, and the hitherto equally unknown actions abroad during Charles the Second's exile and reign.

The wars of Mountcashel's (the old) Brigade in 1690-1, under St. Ruth in Savoy, occupy many interesting pages, and the first campaigns of the New Brigade, with the death of Sarsfield and Mountcashel, are carefully narrated. The largest part of the work is occupied with the wars of the Spanish succession, and contains minute narratives of the battles and sieges of Cremona, Spire, Luzzaca, Bleinheim, Cassano, Ramilies, Almanza, Alcira, Malplaquet, and Denain, with the actions of the Irish in them.

Here are great materials for our future History of Ireland.

THE SPEECHES OF GRATTAN.[*]

OF the long line of Protestant patriots Grattan is the first in genius, and first in services.
He had a more fervid and more Irish nature
than Swift or Flood, and he accomplished what
Swift hardly dreamed, and Flood failed in—an
Irish constitution. He had immeasurably more
imagination than Tone ; and though he was far
behind the great Founder of the United Irishmen
in organising power, he surpassed him in inspiration. The statues of all shall be in our forums,
and examples of all in our hearts, but that of
Grattan shall be pre-eminent. The stubborn
and advancing energy of Swift and Flood may
teach us to bear up against wrong; the principles
of Tone may end in liberation ; but the splendid
nationality of Grattan shall glorify us in every
condition.

The speeches of Grattan were collected and
his memoirs written by his son. The latter is
an accessible and an invaluable account of his
life ; but the speeches were out of print, not
purchaseable under five or six guineas, and then
were unmanageably numerous for any but a

* The Select Speeches of the Right Hon. Henry
Grattan. To which is added his Letter on the Union,
with a Commentary on his Career and Character. By
Daniel Owen Madden, Esq., of the Inner Temple.
Dublin, James Duffy, 1845. 8vo, pp. 534.

professed politician. Mr. Madden's volume gives
for a trifle all Grattan's most valuable speeches,
with a memoir sufficient to explain the man and
the orator.

On the speeches of Grattan here published we
have little to say. They are the finest specimens
of imaginative eloquence in the English, or in
any language. There is not much pathos, and
no humour in them, and in these respects Grattan is far less of an Irishman, and of an orator,
too, than Curran ; but a philosophy, penetrating
constitutions for their warnings, and human
nature for its guides—a statesman's (as distinguished from an antiquarian's) use of history
—a passionate scorn and invective for the base,
tyrannical, and unjust—a fiery and copious zeal
for liberty and for Ireland, and a diction and
cadence almost lyrical, made Grattan the sudden achiever of a Revolution, and will make
him for ever one of the very elements of Ireland.

No other orator is so uniformly animated.
No other orator has brightened the depths of
political philosophy with such vivid and lasting
light. No writer in the language, except Shakspeare, has so sublime and suggestive a diction.
His force and vehemence are amazing—far beyond Chatham, far beyond Fox, far beyond any
orator we can recal.

To the student of oratory Grattan's speeches
are dangerously suggestive—overpowering spirits
that will not leave when bid. Yet, with all this
terrible potency, who would not bask in his
genius, even at the hazard of having his light

for ever in your eyes. The brave student will rather exult in his effulgence—not to rob, not to mimic it—but to catch its inspiration, and then go on his way resolved to create a glory of his own which, however small, being genuine, shall not pale within its sphere.

To give a *just* idea of Grattan's rush and splendour to any one not familiar with his speeches is impossible; but *some* glimmer may may be got by one reading the extracts we shall add here. We shall take them at random, as we open the pages in the book, and leave the reader, untaught in our great orator, to judge, if chance is certain of finding such gems, what would not judicious care discover! Let him use that care again and again :—

"Sir, we may hope to dazzle with illumination, and we may sicken with addresses, but the public imagination will never rest, nor will her heart be well at ease: never! so long as the parliament of England exercises or claims a legislation over this country : so long as this shall be the case, that very free trade, otherwise a perpetual attachment, will be the cause of new discontent; it will create a pride to feel the indignity of bondage; it will furnish a strength to bite your chain, and the liberty withheld will poison the good communicated.

"The British minister mistakes the Irish character; had he intended to make Ireland a slave, he should have kept her a beggar; there is no middle policy; win her heart by the restoration of her right, or cut off the nation's right hand; greatly emancipate, or fundamentally destroy. We may talk plausibly to England, but so long as she exercises a power to bind this country, so long are the nations in a state of war; the claims of the one go against the liberty of the other, and the sentiments of the latter go to oppose those claims to the last drop of her blood. The English opposition, therefore, are right; mere trade will not satisfy Ireland :—they judge of us by other great nations, by the nation whose political life has been a struggle for liberty; they judge of us with a true knowledge, and just deference, for our character : that a country enlighted as Ireland, chartered as Ireland, armed as Ireland, and injured as Ireland, will be satisfied with nothing less than liberty.

"Impracticable! impracticable! impracticable, a zealous divine will say ; any alteration is beyond the power and wisdom of parliament; above the faculties of man to make adequate provision for 900 clergymen, who despise riches. Were it to raise a new tax for their provision, or for that of a body less holy, how easy the task! how various the means! but, when the proposal is to diminish a tax already established, an impossibility glares us in the face, of a measure so contrary to our practices both in church and state."

We were wrong in saying there was no humour in Grattan. Here is a passage humorous enough, but it is scornful, rhetorical humour :—

"It does not affect the doctrine of our religion; it does not alter the church establishment; it does not affect the constitution of episcopacy. The modus does not even alter the mode of their provision, it only limits the quantum, and limits it on principles much less severe than that charity which they preach, or that abstinence which they inculcate. Is this innovation?—as if the Protestant religion was to be propagated in Ireland, like the influence of a minister, by bribery ; or like the influence of a county candidate, by money ; or like the cause of a potwalloping canvasser, by the weight of the purse ; as if Christ could not prevail over the earth unless Mammon took him by the hand. Am I to understand that if you give the parson 12s. in the acre for potatoes, and 10s. for wheat, the Protestant religion is safe on its rock ? But if you reduce him to 6s. the acre for potatoes and wheat, then Jupiter shakes the Heavens with his thunder, Neptune rakes up the deep with his trident, and Pluto leaps from his throne! See the curate—he rises at six to morning prayers; he leaves company at six for evening prayer; he baptizes, he marries, he churches, he buries, he follows with pious offices his fellow-creature from the cradle to the grave; for what immense income! what riches to reward these inestimable services? (Do not depend on the penury of the laity, let his own order value his deserts;) 50*l.* a year! 50*l.*! for praying, for christening, for marrying, for churching, for burying, for following with Christian offices his fellow-creature from cradle to grave; so frugal a thing is devotion, so cheap religion, so easy the terms on which man may worship his Maker, and so small the income, in the opinion of ecclesiastics, sufficient for the duties of a clergyman, as far as he is connected at all with the Christian religion.

*   *   *   *   *   *

"By this trade of parliament the King is absolute; his will is signified by both houses of parliament, who are now as much an instrument in his hand as a bayonet in the hands of a regiment. Like a regiment we have our adjutant, who sends to the infirmary for the old and to the brothel for the young, and men thus carted, as it were, into this house, to vote for the minister, are called the representatives of the people! Suppose General Washington to ring his bell, and order his servants out of livery to take their seats in Congress—you can apply this instance.

"It is not life but the condition of living—the slave is not so likely to complain of the want of property as the proprietor of the want of privilege. The human mind is progressive—the child does not look back to the parent that gave him being, nor the proprietor to the people that gave him the power of acquisition, but both look forward—the one to provide for the comforts of life, and the other to obtain all the privileges of property."

But we have fallen on one of his most marvellous passages, and we give it entire:—

"I will put this question to my country; I will suppose her at the bar, and I will ask her, will you fight for ,

Union as you would for a constitution? Will you fight
for that Lords, and that Commons, ho, in the last
century, took away your trade, and, in the present,
your constitution, as for that King, Lords, and Commons, who have restored both? Well, the minister has
destroyed this constitution; to destroy is easy. The
edifices of the mind, like the fabrics of marble, require
an age to build, but ask only minutes to precipitate;
and, as the fall of both is an effort of no time, so neither
is it a business of any strength—a pick-axe and a common labourer will do the one—a little lawyer, a little
pimp, a wicked minister the other.

"The constitution, which, with more or less violence,
has been the inheritance of this country for six hundred
years—that *modus tenendi parliamentum*, which lasted
and outlasted of Plantagenet the wars, of Tudor the
violence, and of Stuart the systematic falsehood—the
condition of our connexion—yes, the constitution he destroys is one of the pillars of the British empire. He
may walk round it and round it, and the more he contemplates the more must he admire it—such a one as
had cost England of money millions and of blood a
deluge, cheaply and nobly expended—whose restoration
had cost Ireland her noblest efforts, and was the habitation of her loyalty—we are accustomed to behold the
kings of these countries in the keeping of parliament—
I say of her loyalty as well as of her liberty, where she
had hung up the sword of the Volunteer—her temple of
fame as well as of freedom—where she had seated herself, as she vainly thought, in modest security and in a
long repose.

"I have done with the pile which the minister batters,
I come to the Babel which he builds; and as he throws
down without a principle, so does he construct without
a foundation. This fabric he calls a Union, and to this his
fabric, there are two striking objections—first, it is no
Union; it is not an identification of people, for it excludes the Catholics; secondly, it is a consolidation of
the Irish legislatures; that is to say, a merger of the
Irish parliament, and incurs every objection to a Union,
without obtaining the only object which a Union pro-
fesses; it is an extinction of the constitution, and an

exclusion of the people. Well! he has overlooked the
people as he has overlooked the sea. I say he excludes
the Catholics, and he destroys their best chance of admission—the relative consequence. Thus he reasons,
that hereafter, in course of time (he does not say when),
if they behave themselves (he does not say how), they
may see their subjects submitted to a course of discussion
(he does not say with what result or determination);
and as the ground for this inane period, in which he
promises nothing, and in which, if he did promise much,
at so remote a period he could perform nothing, unless
he, like the evil he has accomplished, be immortal. For
this inane sentence, in which he can scarcely be said to
deceive the Catholic, or suffer the Catholic to deceive
himself, he exhibits no other ground than the physical
inanity of the Catholic body accomplished by a Union,
which, as it destroys the relative importance of Ireland,
so it destroys the relative proportion of the Catholic inhabitants, and thus they become admissible, because
they cease to be anything. Hence, according to him,
their brilliant expectation: ' You were,' say his advo-
cates, and so imports his argument, ' before the Union
as three to one, you will be by the Union as one to
four.' Thus he founds their hopes of political power on
the extinction of physical consequence, and makes the
inanity of their body and the non-entity of their country,
the pillars of their future ambition."

We now return to the memoir by Mr. Madden. It is not the details of a life meagre for
want of space, and confused for want of principles, as most little biographies are ; it is an estimate, a profound one of Grattan's original
nature, of the influences which acted on him
from youth to manhood, of his purposes, his
principles, and his influence on Ireland.

Henry Grattan was twenty-nine years of age
when he entered on politics, and in seven years
he was the triumphant leader of a people free

and victorious after hereditary bondage. He
entered parliament educated in the metaphysical
and political philosophy of the time, injured by
its cold and epigrammatic verse and its artificial
tastes—familiar with every form of aristocratic
life from Kilkenny to London—familiar, too,
with Chatham's oratory and principles, and with
Flood's views and example. He came when
there were great forces rushing through the
land—eloquence, love of liberty, thirst for
commerce, hatred of English oppression, im-
patience, glory, and, above all, a military array.
He combined these elements, and used them to
achieve the Revolution of '82. Be he for ever
honoured!

Mr. Madden defends him against Flood on
the question of Simple Repeal. Here is his
reasoning:—

"It is an easy thing now to dispose of the idle question
of simple repeal. In truth, there was nothing whatever
deserving of attention in the point raised by Mr. Flood.
The security for the continuance of Irish freedom did
not depend upon an English act of parliament. It was
by Irish *will* and not at English pleasure that the new
constitution was to be supported. The transaction between the countries was of a high political nature, and
it was to be judged by political reason, and by states-
manlike computation, and not by the petty techni-
calities of the court of law. The revolution of 1782, as
carried by Ireland, and assented to by England (in re-
pealing the 6th George the First), was a political compact—proposed by one country, and acknowledged by
the other in the face of Europe: it was not (as Mr.
Flood and his partisans construed the transaction) of the
nature of municipal right, to be enforced or annulled by
mere judical exposition."

This is unanswerable, but Grattan should have gone further. The Revolution was effected mainly by the Volunteers, whom he had inspired; arms could alone have preserved the constitution. Flood was wrong in setting value on one form—Grattan in relying on any; but both before, and after, '82 Flood seems to have had glimpses that the question was one of might, as well as of right, and that national laws could not last under such an alien army.

Taken as military representatives, the Convention at the Rotundo was even more valuable than as a civic display. Mr. Madden censures Grattan for having been an elaborate neutral during these Reform dissensions; but that the result of *such* neutrality ruined the Convention proves a comparative want of power in Flood, who could have governed that Convention in spite of the rascally English and the feeble Irish Whigs. Oh! had Tone been in that council!

In describing Grattan's early and enthusiastic and ceaseless advocacy of Catholic liberty, Mr. Madden has a just subject for unmixed eulogy. Let no one imagine that the interest of these Emancipation speeches has died with the achievement of what they pleaded for; they will ever remain divinest protests against the vice and impolicy of religious ascendency, of sectarian bitterness, and of bigot separation.

For this admirable beginning of the design of giving Ireland its most glorious achievement— the speeches of its orators—to contemplate, the country should be grateful; but if there can be anything better for it to hear than can be had in Grattan's speeches, it is such language as this from his eloquent editor :

"Reader! if you be an Irish Protestant, and entertain harsh prejudices against your Catholic countrymen—study the works and life of Grattan—learn from him, for none can teach you better, how to purify your nature from bigotry. Learn from him to look upon all your countrymen with a loving heart—to be tolerant of infirmities, caused by their unhappy history—and, like Grattan, earnestly sympathise with all that is brave and generous in their character.

"Reader! if you be an Irish Catholic, and that you confound the Protestant religion with tyranny—learn from Grattan, that it is possible to be a Protestant, and have a heart for Ireland and its people. Think that the brightest age of Ireland was when Grattan—a steady Protestant—raised it to proud eminence; think also that in the hour of his triumph, he did not forget the state of your oppressed fathers, but laboured through his virtuous life, that both you and your children should enjoy unshackled liberty of conscience.

"But reader! whether you be Protestant or Catholic, and whatever be your party, you will do well as an Irishman to ponder upon the spirit and principles which governed the public and private life of Grattan. Learn from him how to regard your countrymen of all denominations. Observe, as he did, how very much that is excellent belongs to both the great parties into which Ireland is divided. If (as some do) you entertain dispiriting views of Ireland, recollect that any country, containing such elements as those which roused the genius of Grattan, never need despair. *Sursum corda.* Be not disheartened.

"Go—go—my countrymen—and, within your social sphere, carry into practice those moral principles which Grattan so eloquently taught, and which he so remarkably enforced by his well-spent life. He will teach you to avoid hating men on account of their religious professions, or hereditary descent. From him you will learn principles which, if carried out, would generate a new state of society in Ireland."

MEMORIALS OF WEXFORD.

'TWIXT Croghan-Kinshela, and Hook Head, 'twixt Carnsore and Mount-Leinster, there is as good a mass of men as ever sustained a state by honest franchises, by peace, virtue, and intelligent industry; and as stout a mass as ever tramped through a stubborn battle. There is a county where we might seek more of stormy romance, and there is a county where prospers a shrewder economy, but no county in Ireland is fitter for freedom than Wexford.

They are a peculiar people—these Wexford men. Their blood is for the most part English and Welsh, though mixed with the Danish and the Gaelic, yet they are Irish in thought and feeling. They are a Catholic people, yet on excellent terms with their Protestant landlords. Outrages are unknown, for though the rents are high enough, they are not unbearable by a people so idustrious and skilled in farming.

Go to the fair and you will meet honest dealing, and a look that heeds no lordling's frown— for the Wexford men have neither the base bend nor the baser craft of slaves. Go to the hustings, and you will see open and honest voting; no man shrinking or crying for concealment, or extorting a bribe under the name of "his expenses." Go to their farms, and you will see a snug homestead, kept clean, prettily sheltered (much what you'd see in Down), more green crops than even in Ulster, the National School and the Repeal Reading-room well filled, and every religious duty regarded.

Wexford is not all it might be, or all that, with more education and the life-hope of nationality, it will be—there is something to blame and something to lament, here a vice sustained, and there a misfortune lazily borne ; yet, take it for all in all, it is the most prosperous, it is the pattern county of the South ; and when we see it coming forward in a mass to renew its demand for native government, it is an omen that the spirit of the people outlives quarrels and jealousies, and that it has a rude vitality which will wear out its oppressors.

Nor are we indifferent to the memories of Wexford. It owes much of its peace and prosperity to the war it sustained. It rose in '98 with little organisation against intolerable wrong; and though it was finally beaten by superior forces, it taught its aristocracy and the government a lesson not easily forgiven, to be sure, but far harder to be forgotten—a lesson that popular anger could strike hard as well as sigh deeply ; and that it was better to conciliate than provoke those who even for an hour had felt their strength. The red rain made Wexford's harvest grow. Their's was no treacherous assassination—their's no stupid riot—their's no pale mutiny. They rose in mass and swept the country by sheer force.

Nor in their sinking fortunes is there anything

to blush at. Scullabogue was not burned by the fighting men.

Yet, nowhere did the copper sun of that July burn upon a more heart-piercing sight than a rebel camp. Scattered on a hill-top, or screened in a gap, were the grey-coated thousands, their memories mad at burned cabins, and military whips, and hanged friends; their hopes dimmed by partial defeat; their eyes lurid with care; their brows full of gloomy resignation. Some have short guns, which the stern of a boat might bear, but which press through the shoulder of a marching man; and others have light fowling pieces, with dandy locks—troublesome and dangerous toys. Most have pikes, stout weapons, too; and though some swell to handspikes, and others thin to knives, yet, for all that, fatal are they to dragoon or musketeer if they can meet him in a rush; but how shall they do so? The gunsmen have only a little powder in scraps of paper or bags, and their balls are few and rarely fit. They have no potatoes ripe, and they have no bread—their food is the worn cattle they have crowded there, and which the first skirmish may rend from them. There are women and children seeking shelter, seeking those they love; and there are leaders busier, feebler, less knowing, less resolved than the women and the children.

Great hearts! how faithful ye were. How ye bristled up when the foe came on, how ye set your teeth to die as his shells and round-shot fell steadily; and with how firm a cheer ye dashed at him, if he gave you any chance at all of a grapple. From the wild burst with which ye triumphed at Oulart hill, down to the faint gasp wherewith the last of your last column died in the corn fields of Meath, there is nothing to shame your valour, your faith, or your patriotism. You wanted arms, and you wanted leaders. Had you had them, you would have guarded a green flag in Dublin Castle, a week after you beat Walpole. Isolated, unorganised, unofficered, half-armed, girt by a swarm of foes, you ceased to fight, but you neither betrayed, nor repented. Your sons need not fear to speak of Ninety-eight.

You, people of Wexford, almost all Repealers, are the sons of the men of '98; prosperous and many, will you only shout for Repeal, and line roads and tie boughs for a holiday? Or will you press your organisation, work at your education, and increase your political power, so that your leaders may know and act on the knowledge, that come what may, there is trust in Wexford?

THE HISTORY OF TO-DAY.

FROM 1793 to 1829—for thirty-six years—the Irish Catholics struggled for Emancipation. *That* Emancipation was but admission to the Bench, the Inner Bar, and Parliament. It was won by self-denial, genius, vast and sustained labours, and lastly by the sacrifice of the forty-shilling freeholders—the poor veterans of the war—and by submission to insulting oaths; yet it was cheaply bought. Not so cheaply, perchance, as if won by the sword; for, on it were expended more treasures, more griefs, more intellect, more passion, more of all which makes life welcome, than had been needed for war; still it was cheaply bought, and Ireland has glorified herself, and will through ages triumph in the victory of '29.

Yet what was Emancipation compared to Repeal?

The one put a silken badge on a few members of one profession; the other would give to all professions and all trades the rank and riches which resident proprietors, domestic legislation, and flourishing commerce, infallibly create.

Emancipation made it possible for Catholics to sit on the judgment seat; but it left a foreign administration, which has excluded them, save in two or three cases, where over-topping eminence made the acceptance of a Judgeship no

promotion ; and it left the local Judges—those
with whom the people has to deal—as partial,
ignorant, and bigotted as ever ; while Repeal
would give us an Irish code and Irish-hearted
Judges in every Court, from the Chancery to
the Petty Sessions.

Emancipation dignified a dozen Catholics with
a senatorial name in a foreign and hostile Legislature. Repeal would give us a Senate, a Militia, an Administration, all our own.

The Penal Code, as it existed since 1793, insulted the faith of the Catholics, restrained their
liberties, and violated the public Treaty of Limerick. The Union has destroyed our manufactures, prohibits our flag, prevents our commerce,
drains our rental, crushes our genius, makes our
taxation a tribute, our representation a shadow,
our name a bye-word. It were nobler to strive
for Repeal than to get Emancipation.

Four years ago, the form of Repeal agitation
began—two years ago, its reality. Have we not
cause to be proud of the labours of these two
years? If life be counted, not by the rising
of suns, or the idle turning of machinery, but
by the growth of the will, and the progress of
thoughts and passions in the soul, we Irishmen
have spent an age since we raised our first cry
for liberty. Consider what we were then, and
what we have done since. We had a People
unorganised—disgusted with a Whig alliance—
beaten in a dishonourable struggle to sustain a
faction—ignorant of each others' will—without
books, without song, without leaders (save one),
without purposes, without strength, without

G

hope. The Corn-Exchange was the faint copy
of the Catholic Association, with a few enthu-
siasts, a few loungers, and a few correspondents.
Opposite to us was the great Conservative party,
with a majority exceeding our whole representation, united, flushed, led by the craftiest of living
statesmen and the ablest of living generals. Oh!
how disheartening it was then, when, day by
day, we found prophecy and exhortation, lay
and labour, flung idly before a distracted People.
May we never pass through that icy ordeal
again!

How different now! The People are united
under the greatest system of organisation ever
attempted in any country. They send in, by
their Collectors, Wardens, and Inspectors, to the
central office of Ireland, the contributions needed
to carry on the Registration of Voters, the public meetings, the publications, the law expenses,
and the organisation of the Association ; and
that in turn carries on registries, holds meetings,
opens Reading-rooms, sends newspapers, and
books, and political instructions, back through
the same channel ; so that the Central Committee
knows the state of every parish, and every parish
receives the teaching and obeys the will of the
Central Committee.

The Whig Alliance has melted, like ice before
the sun, and the strong souls of our People will
never again serve the purposes of a faction.

The Conservative party, without union and
without principle, is breaking up. Its English
section is dividing into the tools of expediency
and the pioneers of a New Generation—its

Irish section into Castle Hacks, and National Conservatives.

Meantime, how much have the Irish People gained and done! They have received, and grown rich under torrents of thought. Song, and sermon, and music, speech and pamphlet, novel and history, essay, and map, and picture, have made the dull thoughtful, and the thoughtful studious, and will make the studious wise and powerful. They have begun a system of self-teaching in their Reading-rooms. If they carry it, we shall, before two years, have in every parish men able to manufacture, to trade, and to farm—men acquainted with all that Ireland was, is, and should be—men able to serve The Irish Nation in peace and war.

In the teeth, too, of the Government, we held our meetings. They are not for this time, but they were right well in their own time. They showed our physical force to the Continent, to ourselves, to America, to our rulers. They showed that the People would come and go rapidly, silently, and at bidding, in numbers enough to recruit a dozen armies. These are literal facts. Any one monster meeting could have offered little resistance in the open country to a regular army, but it contained the materials—the numbers, intelligence, and obedience—of a conquering host. Whenever the impression of their power grows faint, we shall revive them again.

The toleration of these meetings was the result of fear; the prosecution of their chiefs sprung from greater fear. That prosecution was begun audaciously, was carried on meanly and with virulence, and ended with a charge and a verdict which disgraced the law. An illegal imprisonment afforded a glorious proof that the People could refrain from violence under the worst temptation; that their leaders were firm; and, better than all, that had these leaders been shot, not prisoned, their successors were ready. Such an imprisonment served Ireland more than an acquittal, for it tried her more; and then came the day of triumph, when the reluctant constitution liberated our chiefs, and branded our oppressors.

This is a history of two years never surpassed in importance and honour. This is a history which our sons shall pant over and envy. This is a history which pledges us to perseverance. This is a history which guarantees success.

Energy, patience, generosity, skill, tolerance, enthusiasm, created and decked the agitation. The world attended us with its thoughts and prayers. The graceful genius of Italy and the profound intellect of Germany paused to wish us well. The fiery heart of France tolerated our unarmed effort, and proffered its aid. America sent us money, thought, love—she made herself a part of Ireland in her passions and her organisation. From London to the wildest settlement which throbs in the tropics, or shivers nigh the Pole, the empire of our misruler was shaken by our effort. To all earth we proclaimed our wrongs. To man and God we made oath that we would never cease to strive till an Irish Nation stood supreme on this island. The genius which roused and organised us, the energy which laboured, the wisdom that taught, the manhood which rose up, the patience which obeyed, the faith which swore, and the valour that strained for action, are here still, experienced, recruited, resolute.

The future shall realise the promise of the past.

THE RESOURCES OF IRELAND.

BISHOP BERKELEY put, as a query, could the Irish live and prosper if a brazen wall surrounded their island? The question has been often and vaguely replied to.

Dr. Kane has at length answered it, and proved the affirmative. Confining himself strictly to the *land* of our island (for he does not enter on the subjects of fisheries and foreign commerce,) he has proved that we possess *physical* elements for every important art. Not that he sat down to prove this. Taste, duty, industry, and genius, prompted and enabled him gradually to acquire a knowledge of the physical products and powers of Ireland, and his mastery of chemical and mechanical science enabled him to see how these could be used.

* The Industrial Resources of Ireland, by Robert Kane, M.D., Secretary to the Council of the Royal Irish Academy, Professor of Natural Philosophy to the Royal Dublin Society, and of Chemistry to the Apothecaries' Hall of Ireland. Dublin: Hodges and Smith, 21, College-green.

Thus qualified, he tried, in the Lecture-room of the Dublin Society, to communicate his knowledge to the public. He was as successful as any man lecturing on subjects requiring accurate details could be; and now he has given, in the volume before us, all his lectures, and much more. He, then, is no party pamphleteer, pandering to the national vanity; but a philosopher, who garnered up his knowledge soberly and surely, and now gives us the result of his studies. There was, undoubtedly, a good deal of information on the subjects treated of by Dr. Kane scattered through our topographical works and parliamentary reports, but that information is, for the most part, vague, unapplied, and not tested by science. Dr. Kane's work is full, clear, scientific, exact in stating places, extent, prices, and every other working detail, and is a manual of the whole subject.

In such interlaced subjects as industrial resources we must be content with practical classifications.

Dr. Kane proceeds in the following order:— First, he considers the *mechanical* powers of the country—viz., its fuel and its water powers. Secondly, its *mineral* resources—its iron, copper, lead, sulphur, marble, slates, &c. Thirdly, the agriculture of the country in its first function— the raising of food, and the modes of cropping, manuring, draining, and stacking. Fourthly, agriculture in its secondary use, as furnishing staples for the manufacture of woollens, linens, starch, sugar, spirits, &c. Fifthly, the modes of carrying internal trade by roads, canals, and rail-

ways.   Sixthly, the cost and condition of skilled
and unskilled labour in Ireland.   Seventhly, our
state as to capital.   And he closes by some
earnest and profound thoughts on the need of
industrial education in Ireland.

Now, let us ask the reader what he knows
upon any or all of these subjects; and whether
he ought, as a citizen, or a man of education, or
a man of business, to be ignorant of them?   Such
ignorance as exists here must be got rid of, or
our cry of "Ireland for the Irish" will be a whine
or a brag, and will be despised as it deserves.
We must know Ireland from its history to its
minerals, from its tillage to its antiquities, before
we shall be an Irish nation, able to rescue and
keep the country.   And if we are too idle, too
dull, or too capricious to learn the arts of strength,
wealth, and liberty, let us not murmur at being
slaves.

For the present, we shall confine ourselves to
the subjects of the mechanical powers and minerals of Ireland, as treated by Dr. Kane.

The first difference between manufactures now,
and in *any* former time, is the substitution of
machines for the hands of man.   It may, indeed,
be questioned whether the increased strength
over matter thus given to man compensates for
the ill effects of forcing people to work in crowds ;
of destroying small and pampering large capi-
talists, of lessening the distribution of wealth
even by the very means which increase its pro-
duction.

We sincerely lament, with Lord Wharncliffe,

the loss of domestic manufactures; we would prefer one house-wife skilled in the distaff and the dairy—home-bred, and home-taught, and home-faithful—to a factory full of creatures who live amid the eternal roll, and clash, and glimmer of spindles and rollers, watching with aching eyes the thousand twirls, and capable of but one act—tying the broken threads. We abhor that state; we prefer the life of the old times, or of modern Norway.

But, situated as we are, so near a strong enemy, and in the new highway from Europe to America, it may be doubted whether we can retain our simple domestic life. There is but one chance for it. If the Prussian Tenure Code be introduced, and the people turned into small proprietors, there is much, perhaps every hope of retaining or regaining our homestead habits, and such a population need fear no enemy.

If this do not come to pass, we must make the best of our state, join our chief towns with railways, put quays to our harbours, mills on our rivers, turbines on our coasts, and under restrictions and with guarantees set the steam-engine to work at our flax, wool, and minerals.

The two great mechanical powers are fire and water. Ireland is nobly endowed with both.

We do not possess as ample fields of flaming coal as Britain; but even of that we have large quantities, which can be raised at about the same rate at which English coal can be landed on our coast.

The chief seats of flaming coal in Ireland are

to the west of Lough Allen, in Connaught, and around Dungannon, in Tyrone. There is a small district of it in Antrim.

The stone coal. or anthracite, which having little gas, does not blaze, and having much sulphur is disagreeable in a room, and has been thought unfit for smelting, is found—first, in the Kilkenny district, between the Nore and Barrow—secondly, from Freshford to Cashel; and thirdly, in the great Munster coal country, cropping up in every barony of Clare, Limerick, Cork, and Kerry. By the use of vapour with it, the anthracite appears to be freed from all its defects as a smelting and engine coal, and being a much more pure and powerful fuel than the flaming coal, there seems no reason to doubt that in it we have a manufacturing power that would supply as for generations.

Our bogs have not been done justice to. The use of turf in a damp state turns it into an inferior fuel. Dried under cover, or broken up and dried under pressure, it is more economical, because far more efficient. It is used now in the Shannon steamers, and its use is increasing in mills. For some purposes it is peculiarly good—thus, for the finer iron works, turf, and turf-charcoal are even better than wood, and Dr. Kane shows that the precious Baltic iron, for which from 15l. to 35l. per ton is given, could be equalled by Irish iron smelted by Irish turf for six guineas per ton.

Dr. Kane proves that the cost of fuel, even if greater in Ireland, by no means precludes us from competing with England; he does so by showing that the cost of fuel in English factories is only from 1 to 1½ per cent., while in Ireland it would be only 2½ to 3½ per cent.—a difference greatly overbalanced by our cheaper labour, labour being over 33 per cent. of the whole expense of a factory.

Here is the analysis of the cost of producing cotton in England in 1830:—

Cotton wool	£8,244,693	or per cent.	26·27
Wages	10,419,000	"	33·16
Interest on capital ...	3,400,000	"	10·84
Coals	339,680	"	1·08
Rent, taxes, insurance, other charges and profit	8,935,320	"	28·65
	£31,338,693		100·00

In water-power we are still better off. Dr. Kane calculates the rain which falls on Ireland in a year at over 100 billion cubic yards; and of this he supposes two-thirds to pass off in evaporation, leaving one-third, equal to near a million and a half of horse power, to reach the sea. His calculations of the water-power of the Shannon and other rivers are most interesting. The elements, of course, are the observed fall of rain by the gauge in the district, and the area of the catchment (or drainage) basins of each river and its tributaries. The chief objection to water-power is its irregularity. To remedy this he proposes to do what has increased the water-power on the Bann five-fold, and has made the wealth of Greenock—namely, to make mill-lakes by damming up valleys, and thus controlling and equalising the supply of water, and letting none go waste. His calculations of the relative merits of undershot, overshot, breast, and turbine wheels, are most valuable, especially of the last, which is a late and successful French contrivance, acting by pressure. He proposes to use the turbine in coast mills, the tide being the motive power; and, strange as it sounds, the experiments seem to decide in favour of this plan.——

" The Turbine was invented by M. Fourneyron. Coals being abundant, the steam-engine is invented in England; coals being scarce, the water-pressure engine and the turbine are invented in France. It is thus the physical condition of each country directs its mechanical genius. The turbine is a horizontal wheel furnished with curved float-boards, on which the water presses from a cylinder which is suspended over the wheel, and the base of which is divided by curved partitions, that the water may be directed in issuing, so as to produce upon the curved float boards of the wheel its greatest effect. The best curvature to be given to the fixed partitions and to the float-boards is a delicate problem, but practically it has been completely solved. The construction of the machine is simple, its parts not liable to go out of order; and as the action of the water is by pressure, the force is under the most favourable circumstances for being utilized.

" The effective economy of the turbine appears to equal that of the overshot wheel. But this economy in the turbine is accompanied by some conditions which render it peculiarly valuable. In a water wheel you cannot have great economy of power without very slow motion, and hence where high velocity is required at the working point, a train of mechanism is necessary, which causes a material loss of force. Now, in the turbine the greatest economy is accompanied by rapid motion, and hence the connected machinery may be rendered much less complex. In the turbine also a change in the height of the head of water alters only the power of the machine in that proportion, but the whole quantity of water is economized to the same degree. Thus if a turbine be working with a force of ten horses, and that its supply of water be suddenly doubled, it becomes of twenty horse power; if the supply be reduced to one-half, it still works five horse power: whilst such sudden and extreme change would altogether disarrange water wheels, which can only be constructed for the minimum, and allow the overplus to go to waste."

Our own predilection being in favour of water-power—as cheaper, healthier, and more fit for Ireland than steam—gave the following peculiar interest in our eyes:—

"I have noticed at such length the question of the cost of fuel and of steam power, not from my own opinion of its ultimate importance, but that we might at once break down that barrier to all active exertion which indolent ignorance constantly retreats behind. The cry of, 'what can we do? consider England's coal mines,' is answered by showing that we have available fuel enough. The lament that coals are so dear with us and so cheap in England, is, I trust, set at rest by the evidence of how little influential the price of fuel is. However, there are other sources of power besides coals; there are other motive powers than steam. Of the 83,000 horse power employed to give motion to mills in England, 21,000, even in the coal districts, are not moved by fire but by fire water. The force of gravity in falling water can spin and wave as well as the elasticity of steam; and in this power we are not deficient. It is necessary to study its circumstances in detail, and I shall, therefore, next proceed to discuss the condition of Ireland with regard to water power."

Dr. Kane proves that we have at Arigna an *inexhaustible* supply of the richest iron ore, with coals to smelt it, lime to flux it, and infusible sand-stone and fire-clay to make furnaces of on the spot. Yet not a pig or bar is made there now. He also gives in great detail the extent, analysis, costs of working, and every other leading fact, as to the copper mines of Wicklow, Knockmahon, and Allihies; the lead, gold, and sulphur mines of Wicklow; the silver mines of Ballylichey, and details of the building materials and marbles.

He is everywhere precise in his industrial and scientific statements, and beautifully clear in his style and arrangement.

Why, then, are we a poor province? Dr Kane quotes Forbes, Quetelet, &c., to prove the physical strength of our people. He might have quoted every officer who commanded them to prove their courage and endurance; nor is there much doubt expressed even by their enemies of their being quick and inventive. Their soil is productive—the rivers and harbours good—their fishing *opportunities* great—so is their means of making internal communications across their great central plains. We have immense water, and considerable fire power; and, besides the minerals necessary for the arts of peace, we are better supplied than almost any country with the finer sorts of iron, charcoal, and sulphur, wherewith war is now carried on. Why is it, with these means of amassing and guarding wealth, that we are so poor and paltry? Dr. Kane seems to think we are so from industrial education. He is partly right. The remote causes were repeated foreign invasion, forfeiture, and tyrannous laws. Ignorance, disunion, self-distrust, quick credulity, and caprice, were the weaknesses engendered in us by misfortune and misgovern-

H

ment; and they were then the allies of oppression; for, had we been willing, we had long ago been rich and free. Knowledge is now within our reach, if we work steadily; and strength of character will grow upon us, by every month of perseverance and steadiness in politics, trade, and literature.

IRISH TOPOGRAPHY.

COMPLAINTS had frequently been made of the inequality of the grand jury taxation before any attempt was made to remedy it. The committee on grand jury presentments, in their report, dated 12th June, 1815, stated that these complaints were well founded, and recommended " that some mode should be devised for rendering such assessments more equal, the defect appearing to them to arise, in a great degree, from the levy being made in reference to old surveys (which were taken on the measure of land which was deemed profitable at the time of such surveys), which, of course, cannot comprehend the great improvements which have taken place in Ireland since the period at which these surveys took place."

Though some of the evidence given before that committee displays a remarkable ignorance of this and many other facts, yet the fact itself of the oppressive inequality was put beyond doubt by the evidence of Daniel Mussenden, Esq.,

C. P. Leslie, Esq., Right Hon. Denis Browne,
Colonel Crosbie, General Archdall, &c.

It appears, from their evidence, that the grand
jury cess was in some places distributed in equal
shares over districts of a size and value often dif-
ferring as one from six, and in other places distributed in unequal shares, bearing no obvious
proportion to the size or value of the different
districts.

These districts were generally called townlands, sometimes ploughlands, cartrons, carvas,
tates, &c. Most of the witnesses fancied that
these divisions had been originally equal, and
made by James I., or Strafford, Sir W. Petty, or
William III.

Mr. Mussenden suggested that they were made
by the old Irish. It is possible that the Connaught divisions may have been affected by the
Strafford survey, now lost; Ulster by the settlement in James's time, and many parts of Munster, Leinster, and Connaught, by the forfeitures
and divisions in William's, Cromwell's, Charles's,
James's, and Elizabeth's times, or even by those
of earlier date. With respect to these, we would
remark that the forfeitures were according to
previous divisions, and so the grants generally
were.

Some of the townlands, from their names, seem
to have been household lands of princes, other
hospitality lands attached to the caravanserais
which the ancient Irish so liberally endowed;
but most of them must be accounted for in other
ways. If these divisions grew marked in the
middle ages, we should be disposed to say that

each was the possession of a large family or small
sept, by the aggregation of many of which the
great princedoms were made up. If these names
and divisions are of older date (as we believe),
then they either originated in, or were used for,
the annual distribution of lands which was customary under the Brehon law ; and in either
case were likely to have been continued during
the middle ages for family purposes.

And here we would remark that this annual
distribution of land has been foolishly censured.
The Irish then lived partly as hunters—chiefly
as shepherds and herds—very little as tillers.
The annual distribution of grazing land seems
not so unreasonable, nor could it have been attended with the wasteful and disastrous results
supposed to result from changeful tenures of tillage lands.

In a second report, in 1818, the Grand Jury
Presentment Committee urged the immediate and
complete alteration of the system, and, in 1819,
a bill for the survey and valuation of Ireland
was brought in. But this bill was soon abandoned.

In 1824 the subject was taken up in good earnest. The Commons resolved that " it is expedient, for the purpose of apportioning more
equally the local burthens of Ireland, to provide
for a general survey and valuation of that part
of the United Kingdom." Accordingly it voted
£5,000 towards a trigonometrical survey, and
appointed an active and fair committee " to consider of the best mode of apportioning more
equally the local burthens collected in Ireland,

and to provide for a general survey and valuation of that part of the United Kingdom."

The committee sat and received the evidence of Major Colby (now, and then, head of the survey in both kingdoms), Lieutenant Colonel Keane, Mr. Spring Rice, (now Lord Monteagle), Mr. Leslie Foster (late Baron of the Exchequer), Mr. John Wilson Croker, Mr. Richard Griffiths (since intrusted with the valuation of Ireland), Messrs. Bald, Nimmo, Edgeworth, and Aher, civil engineers, Captain Kater, and many others. It reported on the 21st of June, 1824.

The report states that the grand jury taxes for the preceding year were over £750,000, and that the assessment of this was most unequal and unjust, for the reasons before stated.

The committee speak separately on the survey and valuation.

The most material part of their *Report on the Survey* is as follows :—

They state the surface of Ireland at about twelve millions Irish, or twenty millions English, acres, divided in four provinces, thirty-two counties at large, eight counties of cities or towns or other independent jurisdictions, two hundred and fifty-two baronies, about two thousand four hundred parishes, and an immense number of townlands or minor sub-divisions.

The existing surveys they describe as few and defective. They omit any notice of the survey of Ulster made in 1618–19, under royal commission, by Pymar and others, and printed in the first part of Harris's collection of tracts on Ireland, entitled *Hibernica.*

They state, on Mr. Nimmo's authority, that " Strafford's Survey of the Forfeited Lands" was a memoir, terrier, or written description, accompanied by outline maps, and that all these documents have perished.

Mr. Hardiman, in a paper on Irish maps, printed in the fourteenth volume of the *Transactions of the Irish Academy*, states that surveys had been made of Ireland by the Irish monarchs, that fragments of these remain, and that in one of them, by Fenton, some allusion to a map seems to be made. If such ever existed, it no longer does.

The earliest published map of Ireland, according to Mr. Nimmo, is that in the " Itinerary of Antonine," published by Ricardus Corinensis in the fourteenth century, and taken from the table of latitudes and longitudes, made by Ptolemy. Ware notices that Ptolemy places Mona, Man, &c., among the isles of Ireland, and adds that Macianus (in Periplo) says that Ireland had sixteen provinces, fifteen famous cities, five noted promontories, and six eminent islands.

Mercator and Hondius published an inferior map, taken chiefly from Norse and Danish authorities. Mr. Bald refers to a map of Ireland of the fourteenth century, contained in " Arrowsmith's Memoir;" but whether this is Ricardus's or not, we do not know—neither can we get in Dublin " Arrowsmith's Memoir," or " Ricardus's map." But Bertram, who re-printed Ricardus, Nennius, and Gildas, in 1755, gives an original and highly interesting map of Ireland. Mercator was only copied until Elizabeth's time, when a map fourteen English miles to one inch, was published.

Then follow Speed's in 1610, of Ireland and of the four provinces, Richard Blome's and Strafford's, before alluded to.

In the State Papers (temp. Henry VIII.) there are three Irish maps, for the first time printed from old MSS. maps. The first of these is a map of Munster, the date of which is only shown by its being noted in Lord Burleigh's hand. The second is a map of all Ireland, made by John Goghe in 1557; and the third is also a map of Ireland, made by John Morden, for the Earl of Salisbury, in 1609. All these contain clan names; one of them has the arms of the principal families, and they all, besides written names, contain topographical maps of much antiquarian value.

In the *Pacata Hibernia,* edited by Stafford in 1633, there are maps of Ireland, of Munster, and fifteen plans of different places in Munster, roughly engraved, but usefully drawn as picture-maps or panoramas—the best style for small plans at least, and lately revived on the continent in the panoramas of Switzerland, the Rhine, &c.

Danville contains a map of ancient Ireland, and he and Beaufort, and many others published, made up maps of Ireland in the middle ages. Ware, too, in his antiquities, prints a map of ancient Ireland, made from Ptolemy, Camden, and in one place from Orosius.

We now come to the celebrated Down Survey. It was executed by Sir William Petty, Physician-General, under a commission, dated 11th De-

cember, 1654, at the payment of 20*s.* a-day and
1*d.* an acre. Petty got a lot of Cromwellian soldiers into training in two months, and then surveyed all the forfeited lands. These soldiers used
the chain and circumferentor, and their measurements were sent to Dublin, and there plotted or
laid *down* on paper, whence the work is called
The Down Survey.

This Survey contained both barony and parish
maps of two-thirds of Ireland ; the former on a
scale of forty perches to an inch, containing
parish and townland boundaries, mountain and
bog marks, &c. 1430 maps remain in the Record Tower—of these 260 are baronial, 1170
parochial. 130 baronial maps are perfect, 67
partially burned, 2 or 3 are " missing." 780 parochial are perfect, 391 partly burnt in 1711. A
copy of the baronial maps exists in Paris in the
King's Library, having been taken by a privateer
when on their way to England for Sir W. Petty,
and tracings of these were made by General
Vallancey and Major Taylor. In the Queen's
Inns is copied his account of this survey. All
Petty's maps have marginal descriptions and references to the "Book of Distributions" of the
forfeitures. These maps are evidence between
the crown and subject, and between two subjects
holding as grantees from the crown by that distribution. There are some maps relating to, or
part of this, said to be in the Landsdowne Collection.

Sir William Petty published a folio " County
Atlas"—so did Mr. Pratt. A miniature "County
Atlas" was printed in London, in 1720, by

Rowles, taken from Petty and Pratt. The latest "County Atlas" is the meagre one published with Lewis's "Topographical Dictionary."

The next official survey was that of the lands forfeited in William's time, composing about two millions acres. It is lodged in the vice-treasurer's office.

The following lists of maps and surveys was given in by Mr. Bald as part of his evidence :—

"A map of Ireland in 1716, by Thomas Bakewill, who also issued a map of the city of Dublin.

Herman Moll gave a map of Ireland.

Ortelinus (Charles O'Connor's) map of Ireland, with the names of the septs at the beginning of the 17th century.

Ditto, improved, containing proprietors' names in 1777, (Note too, that this has been re-printed in Madden's United Irishmen—2nd series.)

Ireland, by Pratt, six sheets.

Ditto,   J. Rocque, four sheets.

Ditto,   C. Bowles, four sheets.

Ditto,   Jeffries, one sheet.

Ditto,   Kitchin, one sheet.

Ditto,   Major Taylor, one sheet, 1793.

Ditto,   Beaufort, two sheets, 1793, accompanied by a very bad memoir.

Ditto,   Arrowsmith, four sheets, 1811, reprinted frequently since.

Taylor and Skinner's map of Irish roads, in 1777.

We may add, Ireland, by Overdon and Morgan; do., by Senex, &c., in 1711.

COUNTY MAPS OF IRELAND.

County of Dublin, published in 1760, by John Rocque, scale not quite six inches to three English miles.

Survey of the county of Dublin, by William Duncan, principal draughtsman to the quarter-master-general of Ireland, published in 1821, scale three inches to one mile, and has been constructed on trigonometrical principles.

County of Louth, surveyed by Taylor and Skinner in 1777, scale two inches to one mile.

A survey of Louth, by Mr. John M'Neill.

County of Armagh, surveyed by John Rocque, scale two inches to one mile; states the impossibility of finding the barony bounds, and had recourse to Sir William Petty's surveys.

Wexford, surveyed by Valentine Gill, four sheets.

Westmeath, by Wm. Larkin, since 1800			
Meath,	do.	do.	Scale of the
Waterford,	do.	do.	published
Leitrim,	do.	do.	maps, two
Sligo,	do.	do.	inches to
Galway,	do.	do.	one mile.
Cavan,	do.	do.	

All Mr. Larkin's county surveys were protracted from a scale of four inches to one Irish mile, but do not appear to have been constructed from triangular measurements.

Cork, surveyed by Edwards and Savage in 1811.

Londonderry, by the Rev. G. V. Sampson in 1813, accompanied by a statistical memoir; sections on the map, scale two inches to one mile.

Longford, surveyed by William Edgeworth. This map was constructed from trigonometrical data.

Roscommon, by Messrs. Edgeworth and Griffiths. This survey has been done trigonometrically. The engraving was executed in a most superior manner.

County of Down, scale one inch to a mile; published in 1755. Hills drawn in profile; no surveyor's name to the map; it has soundings along the coast.

County of Down, by Williamson, 1810.

Antrim, by John Lendrick, in 1780.

Kildare, by Major Alexander Taylor, in 1783. Scale one inch and half to a mile.

Kerry, by Pelham.

Ditto, by Porter.

Wicklow, by Jacob Neville, in 1760.

Clare, by Henry Pelham, in 1787. Scale one inch and half to the Irish mile.

Kilkenny has been surveyed by Mr. David Aher in town lands.

Limerick, King's County, Donegal, Fermanagh, Monaghan, Carlow, Queen's County, Tipperary, Mayo, and King's County have all been surveyed.

CHARTS.

Chart of Kenmare River, by William Irwin, 1749.

Mr. Murdoch M'Kenzie made a general survey of the whole harbours, bays, and shores of Ireland, on the scale of one inch to an English mile, with general charts, in two volumes. By the date of the variation in 1759, it appears he was engaged about sixteen years. His sailing directions are valuable; and although the outline of the coast is faulty, yet all chart-makers have continued to copy his soundings.

Chart of Dublin Bay, by Scal and Richards, 1765.

Do. of the Shannon, by Cowan, 1795, two inches and a half to an Irish mile.

Do. of Dublin Bay, by Captain Bligh.

Several charts of the harbours on the east coast of Ireland have been published by the Fishery Board; they were surveyed under the direction of Mr. Nimmo, and are among the finest engraved specimens of our hydrographic surveys yet published.

Chart of Lough Derg, by Longfield and Murray.

Chart of Lough Ree."

Rocque was a pupil of Cassini, the astronomer and topographist, and came to Ireland in 1752. Mr. Nimmo states that he founded a class of surveyors and valuators, represented in 1824 by Messrs. Brassington, Sherrard, &c.; highly respectable, but who, not having much science, use only the circumferentor, chain and level. He added that the hydrographical survey of Dublin Coast, by Scale and Richards' pupils of that old French school was "respectable."

The survey of the forfeited estates in Scotland founded a school with more science, using the theodolite, &c. Among its pupils were Messrs.

Taylor, who, with Skinner, surveyed the roads of Ireland, Scotland, and part of England, and by others of this school the post-office road surveys were made.

Messrs. Nimmo and Bald, Scotchmen, Vignoles, an Englishman, and Messrs. Griffiths, Edgeworth, Aher, and M'Neill, Irishmen, and all men of very high abilities and science, bring down the pedigree of civil topography in Ireland to our time.

Among the greatest topographical works of these men were the BOG MAPS (four inches to the mile) ; Mr. Nimmo's coast and harbour surveys for the Fishery Board ; Mr. Vignoles' surveys for the Railway Commission, and Mr. Bald's superb map of Mayo, on a scale of four inches to the mile, shaded, lithographed beautifully in Paris, and accompanied by raised models of the actual shape of parts of the county. Numerous other surveys and maps were made by these gentlemen, and by Mr. Griffiths, &c., for the Board of Works, the Woods and Forests, the Shannon Commissioners, and various other public departments.

The Ordnance made a slight military survey by order of the Irish Parliament. At the head of it was General Vallancey, assisted by Colonel Tarrant and Major Taylor ; but the witnesses in 1824 treat it slightingly.

The present survey has, besides its own unrivalled maps, given materials for several others. Amongst these are the maps in the census report, shaded to represent the density of population, the diffusion of houses, of stock, and of know-

ledge. Indeed, Captain Larcom's application of
the electrotype to the multiplication of the cop-
per-plates enables him to represent on a map any
single attribute of the country separately, with
little trouble or expense. The materials for
single and double sheet maps of the Useful Knowledge Society, price 6d. and 1s., were supplied
from the Survey-office. The Railway Commissioners' general map was also made at Mountjoy.*
This is the only large-sized map of Ireland,
shaded according to the slopes of the land, possessed of any accuracy. We can testify to this
accuracy. It is published in six sheets for £1
uncoloured. It is also issued at a higher price
coloured geologically. For those who have more
time and energy than money to spare, we know
no better in-door way of studying Irish geology
than to buy this map uncoloured, and to put in
the geological colouring from another copy.

The reader is, probably, wearied enough of
this catalogue, and yet if he be a young student
of his country's state or history, this catalogue
will be most useful to him. If he be master, not
apprentice, he will see how rude and imperfect
this list is. We must ask him to forgive these
crudities, and send us (as he well can) something
better, and we shall be glad to use it for ourselves and the public. For a list of maps of Ireland,
and parts of it chiefly in MSS., in Trinity College, Dublin, we must refer the reader to Mr.
Hardiman's valuable paper in the 14th volume
of the Transactions of the Royal Irish Academy.

* The late Mountjoy Barracks, in the Phœnix Park,
Dublin.

THE VALUATION OF IRELAND.

THE Committee of 1824 was but meagerly supplied with evidence as to foreign surveys. They begin that subject with a notice of the Survey of England, made by order of William the Conqueror, and called the Doomsday Book. That book took six years to execute, and is most admirably analysed by Thierry.

The following is their summary account of some modern surveys :—

"In France, the great territorial survey or *cadastre*, has been in progress for many years. It was first suggested in 1763, and after an interval of thirty years, during which no progress was made, it was renewed by the government of that day, and individuals of the highest scientific reputation, M. M. Lagrange, Laplace, and Delambre, were consulted, with respect to the best mode of carrying into effect the intention of government. Subsequent events suspended any effectual operations in the French *cadastre* till the year 1802, when a school of topographical engineering was organised.— The operations now in progress were fully commenced in 1808. The principle adopted, is the formation of a central commission acting in conjunction with the local authorities ; the classification of lands, according to an ascertained value, is made by three resident proprietors of land in each district, selected by the municipal council, and by the chief officer of revenue. ' In the course of thirteen years, one third only of each department had been surveyed, having cost the state £120,000 per annum. At the rate at which it is carried on, it may be computed as likely to require for its completion, a total sum of £4,680, 000, or an acreable charge of 8½*d*.'

The delay of the work as well as the increase of expense, seem to have been the result of the minuteness of the survey, which extends to every district field; a minuteness which, for many reasons, your committee consider both unnecessary and inexpedient to be sought for, in the proposed Survey of Ireland.

"The survey of Bavaria is of modern date, but of equal minuteness. It is commenced by a primary triangulation, and principal and verification bases; it is carried on to a second triangulation, with very accurate instruments, so as to determine 'all the principal points; the filling up the interior is completed by a peculiar species of plane table; and in order to do away with the inaccuracies of the common chain, the triangulation is carried down on paper to the most minute corners of fields.' *The map is laid down on a scale of* 12 *inches to the mile, or one-five-thousandth part of the real size : and as it contains all that is required in the most precise survey of property, it is used in the purchase and sale of real estates.*

"The cadastre of Savoy and Piedmont began in 1729, and is stated to have at once afforded the government the means of apportioning justly all the territorial contributions, and to have put an end to litigations between individuals, by ascertaining, satisfactorily, the bounds of properties.

"The Neapolitan survey under Visconti, and that of the United States under Heslar, are both stated to be in progress; but your committee have not had the means of ascertaining on what principles they are conducted."

The Committee adopted a scale for the maps of six inches to a statute mile, believing, apparently with justice, that a six-inch scale map, if perfectly well executed, would be minute enough for buyers and sellers of land, especially as the larger holdings are generally townlands, the bounds of which they meant to include. And, wherever a greater scale was needed, the pentagraph afforded a sufficiently accurate plan of forming maps to it. They, in another point, *proposed* to differ from the Bavarian Survey, in omitting field boundaries, as requiring too much time and expense; but they stated that barony, parish, and townland boundaries were essential to the utility of the maps. They also seemed to think that for private purposes their utility would much depend on their being accompanied, as the Bavarian maps were, by a memoir of the number of families, houses, size, and description of farms, and a valuation. And for this purpose they printed all the forms. The valuation still goes on of the townlands, and classes of soil in each. The Statistical Memoir has, unfortunately, been stopped, and no survey or valuation of farms, or holdings as such, has been attempted. We would *now* only recall attention to the design of the Committee of 1824 on the subject.

They proposed to leave the whole Survey to the Board of Ordnance, and the Valuation to Civil Engineers.

The Valuation has been regulated by a series of acts of Parliament, and we shall speak of it presently.

The Survey commenced in 1826, and has gone on under the superintendence of Colonel Colby, and the local control of Captain Larcom.

The following has been its progress :— First, a base line of about five miles was measured on the flat shore of Lough Foyle, and from thence triangular measurements were made by the theodolite and over the whole country, and all the chief points of mountain, coast, &c., ascertained. How accurately this was done has been proved

by an astronomical measurement of the distance
from Dublin to Armagh (about seventy miles),
which only differed four feet from the distance
calculated by the Ordnance triangles.

Having completed these large triangles, a detailed survey of the baronies, parishes, and townlands of each county followed. The field books
were sent to the central station at Mountjoy, and
sketched, engraved on copper, and printed there.
The first county published was Derry, in 1833,
and now the townland survey is finished, and all
the counties have been engraved and issued except Limerick, Kerry, and Cork.

The Survey has also engraved a map of Dublin City on the enormous scale of five feet to a
statute mile. This map represents the shape and
space occupied by every house, garden, yard,
and pump in Dublin. It contains antiquarian
lettering. Every house, too, is numbered on the
map. One of its sheets, representing the space
from Trinity College to the Castle, is on sale,
as we trust the rest of it will be.

Two other sets of maps remain to be executed.
First—Maps of the towns of Ireland, on a scale
of five feet to the mile. Whatever may be said
in reply to Sir Denham Norreys' demand for a
survey of holdings in rural districts does not apply to the case of towns, and we therefore trust
that the holdings will be marked and separately
valued in towns.

The other work is a general *shaded* map of
Ireland, on a scale of one inch to the statute
mile. At present, as we elsewhere remarked,
the only tolerable shaded map of Ireland is that

of the Railway Commission, which is on a scale
of one inch to four statute miles. Captain Larcom proposes, and the Commission on the Ordnance Memoir recommend, that contour lines
should be the skeleton of the shading. If this
plan be adopted the publication cannot be for
some years; but the shading will have the accuracy of machine work instead of mere hand skill.
Contours are lines representing series of levels
through a country, and are inestimable for draining, road making, and military movements. But
though easily explained to the eye, we doubt our
ability to teach their meaning by words only.

To return to the townland or six-inch survey.
The names were corrected by Messrs. Petrie,
O'Donovan, and Curry, from every source accessible in *Ireland*. Its maps contain the county,
barony, parish, townland, and glebe boundaries,
names and acreage; names and representations of
all cities, towns, demesnes, farms, ruins, collie-
ries, forges, limekilns, tanneries, bleachgreens,
wells, &c., &c.; also of all roads, rivers, canals,
bridges, locks, weirs, bogs, ruins, churches,
chapels; they have also the number of feet of
every little swell of land, and a mark for every
cabin.

Of course these maps run to an immense number. Thus for the county of Galway there are
137 double folio sheets, and for the small county
of Dublin 28. Where less than half the sheet is
covered with engraving (as occurs towards the
edges of a county) the sheet is sold uncoloured
for 2*s.* 6*d.*; where more than half is covered the
price is 5*s.*

In order to enable you to find any sheet so as to know the bearings of its ground on any other, there is printed for each county an index map, representing the whole county on one sheet. This sheet is on a small scale (from one to three miles to an inch), but contains in smaller type the baronies and parishes, roads, rivers, demesnes, and most of the information of general interest. This index map is divided by lines into as many oblong spaces as there are maps of the six-inch scale; and the spaces are numbered to correspond with the six-inch map. On the sides of the index maps are tables of the acreage of the baronies and parishes; and examples of the sort of marks and type used for each class of subjects in the *six-inch* maps. Uncoloured, the index map, representing a whole county, is sold for 2s. 6d.

Whenever those maps are re-engraved, the Irish words will, we trust, be spelled in an Irish and civilised orthography, and not barbarously, as at present.

It was proposed to print for each county one or more volumes, containing the history of the district and its antiquities, the numbers, and past and present state and occupations of the people, the state of its agriculture, manufactures, mines, and fisheries, and what means of extending there existed in the county, and its natural history, including geology, zoology, &c. All this was done for the town of Derry, much to the service and satisfaction of its people. All this ought to be *as fully* done for Armagh, Dublin, Cork, and every other part of Ireland.

The commissioners recommend that the geology of Ireland (and we would add natural history generally) should be investigated and published, not by the topographical surveyors nor in counties, but by a special board, and for the whole of Ireland; and they are right, for our plants, rocks, and animals are not within civil or even obvious topographical boundaries, and we have plenty of Irishmen qualified to execute it. They also advise that the statistics should be entrusted to a statistical staff, to be permanently kept up in Ireland. This staff would take the census every ten years, and would in the intervals between the beginning and ending of each census have plenty of statistical business to do for parliament (Irish or Imperial) and for public departments. If we are ever to have a registry of births, deaths (with the circumstances of each case), and marriages, some such staff will be essential to inspect the registry, and work up information from it. But the history, antiquities, and industrial resources, the commissioners recommend to have published in county volumes. They are too solicitous about keeping such volumes to small dimensions; but the rest of their plans are admirable.

The value of this to Ireland, whether she be a nation or a province, cannot be overrated. From the farmer and mechanic to the philosopher, general, and statesman, the benefit will extend, and yet so careless or so hostile are ministers that they have not conceded it, and so feeble by dulness or disunion are Irishmen and Irish members, that they cannot extort even this.

We now come to the last branch of the subject—

THE VALUATION.

The Committee of 1824 recommended only principles of Valuation. They were three, viz.:—

" § 1. A fixed and uniform principle of valuation applicable throughout the whole work, and enabling the valuation not only of townlands but that of counties, to be compared by one common measure. § 2. A central authority, under the appointment of government, for direction and superintendence, and for the generalisation of the returns made in detail. § 3. Local assistance, regularly organised, furnishing information on the spot, and forming a check for the protection of private rights."

Accordingly on the 5th of July, 1825, an act was passed requiring, in the first instance, the entry in all the grand jury records of the names and contents of all parishes, manors, townlands, and other divisions, and the proportionate assessments. It then went on to authorise the Lord Lieutenant to appoint surveyors to be paid out of the Consolidated Fund. These surveyors were empowered to require the attendance of cess collectors and other inhabitants, and with their help to examine, and ascertain, and mark the " reputed boundaries of all and every or any barony, half barony, townland, parish, or other division or denomination of land," howsoever called. The act also inflicted penalties on persons removing or injuring any post, stone, or other mark made by the surveyors ; but we believe there has been no occasion to enforce these clauses, the good sense and good feeling of the people being ample securities against such wanton crime. Such survey was not to affect the rights of owners, yet from it lay an appeal to the Quarter Sessions.

This, as we see, relates to *civil boundaries*, not *valuations*.

In May, 1820, another act was passed directing the Ordnance officers to send copies of their maps, as fast as finished, to the Lord Lieutenant, who was to appoint " *one* Commissioner of Valuation for *any* counties;" and to give notice of such appointment to the grand jury of every such county. Each grand jury was then to appoint an Appeal Committee for each barony, and a Committee of Revision for the whole county. This Commission of Valuation was then to appoint from three to nine fit valuators in the county, who, after trial by the Commissioner, were to go in parties of three and examine all parts of their district, and value such portion of it, and set down such valuation in a parish field book, according to the following average prices :—

" SCALE OF PRICES.

"Wheat, at the general average price of 10s. per cwt., of 112lbs.

"Oats, at the general average price of 6s. per cwt., of 112lbs.

"Barley, at the general average price of 7s. per cwt., of 112lbs.

"Potatoes, at the general average price of 1s. 7d. per cwt., of 112lbs.

"Butter, at the general average price of 69s. per cwt., of 112lbs.

"Beef, at the general average price of 33s. per cwt., of 112lbs.

"Mutton, at the general average price of 34s. 6d. per cwt., of 112lbs.

"Pork, at the general average price of 25s. 6d. per cwt., of 112lbs.

"That is, having examined each tract—say a hill, a valley, an inch, a reclaimed bit, and by digging and looking at the soil, they were to consider what crop it could best produce, considering its soil, elevation, nearness to markets, and then estimating crops at the foregoing rate, they were to say how much per acre the tract was, in their opinion, worth.

"From this Parish Field Book the Commissioner was to make out a table of the parishes and townlands, &c., in each barony, specifying the average and total value of houses in such subdivisions, and to forward it to the high constable, who was to post copies thereof. A vestry of twenty pound freeholders and twenty shilling cesspayers was to be called in each parish, to consider the table. If they did not appeal, the table was to stand confirmed; if they did appeal, the grand jury committee of appeal, with the valuation commissioner as chairman, were to decide upon the appeal; but if the assessor were dissatisfied the appeal was to go to the committee of revision. The same committee were then to revise the *proportionate* liabilities of *baronies*, subject to an appeal to the Queen's Bench. The valuation so settled was to be published in the *Dublin Gazette*, and thenceforward all *grand jury* and *parish* rates and cesses were to be levied in the *proportions* thereby fixed. But no land theretofore exempt from any rate was thereby made liable. The expenses were to be advanced from the consolidated fund, and repaid by presentment from the county."

It made the *proportionate* values of parishes and townlands, pending the baronial survey, and the baronial valuation, to bind after revision and publication in some newspaper circulating in the county; but *within three years* there was to be a second revision, after which they were to be published in the *Dublin Gazette*, &c., and be

final as to the *proportions* of all parish or grand
jury rates to be paid by all baronies, parishes,
and townlands. It also directed the annexation
of detached bits to the counties respectively surrounding them, and it likewise provided for the
use of the valuation maps and field books in
applotting the grand jury cess charged on the
holders of lands, but such valuation to be merely
a guide and not final. From the varying size
and value of holdings this caution was essential.

Under this last act the valuation has been continued, as every reader of the country papers
must have seen by Mr. Griffith's Notices, and is
now complete in twenty counties, forward in six,
begun in four, and not yet begun in Cork, Kerry,
Limerick, or Dublin.

Mr. Griffith's instructions are clear and full,
and we strongly recommend the study of them,
and an adherence to their forms and classifications, to valuators of all private and public properties, so far as they go. He appointed two
classes of valuators—Ordinary Valuators to make
the first valuation all over each county, and
Check Valuators to re-value patches in every
district, to test the accuracy of the ordinary valuators.

The ordinary valuator was to have two copies
of the Townland (or 6-inch) Survey. Taking a
sheet with him into the district represented on
it, he was to examine the quality of the soil in
lots of from fifty to thirty acres, or still smaller
bits, to mark the bounds of each lot on the survey map, and to enter in his field book the value
thereof, with all the special circumstances spe-

cially stated. The examination was to include digging to ascertain the depth of the soil and the nature of the subsoil. All land was to be valued at its agricultural worth, supposing it liberally set, leaving out the value of timber, turf, &c. Reductions were to be made for elevation above the sea, steepness, exposure to bad winds, patchiness of soil, bad fences, and bad roads. Additions were to be made for neighbourhood of limestone, turf, sea, or other manure, roads, good climate and shelter, nearness to towns.

The following classification of soils was recommended :—

ARRANGEMENT OF SOILS.

" All soils may be arranged under four heads, each representing the characteristic ingredients, as 1. Argillaceous, or clayey; 2. Silicious, or sandy; 3. Calcareous, or limy ; 4. Peaty.

" For practical purposes it will be desirable to subdivide each of these classes :—

" Thus argillaceous soils may be divided into three varieties, viz. :—Clay, clay loam, and argillaceous alluvial.

" Of silicious soils there are four varieties, viz. :—Sandy, gravelly, slaty, and rocky.

" Of calcareous soils we have three varieties, viz. :—Limestone, limestone gravel, and marl.

" Of peat soils two varieties, viz. :—Moor, and peat, or bog.

" In describing in the field book the different qualities of soils, the following explanatory words may be used as occasion may require :—

" *Stiff*—Where a soil contains a large proportion, say one-half, or even more, of tenacious clay, it is called stiff. In dry weather this kind of soil cracks, and opens, and has a tendency to form into large and hard lumps, particularly if ploughed in wet weather.

I

"*Friable*—Where the soil is loose and open, as is generally the case in sandy, gravelly, and moory lands.

"*Strong*—Where a soil contains a considerable portion of clay, and has some tendency to form into clods or lumps, it may be called strong.

"*Deep*—Where the soil exceeds ten inches in depth, the term deep may be applied.

"*Shallow*—Where the depth of the soil is less than eight inches.

"*Dry*—Where the soil is friable, and the subsoil porous, (if there be no springs,) the term dry should be used.

"*Wet*—Where the soil, or subsoil, is very tenacious, or where springs are numerous.

"*Sharp*—Where there is a moderate proportion of gravel, or small stones.

"*Fine or Soft*—Where the soil contains no gravel, but is chiefly composed of very fine sand, or soft, light earth without gravel.

"*Cold*—Where the soil rests on a tenacious clay subsoil, and has a tendency when in pasture, to produce rushes and other aquatic plants.

"*Sandy, or gravelly*—Where there is a large proportion of sand or gravel, through the soil.

"*Slaty*—Where the slaty substratum is much intermixed with the soil.

"*Worn*—Where the soil has been a long time under cultivation, without rest or manure.

"*Poor*—Where the land is naturally of bad quality.

"*Hungry*—Where the soil contains a considerable portion of gravel, or coarse sand, resting on a gravelly subsoil; on such land manure does not produce the usual effect.

"The *colours of soils* may also be introduced, as brown, yellow, blue, grey, red, black, &c.

"Also, where applicable, the words steep, level, shrubby, rocky, exposed, &c., may be used."

Lists of market prices were sent with the field books, and the amounts then reduced to a uniform rate, which Mr. Griffith fixed at 2s. 6d. per

pound over the prices of produce mentioned in
the act.

Rules were also given for valuation of houses,
but we must refer to Mr. Griffith's work for them.

COMMERCIAL HISTORY OF IRELAND.

WHILE the Irish were excluded from English
law and intercourse, England imposed no restrictions on our trade.   The Pale spent its time
tilling and fighting, and it was more sure of its
bellyful of blows than of bread.   It had nothing
to sell, why tax its trade?   The slight commerce
of Dublin was needful to the comforts of the
Norman Court in Dublin Castle.   Why should
it be taxed?   The market of Kilkenny was
guarded by the spears of the Butlers, and from
Sligo to Cork the chiefs and towns of Munster
and Connaught—the Burkes, O'Loghlens, O'Sul-
livans, Galway, Dingle, and Dunbay, carried on
a trade with Spain, and piracy or war against
England.   How *could they* be taxed?

Commercial taxes, too, in those days were hard
to be enforced, and more resembled toll to a rob-
ber than contribution to the state.   Every great
river and pass in Europe, from the Rhine and the
Alps to Berwick and the Blackwater, was affec-
tionately watched by royal and noble castles at
their narrowest points, and the barge anchored
and the caravan halted to be robbed, or, as the
receivers called it, to be taxed.

At last the Pale was stretched round Ireland by art and force. Solitude and peace were in our plains ; but the armed colonist settled in it, and the native came down from his hills as a tenant or a squatter, and a kind of prosperity arose.

Protestant and Catholic, native and colonist, had the same interest—namely, to turn this waste into a garden. They had not, nor could they have had, other things to export than Sydney or Canada have now—cattle, butter, hides, and wool. They had hardly corn enough for themselves ; but pasture was plenty, and cows and their hides, sheep and their fleeces, were equally so. The natives had always been obliged to prepare their own clothing, and, therefore, every creaght and digger knew how to dress wool and skins, and they had found out, or preserved, from a more civilized time, dyes which, to this day, are superior to any others. Small quantities of woollen goods were exported, but our assertion holds good that in our war-times there was no manufacture for export worth naming.

Black Tom Wentworth, the ablest of despots, came here 210 years ago, and found "small beginnings towards a clothing trade." He at once resolved to discourage it. He wrote so to the king on July 25th, 1636, and he was a man true to his enmities. "But," said he, "I'll give them a linen manufacture instead." Now, the Irish had raised flax and made and dyed linen from time immemorial. The saffron-coloured linen shirt was as national as the cloak and birred ; so that Strafford rather introduced the linen manufacture among the new settlers than among the Irish. Certainly he encouraged it, by sending Irishmen to learn in Brabant, and by bringing French and Flemings to work in Ireland.

Charles the Second, doubtless to punish us for our most unwise loyalty to him and his father, assented to a series of acts prohibiting the export of Irish wool, cattle, &c., to England or her colonies, and prohibiting the *direct* importation of several colonial products into Ireland. The chief acts are 12 Charles, c. 4 ; 15 Charles, c. 7 ; and 22 and 23 Charles, c. 26. Thus were the value of land in Ireland, the revenue, and trade, and manufactures of Ireland—Protestant and Catholic—stricken by England.

Perhaps we ought to be grateful, though not to England for these acts. They plundered our pockets, but they guarded our souls from being Anglicised. To France and Spain the produce was sent, and the woollen manufacture continued to increase.

England got alarmed, for Ireland was getting rich. The English lords addressed King William, stating that "the growth and increase of the woollen manufacture in Ireland had long been, and would be *ever*, looked upon with great jealousy by his English subjects, and praying him, by very strict laws, totally to prohibit and suppress the same." The Commons said likewise ; and William answered comfortably—" I shall do all that in me lies to discourage the woollen manufacture in Ireland, and to encourage the linen manufacture there, and to promote the trade of England."

He was as good as his word, and even whipped
and humbugged the unfortunate Irish Parliament
to pass an act, putting twenty per cent. duty on
broad, and ten per cent. on narrow cloths :—

"But it did not satisfy the English parliament, where
a perpetual law was made, prohibiting from the 20th of
June, 1699, the exportation from Ireland of all goods
made or mixed with wool, except to England and Wales,
and with the license of the commissioners of the revenue; duties had been before laid on the importation into
England equal to a prohibition, therefore, this act has
operated as a total prohibition of the exportation."

There was nothing left but to send the wool
raw to England; to smuggle it and cloths to
France and Spain, or to leave the land unstocked.
The first was worst. The export to England de-
clined, smuggling prospered, "wild geese" for
the Brigade, and woollen goods, were run in exchange for claret, brandy, and silks; but not
much land was left waste. Our silks, cottons,
malt, beer, and almost every other article was
similarly prohibited. Striped linens were taxed
thirty per cent., many other kinds of linen were
also interfered with, and twenty-four embargoes
in nineteen years straitened our foreign provision trade. Thus England kept her pledge of
wrath, and broke her promise of service to Ireland.

A vigorous system of smuggling induced her
to relax in some points, and the cannon of the
Volunteers blew away the code.

By the Union she was so drained of money,
and absentee rents and taxes, and of spirit in
every way, that she no longer needs a prohibi-

tory code to prevent our competing with her in any market, Irish or foreign. The Union is prohibition enough, and that England says she will maintain.

Whether it be now possible to create home manufactures, in the old sense of the word— that is, manufactures made in the homes of the workers, is doubted.

In favour of such a thing, if it be possible, the arguments are numberless. Such work is a source of ingenuity and enjoyment in the cabin of the peasant; it rather fills up time that would be otherwise idled, than takes from other work.— Our peasants' wives and daughters could clothe themselves and their families by the winter night work, even as those of Norway do, if the peasants possessed the little estates that Norway's peasants do. Clothes manufactured by hand-work are more lasting, comfortable, and hand-some, and are more natural and national than factory goods. Besides, there is the strongest of all reasons in this, that the factory system seems everywhere a poison to virtue and happiness.

Some invention, which should bring the might of machinery in a wholesome and cheap form to the cabin, seems the only solution of the difficulty.

The hazards of the factory system, however, should be encountered, were it sure to feed our starving millions; but this is dubious.

A Native Parliament can alone judge or act usefully on this momentous subject. An absentee tax and a resident government, and the progress of public industry and education, would enable an Irish Parliament to create vast manufactures there by protecting duties in the first instance, and to maintain them by our general prosperity, or it could rely on its own adjustment of landed property as sufficient to put the People above the need of hazarding purity or content by embarking in great manufactures.

A peasant proprietary could have wealth enough to import wrought goods, or taste and firmness enough to prefer home-made manufactures.

But these are questions for other years. We wish the reader to take our word for nothing, but to consult the writers on Irish trade. Laurence's "Interest of Ireland," (1682;) Browne's "Tracts," (1728;) "Dobbs on Trade," (1729;) Hutchinson's "Commercial Restraints," (1779;) "Sheffield on Irish Trade," (1785;) "Wallace on Irish Trade," (1798;) the various "Parliamentary Reports," and the very able articles on the same subject in the "Citizen."

Do not be alarmed at the list, reader, a month's study would carry you through all but the Reports, and it would be well spent. But if you still shrink, you can ease your conscience by reading Mr. John O'Connell's Report on "The Commercial Injustices," just issued by the Repeal Association. It is an elaborate, learned, and most useful tract.

NATIONAL ART.

No one doubts that if he sees a place or an action he knows more of it than if it had been described to him by a witness. The dullest man, who "put on his best attire" to welcome Cæsar, had a better notion of life in Rome than our ablest artist or antiquary.

Were painting, then, but a coloured chronicle, telling us facts by the eye instead of the ear, it would demand the Statesman's care and the People's love. It would preserve for us faces we worshipped, and the forms of men who led and instructed us. It would remind us, and teach our children, not only how these men looked, but, to some extent, what they were, for nature is consistent, and she has indexed her labours. It would carry down a pictorial history of our houses, arts, costume, and manners, to other times, and show the dweller in a remote isle the appearance of countries and races of his cotemporaries.

As a register of *facts*—as a portrayer of men, singly or assembled—and as a depicter of actual scenery, art is biography, history, and topography, taught through the eye.

So far as it can express facts, it is superior to writing ; and nothing but the scarcity of *faithful* artists, or the stupidity of the public, prevents us from having our pictorial libraries of men and places. There are some classes of scenes—as where continuous action is to be expressed—in which sculpture quite fails, and painting is but a shadowy narrator.

But this, after all, though the most obvious and easy use of Painting and Sculpture, is far indeed from being their highest end.

Art is a regenerator as well as a copyist. As the historian, who composes a history out of various materials, differs from a newspaper reporter, who sets down what he sees—as Plutarch differs from Mr. Grant, and the Abbe Barthelmy from the last traveller in India—so do the Historical Painter, the Landscape Composer (such as Claude or Poussin) differ from the most faithful Portrait, Landscape, or Scene Drawer.

The Painter, who is a master of composition, makes his pencil cotemporary with all times and ubiquitous. Keeping strictly to nature and fact, Romulus sits for him and Paul preaches. He makes Attila charge and Mohammed exhort, and Ephesus blaze when he likes. He tries not rashly, but by years of study of men's character, and dress, and deeds, to make them and their acts come as in a vision before him. Having thus got a design he attempts to realise the vision on his canvass. He pays the most minute attention to truth in his drawing, shading, and colouring, and by imitating the force of nature in his composition, all the clouds that ever floated by him, " the lights of other days," and the forms of the dead, or the stranger, hover over him.

But Art in its highest stage is more than this. It is a creator. Great as Herodotus and Thierry

are, Homer and Beranger are greater. The
ideal has resources beyond the actual. It is infinite, and Art is indefinitely powerful. The
Apollo is more than noble, and the Hercules
mightier than man. The Moses of Michael
Angelo is no likeness of the inspired law-giver,
nor of any other that ever lived, and Raphael's
Madonnas are not the faces of women. As Reynolds says, "the effect of the capital works of
Michael Angelo is, that the observer feels his
whole frame enlarged." It is creation, it is representing beings and things different from our
nature, but true to their own. In this self-con-
sistency is the only nature requisite in works
purely imaginative. Lear is true to his nature,
and so are Mephistopheles, and Prometheus, and
Achilles; but they are not true to human nature;
they are beings created by the poets' minds, and
true to *their* laws of being. There is no commoner blunder in men, who are themselves mere
critics, never creators, than to require consistency
to the nature of us and our world in the works of
poet or painter.

To create a mass of great pictures, statues,
and buildings, is of the same sort of ennoblement
to a people as to create great poems or histories,
or make great codes or win great battles. The
next best, though far inferior, blessing and power
are to inherit such works and achievements.
The lowest stage of all is neither to possess nor
to create them.

Ireland has had some great Painters—Barry
and Forde for example, and many of inferior but
great excellence; and now she boasts high names

—Maclise, Hogan, and Mulready. But their works were seldom done for Ireland, and are rarely known in it. Our portrait and landscape Painters paint foreign men and scenes: and, at all events, the Irish people do not see, possess, nor receive knowledge from their works. Irish history has supplied no subjects for our greatest Artists; and though, as we repeat, Ireland possessed a Forde and Barry, creative Painters of the highest order, the pictures of the latter are mostly abroad; those of the former unseen and unknown. Alas! that they are so few.

To collect into, and make known, and publish in Ireland, the best works of our living and dead Artists, is one of the steps towards procuring for Ireland a recognised National Art. And this is essential to our civilization and renown. The other is by giving education to students and rewards to Artists, to make many of this generation true represcnters, some of them great illustrators and composers, and, perchance, to facilitate the creation of some great spirit.

Something has been done—more remains.

There are schools in Dublin and Cork. But why are those so neglected and imperfect? and why are not similar or better institutions in Belfast, Derry, Galway, Waterford, and Kilkenny? Why is there not a decent collection of casts anywhere but in Cork, and why are they in a garret there? And why have we no gallery of Irishmen's, or any other men's, pictures in Ireland?

The Art-Union has done a great deal. It has helped to support in Ireland artists who should otherwise have starved or emigrated; it has dispersed one (when, oh when, will it disperse another?) fine print of a fine Irish picture through the country, and to some extent interested as well as instructed thousands. Yet it could, and we believe will, do much more. It ought to have Corresponding Committees in the principal towns to preserve and rub up old schools of art and foster new ones, and it might by art and historical libraries, and by other ways, help the cause. We speak as friends, and suggest not as critics, for it has done good service.

The Repeal Association, too, in offering prizes for pictures and sculptures of Irish historical subjects has taken its proper place as the patron of nationality in art; and its rewards for Building Designs may promote the comfort and taste of the people, and the reputation of the country. If artists will examine the rules by which the pictures, statues, and plates remain their property, they will find the prizes not so small as they might at first appear. Nor should they, from interest or just pride, be indifferent to the popularity and fame of success on national subjects, and with a People's Prizes to be contended for. If those who are not Repealers will treat the Association's design kindly and candidly, and if the Repealers will act in art upon principles of justice and conciliation, we shall not only advance national art but gain another field of common exertion.

The Cork School of Art owes its excellence to many causes.

The intense, genial, and Irish character of the

K

people, the southern warmth and variety of clime,
with its effects on animal and vegetable beings,
are the natural causes.

The accident of Barry's birth there, and his great
fame, excited the ambition of the young artists.
An Irishman and a Corkman had gone out from
them, and amazed men by the grandeur and originality of his works of art. He had thrown the
whole of the English painters into insignificance,
for who would compare the luscious common-place
of the Stuart painters, or the melo-dramatic
reality of Hogarth, or the imitative beauty of
Reynolds, or the clumsy strength of West, with
the overbearing grandeur of his works.

But the *present* glories of Cork, Maclise and
Hogan, the greater, but buried, might of Forde,
and the rich promise which we know is springing
there now, are mainly owing to another cause;
and that is, that Cork possesses a gallery of the
finest casts in the world.

These casts are not very many—117 only;
but they are perfect, they are the first from Ca-
nova's moulds, and embrace the greatest works
of Greek art. They are ill placed in a dim and
dirty room—more shame to the rich men of
Cork for leaving them so—but there they are, and
there studied Forde, and Maclise, and the rest,
until they learned to draw better than any moderns, except Cornelius and his living brethren.

In the countries where art is permanent there
are great collections, Tuscany and Rome for example. But, as we have said before, the highest
service done by success in art is not in the possession but in the creation of great works, the

spirit, labour, sagacity, and instruction, needed by the artists to succeed, and flung out by them on their country like rain from sunny clouds.

Indeed there is some danger of a traditionary mediocrity following after a great epoch in art. Superstition of style, technical rules in composition, and all the pedantry of art, too often fill up the ranks vacated by veteran genius, and of this there are examples enough in Flanders, Spain, and even Italy. The schools may, and often do, make men scholastic and ungenial, and art remains an instructor and refiner, but creates no more.

Ireland, fortunately or unfortunately, has every thing to do yet. We have had great artists—we have not their works—we own the nativity of great living artists—they live on the Tiber and the Thames. Our capital city has no school of art— no facilities for acquiring it.

To be sure there are rooms open in the Dublin Society, and they have not been useless, that is all. But a student here cannot learn anatomy, save at the same expense as a surgical student. He has no great works of art before him, no Pantheon, no Valhalla, not even a good museum or gallery.

We think it may be laid down as unalterably true, that a student should never draw from a flat surface. He learns nothing by drawing from the lines of another man—he only mimics. Better for him to draw chairs and tables, bottles and glasses, rubbish, potatoes, cabins, or kitchen utensils, than draw from the lines laid down by other men.

Of those forms of nature which the student can originally consult—the sea, the sky, the earth— we would counsel him to draw from them in the first learning; for though he ought afterwards analyse and mature his style by the study of works of art, from the first sketches to the finished picture, yet, by beginning with nature and his own suggestions, he will acquire a genuine and original style, superior to the finest imitation; and it is hard to acquire a master's skill without his manner.

Were all men cast in a divine mould of strength, and straightness, and gallant bearing, and all women proportioned, graceful, and fair, the artist would need no gallery, at least to begin his studies with.　He would have to persuade or snatch his models in daily life.　Even then, as art creates greater and simpler combinations than ever exist in fact, he should finally study before the superhuman works of his predecessors.

But he has about him here an indifferently-made, ordinary, not very clean, nor picturesquely-clad people; though, doubtless, if they had the feeding, the dress, and the education (for mind beautifies the body) of the Greeks, they would not be inferior, for the Irish structure is of the noblest order.

To give him a multitude of fine natural models, to say nothing of ideal works, it is necessary to make a gallery of statues or casts.　The statues will come in good time, and we hope, and are sure, that Ireland, a nation, will have a national gallery, combining the greatest works of the Celtic and Teutonic races. But at present the most that can be done is to form a gallery.

Our readers will be glad to hear that this great boon is about to be given to Irish Art. A society for the formation of a gallery of casts in Dublin has been founded.

It embraces men of every rank, class, creed, politics, and calling, thus forming another of those sanctuaries, now multiplying in Ireland, where one is safe from the polemic and the partizan.

Its purpose is to purchase casts of all the greatest works of Greece, Egypt, Etruria, ancient Rome, and Europe in the middle ages. This will embrace a sufficient variety of types both natural and ideal to prevent imitation, and will avoid the debateable ground of modern art. Wherever they can afford it the society will buy moulds, in order to assist provincial galleries, and therefore the provinces are immediately interested in its support.

When a few of these casts are got together, and a proper gallery procured, the public will be admitted to see, and artists to study them without any charge. The annual subscription is but 10s., the object being to interest as many as possible in its support.

It has been suggested to us by an artist that Trinity College ought to establish a gallery and museum containing casts of all the ancient statues, models of their buildings, civil and military, and a collection of their implements of art, trade, and domestic life. A nobler institution, a more vivid and productive commentary on the classics could not be.   But if the Board will not do this of themselves, we trust they will see the propriety of assisting this public gallery, and procuring, therefore, special privileges for the students in using it.

But no matter what persons in authority may do or neglect, we trust the public—for the sake of their own pleasure, their childrens' profit, and Ireland's honour—will give it their instant and full support.

ART UNIONS.

ART Unions are a substitute for State patronage. The State can do much for art.   It can furnish teachers and models to a large class, and it can enable an artist to live by great works.   Private patronage does not encourage great works.   They require much time, and occupy a larger space than suits the size of private dwellings.   Their price is immense, not only from the labour they require, but because of the rarity of men able to execute them.   Wherever the arts have flourished, the State has been their chief patron. So it was in Athens where art was a branch of public business.   In Rome, the patronage was even more liberal, if not quite so just.   When arts revived, they were sustained by the monarchs and ecclesiastical corporations of all Europe. But, amongst their earliest, firmest, and wisest friends, were the little republics of Italy and the corporations of the Low Countries.   Even now

there is more art of a high order called out by
the patronage of the little court of Munich than
by any people in the world. When we speak of
high art, we mean art used to instruct and ennoble men; to teach them great deeds whether
historical, religious, or romantic; to awaken their
piety, their pride, their justice, and their valour;
to paint the hero, the martyr, the rescuer, the
lover, the patriot, the friend, the saint, and the
Saviour—nor is it confined to expressing moral
excellence. It expresses intellectual and physical
might—the poet, the orator, the sage, the giant
savage, the falling angel. Whatever can be
painted or sculptured, of strength or sweetness,
of grace or terror, of piety or power—that belongs
to high art.

In prizing State patronage so high, we do not
assume it sufficient to produce great artists.
Public passions, strong thoughts, condensed and
deep education must exist (along with facilities
to learn, and State patronage) to produce great
artists. The perfect success of the little states
of Greece, Italy, and the Low Countries in art,
was owing less to their patronising art than to
the strong passions, the public spirit, the concen-
tration and earnestness of character produced by
local government. Polygamy is not more unnatural and debasing than central government.
We do not hope to see art advance much till
national character is restored by the break up of
two or three of the huge and hateful empires.

Latterly a substitute for state patronage has
been found, or supposed to have been found, in
Art Unions. The clubbed guineas of thousands
form a sum large enough to buy the costliest

pictures. We do not think these Unions can
realise all their more sanguine friends look for.
Some people subscribe to encourage art, most
people to get pictures and prints. There is
therefore a strong inducement among the managers of these institutions to have as many prizes
as possible to distribute. Their motive is excellent. Their desire is to serve artists and satisfy
the public. They are all gratuitous labourers in
this excellent work. But the effect is to break
up the fund into small sums and to prevent Art
Committees from buying great, and, therefore,
costly pictures, and thus to discourage them.
Perhaps even in this respect these committees
are blameless; a petty style existed, and has not
been got rid of, and it may be many years before
they have the opportunity of buying a picture
great in design and execution.

Still these institutions do and have done a
great deal. They have given the guineas of
tens of thousands to support artists who might
otherwise have starved or painted portraits.
They have put hundreds of pictures and thousands of fine prints into houses where a catch-
penny London engraving, or nothing at all,
would have reached. They have created an excitement about art. Men talk of it, read of it,
think of it, and recommend it, who, ten years
ago, would not have heeded its existence. Artists
thus encouraged and honored are improving, and
there, is every hope that by the continuance of
such support, and by the increase of public spirit,
a school of eminent Irish artists will be created
to illustrate their country's history and character,
had to associate their fame with her's.

ILLUSTRATIONS OF IRELAND.

THE most useful premium offered by the Art Union is that for outline illustrations of Irish books. More instruction in art, more service to nationality, would follow from the success of this project than of any other they have attempted.

The preliminary to any excellence in painting is correct drawing. The boldest imagination cannot represent its thought without command over outline. Had Raphael's Madonna crooked eyes, or were the limbs of Angelo's Lazarus not bone and sinew convulsed with returning life, but galvanised blocks (as a pencil untrained to correct outline would have drawn them), not all the light, and shade, and colouring in the world could have made these figures admirable. The prints which glare in our cabins are not more abominable with brick-dust blood, and ochre-skin, than the costlier trash of our drawing-rooms with upright figures that could never stand, eyes that look round corners, arms and necks that seem the work of a carpenter, and bodies, compared to which, gate-posts look animated.

The glare and the prettiness reconcile our ignorant peasants, and our more ignorant gentry, to these deformities; but the same drawings in outline would not be tolerated even by them, ex-

cept as caricatures—dull caricatures. Accustom
people to outline drawings—train their eyes to
judge and admire correct outlines, vigour of
action, strength and beauty of limb, possibility
of attitude, unity of frame and of expression, and
they will cease to value high colours or smooth
graving—they will insist on nature, and faith,
and power in works of art—they will appreciate
the statues of Greece, the paintings of Italy, and
Deutschland—they will demand of their own
artists the excellence they are accustomed to,
and they will recognise and reward that excellence.

National interests would be served in another
way by the publication of such designs. Our history exists chiefly in dry annals or stupid compilations. The original memoirs and letters are little known and hard of access. People think of
our history as a set of political facts, not as the
lives and deaths of men clad in skins, and
armour, and silk, bounding with strength and
beauty, flushed with love, wrinkled with rage, full
of chivalrous ambition.

The Druid in his grove—the Monk in his
abbey—the Creaght on his hill—the Pagan conqueror—the Christian liberator—the Norman
castle with its courted maidens, its iron barons,
and its plumed train—the Irish rath with its
circling trench, and circling woodland, its patri-
arch prince, its Tartar clan, its foster-love, and
its harping bards—the Dane in his galley—the
Viceroy in his council—the Patriot in his fore-
thought—the Martyr in his endurance—the
Hero in his triumph—his passing triumph—who

thought of these till lately?—who clearly sees them now? All these things an artist illustrating Irish history—illustrating Moore, or Keating—illustrating (to give better texts) the publications of the Archæological Society—the tracts in the *Desiderata*, or the *Hibernica*—the *State Papers*—Carte's *Ormond*—Ware's *Antiquities*, or any of the minuter works on our history—can show us.

How suited for countless illustrations are our Irish fictions, from our ancient fairy stories to our modern novels. In *The Collegians, Suil Dhuv, Crohore, The Fetches, The Poor Scholar, The Faction and Party Fight, Valentine M'Clutchy*, there are countless subjects for illustration, ranging from the mildest beauty to the utmost sublimity.

There is one work of fiction which we peculiarly desire to see illustrated, and that is Griffin's *Invasion*. Its great length, its hard words, and its freedom from hot stimulants, moderate its popularity—but there is in it the most exquisite beauty of scene and form, the purest loveliness, the most original heroism of any work we own, and it contains besides invaluable and countless hints on the *appearance* of ancient Ireland. Nor do occasional antiquarian errors materially lessen the value of the book to an illustrator.

Of poetry, Maclise has taken the best subject —*The Melodies ;* nor can we advise any one to compete with him.

But we have wandered. The publication of outlines on our historical and romantic literature would convey a deep and fresh sense of what Ireland was and is, and of what her writers have described or created. These illustrations would instruct the public in the organisation and costume of our races, give new and distinct imagery to orator and writer, and, becoming confluent, would represent Ireland in all her periods—Ireland imaginative, as well as actual and historical.

We entreat our artists as they love their country, as they owe it a service, as they pity its woes and errors, as they are wroth at its sufferings, and as they hope to share and aid its advance, to use this opportunity of raising the taste and cultivating the nationality of Ireland.

We shall only, in addition, repeat the proposal of the Art-Union :—

DRAWING AND COMPOSITION.

"For the best series of not less than five Outline Drawings, illustrative of the works of Irish writers, in poetry, prose, or history, 30*l.*

"Correct drawing, beauty of form and expression, will be especially looked for ; should the committee think it advisable to engrave the outlines selected, a further remuneration will be given to the artist : the drawings, with a sealed letter containing the name and address of the artist, to be forwarded to the Secretary of the Society, Board-room, College-street, Dublin, previous to the 1st of September next."

HINTS FOR IRISH HISTORICAL PAINTINGS.

NATIONAL art is conversant with national subjects. We have Irish artists, but no Irish, no national art. This ought not to continue; it is injurious to the artists, and disgraceful to the country. The following historical subjects were loosely jotted down by a friend. Doubtless, a more just selection could be made by students noting down fit subjects for painting and sculpture, as they read. We shall be happy to print any suggestions on the subject—our own are, as we call them, mere hints with loose references to the authors or books which suggested them. For any good painting, the marked figures must be few, the action obvious, the costume, arms, architecture, postures, historically exact, and the manners, appearance, and rank of the characters, strictly studied and observed. The grouping and drawing require great truth and vigour. A similar set of subjects illustrating social life could be got from the Poor Report, Carleton's, Banim's, or Griffin's Stories, or better still from observation.

The references are vague, but perhaps sufficient.

The Landing of the Milesians.—Keating, Moore's Melodies.

Ollamh Fodhla Presenting his Laws to his People. Keating's, Moore's, and O'Halloran's Histories of Ireland.—Walker's Irish Dress and Arms, and Vallancey's Collectanea.

Nial and his Nine Hostages.—Moore, Keating.

A Druid's Augury.—Moore, O'Halloran, Keating.

A Chief Riding Out of his Fort.—Griffin's Invasion, Walker, Moore.

The Oak of Kildare.—Moore.

The Burial of King Dathy in the Alps, his thinned troops laying stones on his grave.—M'Geoghegan, l'Histoire de l'Irlande (French edition), Invasion, Walker, Moore.

St. Patrick brought before the Druids at Tara.—Moore and his Authorities.

The First Landing of the Danes.—See Invasion, Moore, &c.

The Death of Turgesius.—Keating, Moore.

Ceallachan Tied to the Mast.—Keating.

Murkertach Returning to Aileach.—Archæological Society's Tracts.

Brian Reconnoitring the Danes before Clontarf.

The Last of the Danes Escaping to his Ship.

O'Ruarc's Return.—Keating, Moore's Melodies.

Raymond Le Gros Leaving his Bride.—Moore.

Roderic in Conference with the Normans.—Moore, M'Geoghegan.

Donald O'Brien Setting Fire to Limerick.—M'Geoghegan.

Donald O'Brien Visiting Holycross.—M'Geoghegan.

O'Brien, O'Connor, and M'Carthy, making Peace to Attack the Normans.—M'Geoghegan, Moore.

The Same Three Victorious at the Battle of Thurles.—Moore and O'Connor's Rerum Hibernicarum Scriptores.

Irish Chiefs Leaving Prince John.—Moore, &c.

M'Murrough and Gloster.—Harris's Hibernica, p. 53.

Crowning of Edward Bruce.—Leland, Grace's Annals, &c.

Edgecombe Vainly Trying to Overawe Kildare—Harris's Hibernica.

Kildare "on the Necks of the Butlers."—Leland.

Shane O'Neill at Elizabeth's Court.—Leland.

Lord Sydney Entertained by Shane O'Neill.

The Battle of the Red Coats.—O'Sullivan's Catholic History.

Hugh O'Neill Victor in Single Combat at Clontibret.—Fynes Moryson, O'Sullivan, M'Geoghegan.

The Corleius.—Dymmok's Treatise, Archæological Society's Tracts.

Maguire and St. Leger in Single Combat.—M'Geoghegan.

O'Sullivan Crossing the Shannon.—Pacata Hibernica.

O'Dogherty Receiving the Insolent Message of the Governor of Derry.—M'Geoghegan.

The Brehon Before the English Judges.—Davis's Letter to Lord Salisbury.

Ormond Refusing to give up his Sword.—Carte's Life of Ormond.

Good Lookers on.—Stafford's Letters.

Owen Conolly Before the Privy Council, 1641.—Carey's Vindiciæ.

The Battle of Julianstown.—Temple's Rebellion, and Tichbourne's Drogheda.

Owen Roe Organising the Creaghts.—Carte, and also Belling and O'Neil in the Desiderata Curiosa Hibernica.

The Council of Kilkenny.—Carte.

The Breach of Clonmel.—Do.

Smoking Out the Irish.—Ludlow's Memoirs.

Burning Them.—Castlehaven's Memoirs.

Nagle Before the Privy Council.—Harris's William.

James's Entry into Dublin.—Dublin Magazine for March, 1843.

Bishop King Combining Falsehoods into his Book.

The Bridge of Athlone.—Green Book and Authorities.

St. Ruth's Death.—Do.

The Embarkation from Limerick.—Do.

Cremona.—Cox's Magazine.

Fontenoy.—Do.

Sir S. Rice Pleading against the Violation of the Treaty of Limerick.—Staunton's Collection of Tracts in Ireland.

Molyneux's Book Burned.

Liberty Boys Reading a Drapier's Letter.—Mason's St. Patrick's Cathedral.

Lucas, Surrounded by Dublin Citizens in his Shop.

Grattan Moving Liberty.—Memoirs.

Flood Apostrophising Corruption.—Barrington.

Dungannon Convention.—Wilson Barrington.

Curran Cross-examining Armstrong.—Memoirs.

Curran Pleading Before the Council in Alderman James's Case.

Tone's First Society.—See his Memoirs.

The Belfast Club.—Madden's U.I., 2nd Series, Vol. I.

Tone, Emmet, and Keogh, in the Rathfarnham Garden.

Tone and Carnot.—Tone's Memoirs.

Battle of Oulart.—Hay, Teeling, &c.

First Meeting of the Catholic Association.

O'Connell Speaking in a Munster Chapel.—Wyse's Association.

The Clare Hustings—Proposal of O'Connell.

The Dublin Corporation Speech.

Father Mathew Administering the Pledge in a Munster County.

Conciliation—Orange and Green.

The Lifting of the Irish Flags of a National Fleet and Army.

OUR NATIONAL LANGUAGE.

MEN are ever valued most for peculiar and original qualities. A man who can only talk common-place, and act according to routine, has little weight. To speak, look, and do what your own soul from its depths orders you, are credentials of greatness which all men understand and acknowledge. Such a man's dictum has more influence than the reasoning of an imitative or common-place man. He fills his circle with confidence. He is self-possessed, firm, accurate, and daring. Such men are the pioneers of civilization, and the rulers of the human heart.

Why should not nations be judged thus? Is not a full indulgence of its natural tendencies essential to a *people's* greatness? Force the manners, dress, language, and constitution of Russia, or Italy, or Norway, or America, and you instantly stunt and distort the whole mind of either people.

The language, which grows up with a people, is conformed to their organs, descriptive of their climate, constitution, and manners, mingled inseparably with their history and their soil, fitted beyond any other language to express their prevalent thoughts in the most natural and efficient way.

To impose another language on such a people is to send their history adrift among the accidents of translation—'tis to tear their identity from all places—'tis to substitute arbitrary signs for picturesque and suggestive names—'tis to cut off the entail of feeling, and separate the people from their forefathers by a deep gulf—'tis to corrupt their very organs, and abridge their power of expression.

The language of a nation's youth is the only easy and full speech for its manhood and for its age And when the language of its cradle goes, itself craves a tomb.

What business has a Russian for the rippling language of Italy or India? How could a Greek distort his organs and his soul to speak Dutch upon the sides of Hymetus, or the beach of Salamis, or on the waste where once was Sparta? And is it befitting the fiery, delicate-organed Celt to abandon his beautiful tongue, docile and spirited as an Arab, "sweet as music, strong as the wave"—is it befitting in him to abandon this wild liquid speech for the mongrel of a hundred breeds called English, which, powerful though it be, creaks and bangs about the Celt who tries to use it?

We lately met a glorious thought in the "Triads of Mochmed," printed in one of the Welsh codes by the Record Commission: "There are three things without which there is no country—common language, common judicature, and co-tillage land—for without these a country cannot support itself in peace and social union."

A people without a language of its own is only half a nation. A nation should guard its

language more than its territories—'tis a surer
barrier, and more important frontier, than fortress or river.

And in good times it has ever been thought
so. Who had dared to propose the adoption of
Persian or Egyptian in Greece—how had
Pericles thundered at the barbarian? How
had Cato scourged from the forum him who
would have given the Attic or Gallic speech to
men of Rome? How proudly and how nobly
Germany stopped "the incipient creeping" progress of French! And no sooner had she succeeded, than her genius, which had tossed in a
hot trance, sprung up fresh and triumphant.

Had Pyrrhus quelled Italy, or Xerxes subdued
Greece for a time long enough to impose new
languages, where had been the literature which
gives a pedigree to human genius? Even
liberty recovered had been sickly and insecure
without the language with which it had hunted
in the woods, worshipped at the fruit-strewn
altar, debated on the council-hill, and shouted in
the battle-charge.

There is a fine song of the Fusians, which describes—

"Language linked to liberty."

To lose your native tongue, and learn that of an
alien, is the worst badge of conquest—it is the
chain on the soul. To have lost entirely the
national language is death; the fetter has worn
through. So long as the Saxon held to his German speech, he could hope to resume his land
from the Norman; now, if he is to be free and

locally governed, he must build himself a new
home. There is hope for Scotland—strong hope
for Wales—sure hope for Hungary. The speech
of the alien is not universal in the one ; is gallantly held at bay in the other; is nearly ex-
pelled from the third.

How unnatural—how corrupting 'tis for us,
three-fourths of whom are of Celtic blood, to
speak a medley of Teutonic dialects. If we add
the Celtic Scots, who came back here from the
thirteenth to the seventeenth centuries, and the
Celtic Welsh, who colonised many parts of
Wexford and other Leinster counties, to the
Celts who never left Ireland, probably five-
sixths, or more, of us are Celts. What business
have we with the Norman-Sassenagh ?

Nor let any doubt these proportions because
of the number of English *names* in Ireland.
With a politic cruelty, the English of the Pale
passed an act (3 Edw. IV., chap. 3), compelling
every Irishman within English jurisdiction, "to
go like to one Englishman in apparel, and
shaving off his beard above the mouth," "and
shall take to him an English sirname of one
town, as Sutton, Chester, Trym, Skryne, Corke,
Kinsale ; or colour, as White, Blacke, Browne ;
or art or science, as Smith, or Carpenter; or
office, as Cook, Butler ; and that he and his issue
shall use this name, under pain of forfeiting his
goods yearly."

And just as this parliament before the Reformation, so did another after the Reformation.
By the 28th Henry VIII., c. 15, the dress and
language of the Irish were insolently described

as barbarous by the minions of that ruffian king, and were utterly forbidden and abolished under many penalties and incapacities. These laws are still in force; but whether the Archæological Society, including Peel and O'Connell, will be prosecuted, seems doubtful.

There was also, 'tis to be feared, an adoption of English names, during some periods, from fashion, fear, or meanness. Some of our best Irish names, too, have been so mangled as to require some scholarship to identify them. For these and many more reasons, the members of the Celtic race here are immensely greater than at first appears.

But this is not all; for even the Saxon and Norman colonists, notwithstanding these laws, melted down into the Irish, and adopted all their ways and language. For centuries upon centuries Irish was spoken by men of all bloods in Ireland, and English was unknown, save to a few citizens and nobles of the Pale. 'Tis only within a very late period that the majority of the people learned English.

But, it will be asked, how can the language be restored now?

We shall answer this partly by saying that, through the labours of the Archæological and many lesser societies, it *is* being revived rapidly.

We shall consider this question of the possibility of reviving it more at length some other day.

Nothing can make us believe that it is natural or honourable for the Irish to speak the speech

of the alien, the invader, the Sassenagh **tyrant,**
and to abandon the language of our kings and
heroes. What! give up the tongue of Ollamh
Fodhla and Brian Boru, the tongue of M'Carty,
and the O'Nials, the tongue of Sarsfield's, Curran's, Mathew's, and O'Connell's boyhood, for
that of Strafford and Poynings, Sussex, Kirk,
and Cromwell!

No, oh! no! the "the brighter days shall
surely come," and the green flag shall wave on
our towers, and the sweet old language be heard
once more in college, mart, and senate.

But, even should the effort to save it as the
national language fail, by the attempt we will
rescue its old literature, and hand down to our
descendants proofs that we had a language as fit
for love, and war, and business, and pleasure, as
the world ever knew, and that we had not the
spirit and nationality to preserve it!

Had Swift known Irish, he would have sowed
its seed by the side of that nationality which he
planted, and the close of the last century would
have seen the one as flourishing as the other.
Had Ireland used Irish in 1782, would it not
have impeded England's re-conquest of us?
But 'tis not yet too late.

For *you*, if the mixed speech called English
was laid with sweetmeats on your child's tongue,
English is the best speech of manhood. And yet,
reader, in that case you are unfortunate. The
hills, and lakes, and rivers, the forts and castles,
the churches and parishes, the baronies and
counties around you, have all Irish names—
names which describe the nature of the scenery

or ground, the name of founder, or chief, or priest, or the leading fact in the history of the place. To you these are names hard to pronounce, and without meaning.

And yet it were well for you to know them. That knowledge would be a topography, and a history, and romance, walking by your side, and helping your discourse. Meath tells its flatness, Clonmel the abundant riches of its valley, Fermanagh is the land of the Lakes, Tyrone the country of Owen, Kilkenny the Church of St. Canice, Dunmore the great fort, Athenry the Ford of the Kings, Dunleary the Fort of O'Leary ; and the Phœnix Park, instead of taking its name from a fable, recognises as christener, the "sweet water" which yet springs near the East-gate.

All the names of our airs and songs are Irish, and we every day are as puzzled and ingeniously wrong about them as the man who, when asked for the air, " I am asleep, and don't waken me," called it " Tommy M'Cullagh made boots for me."

The bulk of our history and poetry are written in Irish, and shall we, who learn Italian, and Latin, and Greek, to read Dante, Livy, and Homer in the original—shall we be content with ignorance or a translation of Irish ?

The want of modern scientific words in Irish is undeniable, and doubtless we should adopt the existing names into our language. The Germans have done the same thing, and no one calls German mongrel on that account. Most of these names are clumsy and extravagant ; they are almost all derived from Greek or Latin, and cut as foreign a figure in French and English as they would in Irish. Once Irish was recognised as a language to be learned as much as French or Italian, our dictionaries would fill up, and our vocabularies ramify, to suit all the wants of life and conversation.

These objections are ingenious refinements, however, rarely thought of till after the other and great objection has been answered.

The usual objection to attempting the revival of Irish is, that it could not succeed.

If an attempt were made to introduce Irish, either through the national schools or the courts of law, into the eastern side of the island, it would certainly fail, and the re-action might extinguish it altogether. But no one contemplates this save as a dream of what may happen a hundred years hence. It is quite another thing to say, as we do, that the Irish language should be cherished, taught, and esteemed, and that it can be preserved and gradually extended.

What we seek is, that the people of the upper classes should have their children taught the language which explains our names of persons or places, our older history, and our music, and which is spoken in the majority of our counties, rather than Italian, German, or French. It would be more useful in life, more serviceable to the taste and genius of young people, and a more flexible accomplishment for an Irish man or woman to speak, sing, and write Irish than French.

At present the middle classes think it a sign

of vulgarity to speak Irish—the children are everywhere taught English and English alone in schools—and, what is worse, they are urged by rewards and punishments to speak it at home, for English is the language of their masters. Now, we think the example and exertions of the upper classes would be sufficient to set the opposite and better fashion of preferring Irish; and, even as a matter of taste, we think them bound to do so. And we ask it of the pride, the patriotism, and the hearts of our farmers and shopkeepers, will they try to drive out of their children's minds the native language of almost every great man we had, from Brian Boru to O'Connell—will they meanly sacrifice the language which names their hills, and towns, and music, to the tongue of the stranger?

About half the people west of a line drawn from Derry to Waterford speak Irish habitually, and in some of the mountain tracts east of that line it is still common. Simply requiring the teachers of the National Schools in these Irish-speaking districts to know Irish, and supplying them with Irish translations of the school books, would guard the language where it now exists, and prevent it from being swept away by the English tongue, as the red Americans have been by the English race from New York to New Orleans.

The example of the upper classes would extend and develop a modern Irish literature, and the hearty support they have given to the Archæological Society makes us hope that they will have sense and spirit to do so.

L

But the establishment of a newspaper partly or wholly Irish would be the most rapid and sure way of serving the language. The Irish-speaking man would find, in his native tongue, the political news and general information he has now to seek in English; and the English-speaking man, having Irish frequently before him in so attractive a form, would be tempted to learn its characters, and by-and-by its meaning.

These newspapers in many languages are now to be found everywhere but here. In South America many of these papers are Spanish and English, or French; in North America, French and English; in Northern Italy, German and Italian; in Denmark and Holland, German is used in addition to the native tongue; in Alsace and Switzerland, French and German; in Poland, German, French, and Sclavonic; in Turkey, French and Turkish; in Hungary, Maggar, Sclavonic, and German; and the little Canton of Grison uses three languages in its press. With the exception of Hungary, the secondary language is, in all cases, spoken by fewer persons than the Irish-speaking people of Ireland, and while they everywhere tolerate and use one language as a medium of commerce, they cherish the other as the vehicle of history, the wings of song, the soil of their genius, and a mark and guard of nationality.

O'DONOVAN'S IRISH GRAMMAR.

MR. O'DONOVAN has the reputation (right well earned, we believe) of being the best Celtic scholar alive. He is a man eminently cautious; and disposed, from the highest motives, rather against the pretensions of Gaelic literature. His grammar, begun in 1828, has been gradually ripened while he was engaged on the orthography of the Ordnance Survey, and in editing the best and most learned of the publications of the Archæological Society. It is now published as the class-book, and with the guarantee of the College of St. Columba. His capacity, disposition, and opportunities, and the circumstances of the publication, will, therefore, place his grammar at once, and without question, at the head of Celtic literature.

The work is quite (shall we not say, wonderfully?) free from the vehement style and sweeping assertions, so often and so mischievously carried from the forum to the study, by Irish writers.

One need not be a master, nor even a student of the Irish language, to find interest and knowledge in this work. It is no regiment of rules without reason, illustration, or authority, like most grammars. It is a profound and discursive treatise on the pronunciation, inflections, structure, and prosody of the most perfect of the

Celtic tongues. There is not, we are sure, an antiquarian or philologist in Europe but will grasp it as the long-wished-for key to facts locked in the obscurity of a language, whose best grammarians had only the dialect of their own parishes, and whose most notable grammars were the work of pretenders. .

From the letters of the alphabet to the rules of versification, every portion of the Grammar is argued and illustrated—the argument not frantic speculation on the tongues of Tyre or Babel, but the philosophy of one who has weighed the metaphysics of language in Tooke, Mill, and Harris—the illustrations (drawn out of his own and Mr. Curry's reading and experience), extending from the hymns of the early saints, to the Jacobite ballads, from Cormack's glossary, to the slang of the Munster masons.

You cannot open a page of it without finding some fact or fragment which lightens the history of the country, the customs of the people, and the idiom which they have brought into English. In the chapter on Prepositions alone (running to thirty-eight close pages) there are pleasant materials for long study to any student of Ireland, be he ever so ignorant of Irish.

Yet no one must suppose that this work is merely an antiquarian miscellany, or a philological treatise, or both.

It is a thoroughly practical Irish Grammar. It gives, with care and simplicity, the most perfect forms and rules (according to the best judgment of its author), and then proceeds to explain

the effect of each rule, and the reasons for it to
show the variations from it during different ages
and in distant parts of the island.

These minute details of provincial pronunciation are here given for the first time, and any
one who has ever attempted to learn Irish will
know the value of them.

It has been made a reproach to the Irish language, that it varies from Kerry to Cork, from
Kilkenny to Galway, from Donegal to Armagh,
and from Louth to Antrim. The difference in
this last county is great; but the Gaelic of the
Antrim glens is the Erse, or Albanian dialect,
brought from Argyleshire and the Hebrides during the fourteenth, fifteenth, and sixteenth centuries. It is a prodigal son returned a good
deal the worse for having been so long on the
shaughran!

The variety of dialects in Ireland is hardly
greater than in other countries. We have tried
hopelessly to understand a Zomerzetshire peasant
talking English, and the difference between Yorkshire, Norfolkshire, and Cockneyshire are immense. No two provinces in Germany speak
the one dialect. The Bavarian and the Olden-
burger, the Hessian and the Silesian, are as
wide from each other in dialect as the Kerryman
and the native of Armagh; and the Low Dutch
of Holland and the Danish are as far from the
pure tongue of Frankfort, as Erse and Manx
from the classic speech of Galway.

By the way, let us pause for a moment to give
the original authority for the distinctive qualities

of provincial speaking, with which we are all familiar in a ruder way :—

" The Munsterman has the accent without the propriety.

" The Ulsterman has the propriety without the accent.

" The Leinsterman has neither the propriety nor the accent.

" The Connaughtman has the accent and the propriety."

Mr. O'Donovan gives us a paraphrase of these proverbs, published by Lombard, in his *De Regno* in 1632 ; so that the notion is an old one.

But, talking of dialects, it was only since Luther's Bible that Germany began to have a standard language. Dante took up the speech prevalent about Florence, and founded classic Italian ; but to this hour neither the Venetian, nor the Neapolitan, nor the Sicilian, have abandoned their old dialects. Similar differences exist in France, Spain, and everywhere.

Let us no more hear, then, of *this* objection to Irish ; but trust that the labours of Mr. O'Donovan, Mr. Curry, Mr. Connellan, the Rev. Mr. O'Sullivan, of Bandon, and whoever besides are the best of our Celtic scholars, will be combined to produce such standards as will make this age the founding-time or the epoch of restoration for the Gaelic language.

INSTITUTIONS OF DUBLIN.

JUDGED by the *Directory*, Dublin is nobly supplied with Institutions for the promotion of Literature, Science, and Art ; and, judged by its men, there is mind enough here to make these Institutions prosper, and instruct and raise the country. Yet their performances are far short of these promises, and the causes for ill-success are easily found. We believe these causes could be almost as easily removed.

In the first place, we have too many of these Institutions. Stingy grants from Government and the general poverty of the people render economy a matter of first consequence ; yet we find these societies maintaining a number of separate establishments, at a great expense of rent and salaries.

The consequence, of course, is that none of them flourishes as it ought—museums, meetings, lectures, libraries, and exhibitions are all flittered away, and nothing is done so well, as it might be. Moreover, from the want of any arrangement and order, the same men are dragged from one society to another—few men do much, because all are forced to attempt so many things.

But 'tis better to examine this in detail, and in doing so we may as well give some leading facts as to the chief of these bodies. Take for example, as a beginning, the

INSTITUTIONS FOR THE PROMOTION OF FINE ARTS.

And first there is the Hibernian Academy. It was founded in 1823, received a present of its house, in Abbey-street, and some books and casts, from Francis Johnston (a Dublin architect,) and has the miserable income of 300*l.* a year from the Treasury. It has a drawing-school, with a few casts, no pictures, bad accommodation, and professors whose pay is nearly nominal.

It undoubtedly has some men of great ability and attainments (and some who have neither.); but what can be done without funds, statues, or pictures. To aggravate its difficulties, the Dublin Society has another art school, still worse off as to casts, and equally deficient in pictures. As a place of instruction in the designing of patterns for manufactures and the like, the Dublin Society school has worked well; and many of the best-paid controllers of design in the English manufactories were educated there; but as a school of fine arts it does little; and no wonder. Another branch of the Hibernian Academy's operations is its annual exhibitions of pictures. These exhibitions attract crowds who would never otherwise see a painting, promote thought on art, and procure patronage for artists. In this, too, the Hibernian Academy has recently found a rival in the Society of Irish Artists established in 1842, which has an annual exhibition in College-street, and pays the expenses of the exhibition out of the admission fees, as does the Hibernian Academy. We are not attaching blame to the Society of Irish Artists in noticing the fact of its rivalry.

There are three other bodies devoted to the
encouragement of art. One of these is the Art-
Union, founded in 1840, and maintained entirely
by subscriptions to its lottery. It distributes
fine engravings from Irish pictures among all its
members, and pictures and statues, bought in
the exhibitions of the Hibernian Academy, and
of the Society of Irish Artists, among its prize-
holders; and it gives premiums for the works of
native or resident artists. Its operation is as
a patron of art; and, in order to get funds for
this purpose, and also to secure superior works
and a higher competition, it extends its pur-
chases to the best foreign works exhibited here.
It has no collection, and has merely an office in
College-street—in fact, its best permanent possession is its unwearied Secretary. The Society
of Ancient Art was established last year for the
formation of a public gallery of casts from classical and medœval statues, and ultimately for purposes of direct teaching by lectures, &c. It obtained some funds by subscription; but under the
expectation, 'tis said, of a public grant, has done
nothing. Lastly, there is the "Institute of Irish
Architects," founded in 1839 "for the general
advancement of civil architecture, for promoting
and facilitating the acquirement of a knowledge
of the various arts and sciences connected there-
with, for the formation of a Library and Museum, &c."

To us it is very plain that here are too many
institutions, and that the efficiency of all suffers
materially from their want of connection and
arrangement. Some at least, might be amal-

gamated with great advantage, or rather all,
except the Art Union. That is only a club of
purchasers, and any attempt materially to change
its nature would peril its funds. Some such plan
as the following would accomplish all that is
vainly attempted now. Let the Government be
pressed to give 2,000*l.* a year, if the public supply
1,000*l.* a year. Let this income go to a new
Hibernian Academy—the present Hibernian
Academy, Artists' Society, Society of Ancient
Art, the Art Schools of the Dublin Society, and
the Institute of Irish Architects, being merged
in it. This merger could be easily secured
through the inducements secured by the charter,
and by accommodation, salaries, and utility of
the new body. The present property of these
bodies, with some moderate grant, would suffice
for the purchase of a space of ground ample for
the schools, museums, library, lecture-room, and
yards of such an institution.

At the head of it should be a small body
governing and accounting for its finances, but
no person should be a governing member of more
than one of its sections. These sections should
be for Statuary, Painting, Architecture, and
Design Drawing. Each of these sections should
have its own Gallery, and its own Practice Rooms;
but one Library and one public Lecture Room
would suffice for the entire. The architectural
section would also need some open space for its
experiments and its larger specimens. A present
of copies of the British Museum casts, along with
the fund of the Ancient Art Society, would
originate a Cast Gallery, and a few good pictures

could be bought as a commencement of a National Gallery of Painting, leaving the economy of the managers and the liberality of the public gradually to fill it. Collections of native works in canvass and marble, and architectural models could be soon and cheaply procured. The Art Library of the Dublin Society added to that of the Hibernian Academy would need few additions to make it sufficient for the new body.

Such an Institute ought not to employ any but the best teachers and lecturers. It should encourage proficiency by rewards that would instruct the proficient; it should apply itself to cataloguing, preserving, and making known all the works of art in the country; give prizes for artistical works; publish its lectures and transactions; issue engravings of the most instructive works of art; and hold evening meetings, to which ladies would be admitted. It should allow at least 400*l.* a year for the support of free pupils. In connexion with its drawing and modelling schools should be a professorship of anatomy, or, what were better, some arrangement might be made with the College of Surgeons, or some such body, for courses of instruction for its pupils. The training for its pupils in sculpture, painting, and design, should include the study of ancient and modern costumes, zoology, and of vegetable and geological forms. For this purpose books should not be so much relied on as lectures in gardens, museums, and during student excursions. Of course, the architectural pupils should be required to answer at a preliminary examination in mathematics, and should receive special instruction in the building materials, action of climate, &c., in Ireland.

Were the buildings standing, and the society chartered judiciously, the sum we have mentioned would be sufficient. Four professors at from 200*l.* to 300*l.* a year each, four assistants at 100*l.* a year each, a librarian at the same rate, with payments for extra instruction in anatomy, &c. &c., and for porters, premiums, and so forth would not exceed 2,000*l.* a year. So that if 400*l.* were expended on free pupils, there would remain 600*l.* a year for the purchase of works for the galleries.

At present there is much waste of money, great annoyance, and loss of time to the supporters of these institutions, and marvellously little benefit to art. The plan we have proposed would be economical both of time and money; but, what is of more worth, it would give us, what we have not now, a National Gallery of Statuary and Painting—good Exhibition-Rooms for works of art—business-like Lecturers and Lectures—great public excitement about art—and, finally, a great National Academy.

If any one has a better plan, let him say it; we have told ours. At all events, some great change is needed, and there can be no fitter time than this for it.

In any community it is desirable to have Literary Institutions, as well classified as legal offices, and as free from counter-action; but it is especially desirable here now. Our literary class is small, and its duties measureless. The diseased suction of London—the absence of gentry, offices,

and Legislature—the heart-sickness that is on
every thoughtful man without a country—the
want of a large, educated, and therefore book-
buying class—and (it must be confessed) the
depression and distrust produced by rash experiments and paltry failure, have left us with few
men for a great work. Palpably the great remedy is the restoration of our Parliament, bringing back, as it would, the aristocracy and the
public offices, giving society and support to
Writers and Artists, and giving them a country's praise to move and a country's glory to reward them.

But one of the very means of attaining nationality is securing some portion of that literary
force which would gush abundantly from it ; and
therefore, consider it how you will, it is important to increase and economise the exertions of
the literary class in Ireland. Yet the reverse is
done. Institutions are multiplied instead of those
being made efficient which exist ; and men talk
as proudly of the new " Teach'em-everything-in-
no-time-Society" as if its natty laws were a
library, its desk a laboratory and a museum, and
its members fresh labourers, when all they have
done is to waste the time of persons who had
business, and to delude those who had none into
the belief that they were doing good. Ephemeral
things ! which die not without mischief—they
have wasted hours and days of strong men in
spinning sand, and leave depression growing
from their tombs.

It is a really useful deed to rescue from dissipation, or from idle reading, or from mammon-

M

hunting, one strong passionate man or boy, and to set him to work investigating, arranging, teaching. It is an honest task to shame the 'broidered youth from meditation on waistcoats and the display of polka steps into manly pursuits. It is an angel's mission (oftenest the work of love) to startle a sleeping and unconscious genius into the spring and victory of a roused lion. But it is worse than useless to establish new associations and orders without well considering first whether the same machinery do not already exist and rust for want of the very energy and skill which you need, too. There is a bridge in a field near Blarney Castle where water never ran. It was built "at the expense of the county." These men build their mills close as houses in a capital, taking no thought for the stream to turn them.

We have already censured this, in some detail, with reference to societies for the promotion of the Fine Arts, and have urged the formation, out of all these fiddling, clashing bodies, of some one great institution for the promotion of Painting, Sculpture, and Architecture, with a Museum, a Library, a Gallery, and Lecturers, governed by professional minds, great enough to be known and regarded by the people, and popular and strong enough to secure Government support.

Similar defects exist everywhere. Take the Dublin Society for example. Nothing can be more heterogeneous than its objects. We are far from denying its utility. That utility is immense, the institution is native, of old standing (it was founded in 1731), national, and, when it wanted support, our pen was not idle in its behalf.

But we believe its utility greatly diminished by its attempting too many things, and especially by including objects more fitly belonging to other institutions; and on the opposite it is maimed, by the interference of other bodies, in its natural functions. The Dublin Society was founded for the promotion of husbandry and other useful arts. Its labours to serve agriculture have been repeated and extensive, though not always judicious. It has also endeavoured to promote manufactures. It has gardens and museums fitter for scientific than practical instruction, admirable lecturers, a library most generously opened, a drawing school of the largest purposes and of equivocal success, and various minor branches.

The Irish Academy has some of this fault. It endeavours to unite antiquarianism and abstract science. Its meetings are alternately entertained with mathematics and history, and its transactions are equally comprehensive. We yield to none in anxiety for the promotion of antiquarian studies; we think the public and the government disgraced by the slight support given to the academy. We are not a little proud of the honour and strength given to our country by the science of MacCullagh, Hamilton, and Lloyd; but we protest against the attempt to mix the armoury of the ancient Irish, or the Celtic dialects, or the essay on Round Towers, with trigonometry and the calculus, whether in a lecture-room or a book.

Let us just set down, as we find them, some of the Literary and Scientific Institutions. There are the Royal Dublin Society, the Royal Irish Academy (we wish these royalties were dropped —no one minds them), the Irish Archæological Society, the Royal Zoological Society, the Geological Society, the Dublin Natural History Society, the Dublin Philosophical Society, the Royal Agricultural Society, &c., &c. Now, we take it that these bodies might be usefully reduced to three, and if three moderate government grants were made under conditions, rewarding such a classification, we doubt not it would instantly be made.

In the first place, we would divorce from the Irish Academy the scientific department, requiring Trinity College to form some voluntary organization for the purpose. To this non-collegiate philosophers should be admitted, and, thus disencumbered, we would devote the Academy to antiquities and literature—incorporate with it the Archæological Society—transfer to it all the antiques (of which it had not duplicates in Trinity College, the Dublin Society, &c., and enlarge its museum and meeting-room. Its section of "polite literature" has long been a name— it should be made real. There would be nothing inconvenient or strange in finding in its lecture-rooms or transactions, the antiquities and literature of Ireland, diversified by general historical, critical, and æsthetical researches.

The Dublin Society would reasonably divide into two sections. One, for the promotion of husbandry, might be aggrandised by tempting

the Agricultural Society to join it, and should
have a permanent museum, an extensive farm,
premiums, shows, publications, and special lecturers.   The second section, for the encouragement of manufactures, should have its museum,
work-shops, and experiment ground (the last,
perhaps, as the agricultural farm), and its special
lecturers.   The library might well be joint, and
managed by a joint committee, having separate
funds.   The general lecturers on chemistry and
other such subjects might be paid in common.
The drawing-school (save that for pattern and
machine drawing) might be transferred to the
Art Institution ; and the botanic garden and
museum of minerals to a third body we propose.

This third body we would form from a union
of the Zoological, the Geological, the Natural
History and all other such societies, and endow
it with the Botanic and Zoological Gardens—
give it rooms for a general, and for a specially
Irish museum, and for lecture rooms in town,
and supply it with a small fund to pay lecturers,
who should go through the provinces.

We are firmly convinced that this re-arrange-
ment of the Institutions of Dublin is quite practicable, would diminish unproductive expenses,
economise the time, and condense the purposes
of our literary, scientific, and artistical men, and
increase enormously the use of the institutions
to the public.

Of course the whole plan will be laughed at as
fanciful and improbable ; we think it easy, and
we think it will be done.

IRELAND'S PEOPLE, LORDS, GENTRY, COMMONALTY.

WHEN we are considering a country's resources and its fitness for a peculiar destiny, its people are not to be overlooked. How much they think, how much they work, what are their passions, as well as their habits, what are their hopes and what their history, suggest inquiries as well worth envious investigation as even the inside of a refugee's letter.

And there is much in Ireland of that character —much that makes her superior to slavery, and much that renders her inferior to freedom.

Her inhabitants are composed of Irish nobles, Irish gentry, and the Irish people. Each has an interest in the independence of their country, each a share in her disgrace. Upon each, too, there devolves a separate duty in this crisis of her fate. They all have responsibilities ; but the infamy of failing in them is not alike in all.

The nobles are the highest class. They have most to guard. In every other country they are the champions of patriotism. They feel there is no honour for them separate from their fatherland. Its freedom, its dignity, its integrity are as their own. They strive for it, legislate for it, guard it, fight for it. Their names, their titles, their very pride are of it.

In Ireland they are its disgrace. They were first to sell and would be last to redeem it.—

Treachery to it is daubed on many an escutcheon in its heraldry. It is the only nation where slaves have been ennobled for contributing to its degradation.

It is a foul thing this—dignity emanating from the throne to gild the filthy mass of national treason that forms the man's part of many an Irish lord.

We do not include in this the whole Irish peerage. God forbid. There are several of them not thus ignoble. Many of them worked, struggled, sacrificed for Ireland. Many of them were true to her in the darkest times.

They were her Chiefs, Ler ornaments, her sentinels, her safeguards. Alas, that they, too, should have shrunk from their position, and left their duties to humbler, but bolder and better men.

Look at their station in the State. Is it not one of unequivocal shame ? They enjoy the half mendicant privilege of voting for a representative of their order, in the House of Lords, some twice or thrice in their lives. One Irish peer represents about a dozen others of his class, and thus, in his multiplex capacity, he is admitted into fellowship with the English nobility. The borrowed plumes, and delegated authority of so many of his equals raise him to a half-admitted equality with an English nobleman. And, although thus deprived of their inheritance of dignity, they are not allowed even the privilege of a commoner. An Irish lord cannot sit in the House of Commons for an Irish county or city, nor can he vote for an Irish member.

But an Irish lord can represent an English constituency. The distinction is a strange one—unintelligible to us in any sense but one of national humiliation. We understand it thus :—An Irish lord is too mean in his own person, and by virtue of his Irish title, to rank with the British peerage. He can only qualify for that honour by uniting in his the suffrages and titles of ten or twelve others. But—flattering distinction!—he is above the rank of an Irish commoner, nor is he permitted to sully his name with the privileges of that order. And, unspeakable dignity! he may take his stand with a British mob.

There is no position to match this in shame. There is no guilt so despicable as dozing in it without a blush or an effort, or even a dream for independence. When all else are alive to indignity, and working in the way of honour and liberty, they alone, whom it would best become to be earliest and most earnest in the strife, sink back replete with dishonour.

Of those, or their descendants, who, at the time of the Union, sold their country and the high places they filled in her councils and in her glory, for the promise of a foreign title, which has not been redeemed, the shame and the mortification has been, perhaps, too great to admit of any hope in regard to them. Their trust was sacred—their honour unsuspected. The stake they guarded above life they betrayed then for a false bauble ; and it is no wonder if they think their infamy irredeemable, and eternal.

We know not but it is. There are many

however, not in that category. They struggled
at fearful odds, and every risk, against the fate
of their country. They strove when hope had
left them. Wherefore do they stand apart now,
when she is again erect, and righteous, and
daring ? Have they despaired for her greatness,
because of the infidelity of those to whom she
had too blindly trusted ?

The time is gone when she could be betrayed.
This one result is already guaranteed by recent
teaching. We may not be yet thoroughly instructed in the wisdom and the virtue necessary
for the independent maintenance of self-government ; but we have mastered thus much of
national knowledge that we cannot be betrayed.
There is no assurance ever nation gave which
we have not given, or may not give, that our
present struggle shall end in triumph or in national death.

The writers of *The Nation* have never con-
cealed the defects or flattered the good qualities
of their countrymen. They have told them in
good faith that they wanted many an attribute of
a free people, and that the true way to command
happiness and liberty was by learning the arts
and practising the culture that fitted men for
their enjoyment. Nor was it until we saw
them thus learning and thus practising, that our
faith became perfect, and that we felt entitled to
say to all men, here is a strife in which it will be
stainless glory to be even defeated. It is one in
which the Irish nobility have the first interest
and the first stake in their individual capacities.

As they would be the most honoured and benefitted by national success, they are the guiltiest in opposing, or being indifferent to national patriotism.

Of the Irish gentry there is not much to be said. They are divisible into two classes—the one consists of the old Norman race commingled with the Catholic gentlemen, who either have been able to maintain their patrimonies, or who have risen into affluence by their own industry; the other the descendants of Cromwell's or William's successful soldiery.

This last is the most anti-Irish of all. They feel no personal debasement in the dishonour of the country. Old prejudices, a barbarous law, a sense of insecurity in the possessions they know were obtained by plunder, combine to sink them into the mischievous and unholy belief that it is their interest as well as their duty to degrade, and wrong, and beggar the Irish people.

There are among them men fired by enthusiasm, men fed by fanaticism, men influenced by sordidness; but, as a whole, they are earnest thinkers and stern actors. There is a virtue in their unscrupulousness. They speak, and act, and dare as men. There is a principle in their unprincipledness. Their belief is a harsh and turbulent one, but they profess it in a manly fashion.

We like them better than the other section of the same class. These last are but sneaking echoes of the other's views. They are coward patriots and criminal dandies. But, they ought to be different from what they are. We wish them so. We want their aid now—for the country, for themselves, for all. Would that they understood the truth, that they thought justly, and acted uprightly. They are wanted, one and all. Why conceal it—they are obstacles in our way, shadows on our path.

These are called the representatives of the property of the country. They are against the national cause, and, therefore, it is said that all the wealth of Ireland is opposed to the Repeal of the Union.

It is an ignorant and a false boast.

The people of the country are its wealth.— They till its soil, raise its produce, ply its trade. They serve, sustain, support, save it. They supply its armies—they are its farmers, its merchants, its tradesmen, its artists, all that enrich and adorn it.

And after all, each of them has a patrimony to spend, the honourable earning of his sweat, or his intellect, or his industry, or his genius.— Taking them on an average, they must, to live, spend at least £15 each by the year. Multiply it by seven millions, and see what it comes to.

Thirty-five millions annually—compare with that the rental of Ireland ; compare with it the wealth of the aristocracy spent in Ireland, and are they not as nothing?

But a more important comparison may be made of the strength, the fortitude, the patience, the bravery of those the enrichers of the country, with the meanness in mind and courage of those who are opposed to them.

It is the last we shall suggest. It is sufficient for our purpose. To those who do not think it of the highest value, we have nothing to say.

THE STATE OF THE PEASANTRY.

In a climate soft as a mother's smile, on a soil fruitful as God's love, the Irish peasant mourns.

He is not unconsoled. Faith in the joys of another world, heightened by his woe in this, give him hours, when he serenely looks down on the torments that encircle him—the moon on a troubled sky. Domestic love, almost morbid from external suffering, prevents him from becoming a fanatic or a misanthrope, and reconciles him to life. Sometimes he forgets all, and springs into a desperate glee or a scathing anger ; and latterly another feeling—the hope of better days —and another exertion—the effort for redress— have shared his soul with religion, love, mirth, and vengeance.

His consolations are those of a spirit—his misery includes all physical sufferings, and many that strike the soul, not the senses.

Consider his griefs ! They begin in the cradle —they end in the grave.

Suckled by a breast that is supplied from unwholesome or insufficient food, and that is fevered with anxiety—reeking with the smoke of an almost chimneyless cabin—assailed by wind and rain when the weather rages—breathing, when it is calm, the exhalations of a rotten roof, of clay walls, and of manure, which gives his only chance of food—he is apt to perish in his infancy.

Or he survives all this (happy if he have escaped from gnawing scrofula or familiar fever), and, in the same cabin, with rags instead of his mother's breast, and lumpers instead of his mother's milk, he spends his childhood.

Advancing youth brings him labour, and manhood increases it ; but youth and manhood leave his roof rotten, his chimney one hole, his window another, his clothes rags (at best muffled by a holiday *cotamore*)—his furniture a pot, a table, a few hay chairs and rickety stools—his food lumpers and water—his bedding straw and a coverlid—his enemies the landlord, the taxgatherer, and the law—his consolation the priest and his wife—his hope on earth, agitation—his hope hereafter, the' Lord God !

For such an existence his toil is hard—and so much the better—it calms and occupies his mind ; but bitter is his feeling that the toil, which gains for him this nauseous and scanty livelihood, heaps dainties and gay wines on the table of his distant landlord, clothes his children or his harem in satin, lodges them in marble halls, and brings all the arts of luxury to solicit their senses— bitter to him to feel that this green land, which he loves and his landlord scorns, is ravished by him of her fruits to pamper that landlord ; twice bitter for him to see his wife, with weariness in her breast of love, to see half his little brood torn by the claws of want to undeserved graves, and to know that to those who survive him he can only leave the inheritance to which he was heir ; and thrice bitter to him that even his hovel has not the security of the wild beast's den—that

Squalidness, and Hunger, and Disease are insufficient guardians of his home—and that the puff
of the landlord's or the agent's breath may blow
him off the land where he has lived, and send
him and his to a dyke, or to prolong wretched-
ness in some desperate kennel in the next town,
till the strong wings of Death—unopposed lord
of such suburbs—bear them away.

Aristocracy of Ireland, will ye do nothing?—
will ye do nothing for fear? The body who best
know Ireland—the body that keep Ireland within
the law—the Repeal Committee—declare that
unless some great change take place, an agrarian
war may ensue! Do ye know what that is, and
how it would come? The rapid multiplication
of outrages, increased violence by Magistrates,
collisions between the People and the Police, co-
ercive laws and military force, the violation of
houses, the suspension of industry—the conflux
of discontent, pillage, massacre, war—the gentry shattered, the peasantry conquered and de-
cimated, or victorious and ruined (for who could
rule them)—there is an agrarian insurrection!
May Heaven guard us from it!—may the fear
be vain!

We set aside the fear! Forget it! Think of
the long, long patience of the People—their
toils supporting you—their virtues shaming you
—their huts, their hunger, their disease.

To whomsoever God hath given a heart less
cold than stone, these truths must cry day and
night. Oh! how they cross us like *Banshees*
when we would range free on the mountain—
how, as we walk in the evening light amid flow-

ers, they startle us from rest of mind! Ye
nobles! whose houses are as gorgeous as the
mote's (who dwelleth in the sunbeam)—ye strong
and haughty squires—ye dames exuberant with
tingling blood—ye maidens, whom not splendour
has yet spoiled, will ye not think of the poor?—
will ye not shudder in your couches to think how
rain, wind, and smoke dwell with the blanket-
less peasant?—will ye not turn from the sump-
tuous board to look at those hard-won meals of
black and slimy roots on which man, woman,
and child feed year after year?—will ye never
try to banish wringing hunger and ghastly disease from the home of such piety and love?—
will ye not give back its dance to the village—
its mountain play to boyhood—its serene hopes
to manhood?

Will ye do nothing for pity—nothing for love?
Will ye leave a foreign Parliament to mitigate—
will ye leave a native Parliament, gained in your
despite, to redress these miseries—will ye for
ever abdicate the duty and the joy of making the
poor comfortable, and the peasant attached and
happy? Do—if so you prefer; but know that
if you do, you are a doomed race. Once more,
Aristocracy of Ireland, we warn and entreat you
to consider the State of the Peasantry, and to
save them with your own hands.

HABITS AND CHARACTER OF THE
PEASANTRY.*

THERE are (thank God!) four hundred thousand
Irish children in the National Schools.   A few
years, and *they* will be the People of Ireland—
the farmers of its lands, the conductors of its
traffic, the adepts in its arts. How utterly unlike
that Ireland will be to the Ireland of the Penal
Laws, of the Volunteers, of the Union, or of
the Emancipation?

Well may Carleton say that we are in a transi-
tion state.   The knowledge, the customs, the superstitions, the hopes of the People are entirely
changing.   There is neither use nor reason in
lamenting what we must infallibly lose.   Our
course is an open and a great one, and will try us
severely; but, be it well or ill, we cannot resem-
ble our fathers.   No conceivable effort will get
the people, twenty years hence, to regard the
Fairies but as a beautiful fiction to be cherished,
not believed in, and not a few real and human
characters are perishing as fast as the Fairies.

Let us be content to have the past chronicled
wherever it cannot be preserved.

Much may be saved—the Gaelic language and
the music of the past may be handed uncor-
rupted to the future; but whatever may be the

* "Tales and Sketches illustrating the Irish Peasantry." By William Carleton.   James Duffy, Dublin,
1845; 1 vol. 8vo, pp. 393.

substitutes, the Fairies and the Banshees, the
Poor Scholar and the Ribbonman, the Orange
Lodge, the Illicit Still, and the Faction Fight,
are vanishing into history, and unless this generation paints them no other will know what they
were.

It is chiefly in this way we value the work
before us. In it Carleton is the historian of the
peasantry rather than a dramatist. The fiddler
and piper, the seanachie and seer, the match-
maker and dancing-master, and a hundred characters beside are here brought before you,
moving, acting, playing, plotting, and gossip-
ing! You are never wearied by an inventory of
wardrobes, as in short English descriptive fictions; yet you see how every one is dressed;
you hear the honey brogue of the maiden, and
the downy voice of the child, the managed accents of flattery or traffic, the shrill tones of
woman's fretting, and the troubled gush of man's
anger. The moory upland and the corn slopes,
the glen where the rocks jut through mantling
heather, and bright brooks gurgle amid the
scented banks of wild herbs, the shivering cabin
and the rudely-lighted farm-house are as plain in
Carleton's pages as if he used canvass and colours
with a skill varying from Wilson and Poussin,
to Teniers and Wilkie.

But even in these sketches, his power of external description is not his greatest merit. Born
and bred among the people—full of their animal
vehemence—skilled in their sports—as credulous
and headlong in boyhood, and as fitful and varied
in manhood, as the wildest—he had felt with

them and must ever sympathise with them. Endowed with the highest dramatic genius, he has represented their love and generosity, their wrath and negligence, their crimes and virtues, as a hearty peasant—not a note-taking critic.

In others of his works he has created ideal characters that give him a higher rank as a poet (some of them not surpassed by even Shakspeare for originality, grandeur, and distinctness); but here he is a genuine Seanachie, and brings you to dance and wake, to wedding and christening—makes you romp with the girls, and race with the boys—tremble at the ghosts, and frolic with the fairies of the whole parish.

Come what change there may over Ireland, in these "Tales and Sketches" the peasantry of the past hundred years can be for ever lived with.

———

IRISH SCENERY.

WE no more see why Irish people should not visit the Continent, than why Germans or Frenchmen ought not to visit Ireland; but there is a difference between them. A German rarely comes here who has not trampled the heath of Tyrol, studied the museums of Dresden and the frescoes of Munich, and shouted defiance on the bank of the Rhine; and what Frenchman who has not seen the vineyards of Provence and the Bocages of Brittany, and the snows of Jura and

the Pyrenees, ever drove on an Irish jingle?
But our nobles and country gentlemen, our merchants, lawyers, and doctors—and what's worse,
their wives and daughters—penetrate Britain
and the Continent without ever trying whether
they could not defy in Ireland the *ennui* before
which they run over seas and mountains.

The cause of this, as of most of our grievances,
was misgovernment, producing poverty, discom-
fort, ignorance, and misrepresentation. The
people were ignorant and in rags, their houses
miserable, the roads and hotels shocking; we
had no banks, few coaches, and, to crown all,
the English declared the people to be rude and
turbulent, which they were not, as well as
drunken and poor, which they assuredly were.
An Irish landlord, who had ill-treated his own
tenants, felt a conscientious dread of all frieze-
coats, others adopted his prejudices, and a people, who never were rude or unjust to strangers,
were considered unsafe to travel amongst.

Most of these causes are removed. The people
are sober, and are rapidly advancing to knowledge, their political exertions and dignity have
broken away much of the prejudices against
them, and a man passing through any part of
Ireland expects to find woful poverty and strong
discontent, but he does not fear the abduction of
his wife, or attempts to assassinate him on every
lonely road. The coaches, cars, and roads, too,
have become excellent, and the hotels are sufficient for any reasonable traveller. One very
marked discouragement to travelling was the
want of information; the maps were little daubs,

and the guide-books were few and inaccurate. As
to maps we are now splendidly off. The Railway Commissioners' Map of Ireland, aided by
the Ordnance Index Map of any county where
a visiter makes a long stay, are ample. We
have got a good general guide-book in Fraser,
but it could not hold a twentieth of the information necessary to a leisurely tourist; nor,
till the Ordnance Memoir is out shall we have
thorough hand-books to our counties. Meantime
let us not burn the little guides to Antrim, Wicklow, and Killarney, though they are desperately
dull and inexact—let us not altogether prohibit
Mrs. Hall's gossip, though she knows less about
our Celtic people than of the Malays; and let
us be even thankful for Mr. O'Flanagan's volume on the Munster Blackwater (though it is
printed in London), for his valuable stories, for
his minute, picturesque, and full topography,
for his antiquarian and historical details, though
he blunders into making Alaster M'Donnell a
Scotchman, and for his hearty love of the
scenery and people he has undertaken to guide
us through.

And now, reader, in this fine soft summer,
when the heather is blooming, and the sky
laughing and crying like a hysterical bride, full
of love, where will you go—through your own
land or a stranger's? If you stay at home you
can choose your own scenery, and have something to see in the summer, and talk of in the
winter, that will make your friends from the
Alps and Appenines respectful to you.

Did you propose to study economies among

the metayers of Tuscany or the artisans of Belgium, postpone the trip till the summer of '45 or '46, when you may have the passport of an Irish office to get you a welcome, and seek for the state of the linen weavers in the soft hamlets of Ulster—compare the cattle herds of Meath with the safe little holdings of Down, and the well-fought farms of Tipperary, or investigate the statistics of our fisheries along the rivers and lakes and shores of our island.

Had a strong desire come upon you to toil over the glacier, whose centre froze when Adam courted Eve, or walk amid the brigand passes of Italy or Spain—do not fancy that absolute size makes mountain grandeur, or romance, to a mind full of passion and love of strength (and with such only do the mountain spirits walk) the passes of Glenmalure and Barnesmore are deep as Chamouni, and Carn Tual and Slieve Donard are as near the lightning as Mount Blanc.

To the picture-hunter we can offer little, though Vandyke's finest portrait is in Kilkenny, and there is no county without some collection; but for the lover of living or sculptured forms— for the artist, the antiquarian, and the natural philosopher, we have more than five summers could exhaust. Every one can see the strength of outline, the vigour of colour, and the effective grouping in every fair, and wake, and chapel, and hurling-ground, from Donegal to Waterford, though it may take the pen of Griffin or the pencil of Burton to represent them. An Irishman, if he took the pains, would surely find something not inferior in interest to Cologne or

the Alhambra in a study of the monumental
effigies which mat the floors of Jerpoint and
Adare, or the cross in a hundred consecrated
grounds, from Kells to Clonmacnoise—of the
round towers which spring in every barony—of
the architectural perfection of Holycross and
Clare-Galway, and the strange fellowship of
every order in Athassel, or of the military keeps,
and earthen pyramids, and cairns, which tell of
the wars of recent, and the piety of distant centuries. The Entomology, Botany, and Geology
of Ireland are not half explored ; the structure
and distinctions of its races are but just attracting the eyes of philosophers from Mr. Wylde's
tract, and the country is actually full of airs
never noted, history never written, superstitions
and romances never rescued from tradition ; and
why should Irishmen go blundering in foreign
researches when so much remains to be done
here, and when to do it would be more easy,
more honourable, and more useful?

In many kinds of scenery we can challenge
comparison. Europe has no lake so dreamily
beautiful as Killarney ; no bays where the bold-
ness of Norway unites with the colouring of Na-
ples, as in Bantry ; and you might coast the
world without finding cliffs so vast and so terrible as Achill and Slieve League. Glorious, too,
as the Rhine is, we doubt if its warmest admirers
would exclude from rivalry the Nore and the
Blackwater, if they had seen the tall cliffs, and
the twisted slopes, and the ruined aisles, and
glancing mountains, and feudal castles through
which you boat up from Youghal to Mallow, or

glide down from Thomastown to Waterford harbour. Hear what Inglis says of this Avondhu :—

" We have had descents of the Danube, and descents of the Rhine, and the Rhone, and of many other rivers; but we have not in print, as far as I know, any descent of the Blackwater ; and yet, with all these descents of foreign rivers in my recollection, *I think the descent of the Blackwater not surpassed by any of them.* A detail of all that is seen in gliding down the Blackwater from Cappoquin to Youghal would fill a long chapter. There is every combination that can be produced by the elements that enter into the picturesque and the beautiful—deep shades, bold rocks, verdant slopes, with the triumphs of art superadded, and made visible in magnificent houses and beautiful villas, with their decorated lawns and pleasure-grounds."

And now, reader, if these kaleidoscope glimpses we have given you have made you doubt between a summer in Ireland and one abroad, give your country " the benefit of the doubt," as the lawyers say, and boat on our lake or dive into our glens and ruins, wonder at the basalt coast of Antrim, and soften your heart between the banks of the Blackwater.

IRISH MUSIC AND POETRY,

No enemy speaks slightingly of Irish Music, and
no friend need fear to boast of it.   It is without
a rival.

Its antique war-tunes, such as those of O'Byrne,
O'Donnell, Alestrom, and Brian Boru, stream and
crash upon the ear like the warriors of a hundred
glens meeting; and you are borne with them to
battle, and they and you charge and struggle amid
cries and battle-axes and stinging arrows.   Did
ever a wail make man's marrow quiver, and fill
his nostrils with the breath of the grave like the
ululu of the north or the wirrasthrue of Munster ?
Stately are their slow, and recklessly splendid
their quick marches, their "Boyne Water," and
Sios agus sios liom," their "Michael Hoy," and
"Gallant Tipperary."   The Irish jigs and planx-
ties are not only the best dancing tunes, but the
finest quick marches in the world.   Some of them
would cure a paralytic, and make the marble-
legged prince in the Arabian Nights charge like a
Fag-an-Bealach boy.   The hunter joins in every
leap and yelp of the "Fox Chase;" the historian
hears the moan of the penal days in "Drimindhu,"
and sees the embarkation of the Wild Geese in
"Limerick Lamentation;" and ask the lover if
his breath do not come and go, with "Savourneen
Deelish" and "Lough Sheelin."

Varied and noble as our music is, the English-

speaking people in Ireland have been gradually
losing their knowledge of it, and a number of
foreign tunes—paltry scented things from Italy,
lively trifles from Scotland, and German opera
cries—are heard in our concerts, and what is
worse, from our Temperance bands.   Yet we
never doubted that " The Sight Entrancing," or
" The Memory of the Dead," would satisfy even
the most spoiled of our fashionables better than
anything Balfe or Rossini ever wrote ; and, as it
is, " Tow-row-row " is better than *poteen* to the
teetotalers, wearied with overtures and insulted
by " British Grenadiers " and " Rule Britannia."

A reprint of *Moore's Melodies* on lower keys,
and at *much* lower prices, would probably restore
the sentimental music of Ireland to its natural
supremacy.   There are in Bunting but two good
sets of words—" The Bonny Cuckoo," and poor
Campbell's " Exile of Erin."   These and a few
of Lover's and Mahony's songs can alone compete
with Moore.   But, save one or two by Lysaght
and Drennan, almost all the Irish political songs
are too desponding or weak to content a people
marching to independence as proudly as if they
had never been slaves.

The popularity and immense circulation of the
Spirit of the Nation proved that it represented
the hopes and passions of the Irish people.   This
looks like vanity; but as a corporation so numerous
as the contributors to that volume cannot blush,
we shall say our say.   For instance, who did not
admire " The Memory of the Dead ? "   The very
Stamp officers were galvanised by it, and the
Attorney-General was repeatedly urged to sing

N

it for the jury. He refused—he had no music to
sing it to. We pitied and forgave him; but we
vowed to leave him no such excuse next time.
If these songs were half so good as people called
them, they deserved to flow from a million throats
to as noble music as ever O'Neill or O'Connor
heard.

Some of them were written to, and some freely
combined with, old and suitable airs. These we
resolved to have printed with the music, certain
that, thus, the music would be given back to a
people who had been ungratefully neglecting it,
and the words carried into circles where they
were still unknown.

Others of these poems, indeed the best of them,
had no ante-types in our ancient music. New
music was, therefore, to be sought for them. Not
on their account only was it to be sought. We
hoped they would be the means of calling out and
making known a cotemporary music fresh with
the spirit of the time, and rooted in the country.

Since Carolan's death there had been no addition to the store. Not that we were without
composers, but those we have do not compose
Irish-like music, nor for Ireland. Their rewards
are from a foreign public—their fame, we fear,
will suffer from alienage. Balfe is very sweet,
and Rooke very emphatic, but not one passion or
association in Ireland's heart would answer to
their songs.

Fortunately there was one among us (perchance
his example may light us to others) who can smite
upon our harp like a master, and make it sigh
with Irish memories, and speak sternly with

Ireland's resolve. To him, to his patriotism, to his genius, and, we may selfishly add, to his friendship, we owe our ability now to give to Ireland music fit for "The Memory of the Dead" and "The Hymn of Freedom," and whatever else was marked out by popularity for such care as his.

In former editions of the *Spirit* we had thrown in carelessly several inferior verses and some positive trash, and neither paper nor printing were any great honor to the Dublin press. Every improvement in the power of the most enterprising publisher in Ireland has been made, and every fault, within our reach or his, cured—and whether as the first publication of original airs, as a selection of ancient music, or as a specimen of what the Dublin press can do, in printing, paper, or cheapness, we urge the public to support this work of Mr. James Duffy's—and, in a pecuniary way, it is his altogether.

We had hoped to have added a recommendation to the first number of this work, besides whatever attraction may lie in its music, its ballads, or its mechanical beauty.

An artist, whom we shall not describe or he would be known, sketched a cover and title for it. The idea, composition, and drawing of that design, were such as Flaxman might have been proud of. It is a monument to bardic power, to patriotism, to our music and our history. There is at least as much poetry in it as in the best verses in the work it illustrates. If it do nothing else, it will show our Irish artists that refinement and strength, passion and dignity, are as practicable in Irish as in German painting; and the lesson was needed sorely

But if it lead him who drew it to see that our history and hopes present fit forms to embody the highest feelings of beauty, wisdom, truth, and glory in, irrespective of party politics, then, indeed, we shall have served our country when we induced our gifted friend to condescend to sketching "a title-page." We need not describe that design now, as it will appear on the cover of the second number, and on the title-page of the finished volume.

BALLAD POETRY OF IRELAND.

How slow we have all been in coming to understand the meaning of Irish Nationality!

Some, dazzled by visions of Pagan splendour, and the pretensions of pedigree, and won by the passions and romance of the olden races, continued to speak in the nineteenth century of an Irish nation as they might have done in the tenth. They forgot the English Pale, the Ulster Settlement, and the filtered colonization of men and ideas. A Celtic kingdom with the old names and the old language, without the old quarrels, was their hope; and, though they would not repeat O'Neill's comment, as he passed Barrett's castle on his march to Kinsale, and heard it belonged to a Strongbownian, that "he hated the Norman churl as if he came yesterday;" yet they quietly assumed that the Norman and Saxon elements would disappear under the Gaelic genius, like the tracks of cavalry under a fresh crop.

The Nationality of Swift and Grattan was equally partial. They saw that the Government and laws of the settlers had extended to the island—that Donegal and Kerry were in the Pale; they heard the English tongue in Dublin, and London opinions in Dublin—they mistook Ireland for a colony wronged, and great enough to be a nation.

A lower form of nationhood was before the minds of those who saw in it nothing but a parliament in College Green. They had not erred in judging, for they had not tried to estimate the moral elements and tendencies of the country. They were as narrow bigots to the omnipotency of an institution as any Cockney Radical. Could they, by any accumulation of English stupidity and Irish laziness, have got possession of an Irish government, they would soon have distressed every one by their laws, whom they had not provoked by their administration, or disgusted by their dulness.

Far healthier with all its defects, was the idea of those who saw in Scotland a perfect model—who longed for a literary and artistic nationality—who prized the oratory of Grattan and Curran, the novels of Griffin and Carleton, the pictures of Maclise and Burton, the ancient music, as much as any, and far more than most of the political nationalists, but who regarded political independence as a dangerous dream Unknowingly they fostered it. Their writings, their patronage, their talk was of Ireland; yet it hardly occurred to them that the ideal would flow into the practical, or that they, with their dread of agitation, were forwarding a revolution.

At last we are beginning to see what we are, and what is our destiny. Our duty arises where our knowledge begins. The elements of Irish nationality are not only combining—in fact, they are growing confluent in our minds. Such nationality as merits a good man's help, and wakens a true man's ambition—such nationality as could stand against internal faction and foreign intrigue, such nationality, as would make the Irish hearth happy and the Irish name illustrious, is becoming understood. It must contain and represent the races of Ireland. It must not be Celtic, it must not be Saxon—it must be Irish. The Brehon law, and the maxims of Westminster, the cloudy and lightning genius of the Gael, the placid strength of the Sasanach, the marshalling insight of the Norman—a literature which shall exhibit in combination the passions and idioms of all, and which shall equally express our mind in its romantic, its religious, its forensic, and its practical tendencies—finally, a native government, which shall know and rule by the might and right of all; yet yield to the arrogance of none—these are components of *such* a nationality.

But what have these things to do with the "Ballad Poetry of Ireland?" Much every way. It is the result of the elements we have named— it is compounded of all; and never was there a book fitter to advance that perfect nationality to which Ireland begins to aspire. That a country is without national poetry proves its hopeless dulness or its utter provincialism. National poetry is the very flowering of the soul—the greatest evidence of its health, the greatest excellence of its beauty. Its melody is balsam to the senses. It is the playfellow of childhood, ripens into the companion of his manhood, consoles his age. It presents the most dramatic events, the largest characters, the most impressive scenes, and the deepest passions in the language most familiar to us. It shows us magnified, and ennobles our hearts, our intellects, our country, and our countrymen—binds us to the land by its condensed and gem-like history, to the future by examples and by aspirations. It solaces us in travel, fires us in action, prompts our invention, sheds a grace beyond the power of luxury round our homes, is the recognised envoy of our minds among all mankind and to all time.

In possessing the powers and elements of a glorious nationality, we owned the sources of a national poetry. In the combination and joint development of the latter, we find a pledge and a help to that of the former.

This book of Mr. Duffy's,* true as it is to the wants of the time, is not fortuitous. He has prefaced his admirable collection by an Introduction, which proves his full consciousness of the worth of his task, and proves equally his ability to execute it. In a space too short for the most impatient to run by he has accurately investigated the sources of Irish Ballad Poetry, vividly defined the qualities of each, and laboured with perfect success to show that, all naturally

* "Ballad Poetry of Ireland"—Library of Ireland, No. II.

combine towards one great end, as the brooks to
a river, which marches on clear, deep, and single,
though they be wild, and shallow, and turbid,
flowing from unlike regions, and meeting after
countless windings.

Mr. Duffy maps out three main forces which
unequally contribute to an Irish Ballad Poetry.

The *first* consists of the Gaelic ballads.   True
to the vehemence and tendencies of the Celtic
people, and representing equally their vagueness
and extravagance during slavish times, they, nevertheless, remain locked from the middle and
upper classes generally, and from the peasantry
of more than half Ireland, in an unknown language.   Many of them have been translated by
rhymers—few, indeed, by poets.   The editor of
the volume before us, has brought into one house
nearly all the poetical translations from the Irish,
and thus finely justifies the ballad literature of
the Gael from its calumnious friend :—

> "With a few exceptions, all the translations we are
> acquainted with, in addition to having abundance of
> minor faults, are eminently un-Irish.   They seem to
> have been made by persons to whom one of the languages
> was not familiar.   Many of them were confessedly ver-
> sified from prose translations, and are mere English
> poems, without a tinge of the colour or character of the
> country.   Others, translated by sound Irish scholars,
> are bald and literal ; the writers sometimes wanting a
> facility of versification, sometimes a mastery over the
> English language.   The Irish scholars of the last century
> were too exclusively national to study the foreign tongue
> with the care essential to master its metrical resources ;
> and the flexible and weighty language which they had
> not learned to wield hung heavily on them,
>
> > ' Like Saul's plate armour on the shepherd boy,
> >   Eucumbering, and *not* arming them.'

If it were just to estimate our bardic poetry by the specimens we have received in this manner, it could not be
rated highly. But it would manifestly be most unjust.
Noble and touching, and often subtle and profound
thoughts, which no translation could entirely spoil, shine
through the poverty of the style, and vindicate the character of the originals. Like the costly arms and ornaments found in our bogs, they are substantial witnesses
of a distinct civilization ; and their credit is no more
diminished by the rubbish in which they chance to be
found than the authenticity of the ancient *torques* and
skians by their embedment in the mud. When the
entire collection of our Irish Percy—James Hardiman—
shall have been given to a public (and soon may such a
one come) that can relish them in their native dress, they
will be entitled to undisputed precedence in our national
minstrelsy."

About a dozen of the ballads in the volume, are
derived translated from the Irish. It is only in
this way that Clarence Mangan (a name to which
Mr. Duffy does just honour) contributes to the
volume. There are four translations by him
exhibiting eminently his perfect mastery of versification—his flexibility of passion, from loneliest
grief to the maddest humour. One of these,
" The Lament for O'Neill and O'Donnell," is the
strongest, though it will not be the most popular,
ballad in the work.

Callanan's and Ferguson's translations, if not
so daringly versified, are simpler and more Irish
in idiom.

Most, indeed, of Callanan's successful ballads
are translations, and well entitle him to what he
passionately prays for—a minstrel of free Erin
to come to his grave—

" And plant a wild wreath from the banks of the river,
O'er the heart and the harp that are sleeping for ever."

But, we are wrong in speaking of Mr. Ferguson's translations in precisely the same way. His "Wicklow War Song" is condensed, epigrammatic, and crashing as anything we know of, except the "Pibroch of Donnil Dhu."

The *second* source is—the common people's ballads. Most of these "make no pretence to being true to Ireland, but only being true to the *purlieus* of Cork and Dublin;" yet, now and then, one meets a fine burst of passion, and oftener a racy idiom. The "Drimin Dhu," the "Blackbird," "Peggy Bawn," "Irish Molly," "Willy Reilly," and the "Fair of Turloughmore," are the specimens given here. Of these "Willy Reilly" (an old and worthy favourite in Ulster, it seems, but quite unknown elsewhere,) is the best; but it is too long to quote, and we must limit ourselves to the noble opening verse of "Turloughmore" :—

"Come tell me, dearest mother, what makes my father
    stay,
Or what can be the reason that he's so long away?
'Oh! hold your tongue, my darling son, your tears do
    grieve me sore,
I fear he has been murdered in the fair of Turlough-
    more.'"

The *third* and principal source consists of the Anglo-Irish ballads, written during the last twenty or thirty years.

Of this highest class, he who contributes most and, to our mind, best, is Mr. Ferguson. We have already spoken of his translations—his original ballads are better. There is nothing in this volume—nothing in "Percy's Relics," or the

"Border Minstrelsy," to surpass, perhaps to equal,
"Willy Gilliland." It is as natural in structure as
"Kinmont Willie," as vigorous as "Otterbourne,"
and as complete as "Lochinvar." Leaving his
Irish idiom, we get in the "Forester's Com-
plaint" as harmonious versification, and, in the
"Forging of the Anchor," as vigorous thoughts,
mounted on bounding words, as anywhere in
English literature.

We must quote some stray verses from "Willy
Gilliland":—

"Up in the mountain solitudes, and in a rebel ring,
He has worshipped God upon the hill, in spite of church
    and king;
And sealed his treason with his blood on Bothwell bridge
    he hath;
So he must fly his father's land, or he must die the
    death;
For comely Claverhouse has come along with grim
    Dalzell,
And his smoking rooftree testifies they've done their
    errand well.

*   *   *   *   *

"His blithe work done, upon a bank the outlaw rested
    now,
And laid the basket from his back, the bonnet from his
    brow,
And there, his hand upon the Book, his knee upon the
    sod,
He filled the lonely valley with the gladsome word of God;
And for a persecuted kirk, and for her martyrs dear,
And against a godless church and king he spoke up loud
    and clear.

*   *   *   *   *

" ' My bonny mare! I've ridden you when Claver'se
    rode behind,
And from the thumbscrew and the boot you bore me like
    the wind ;
And, while I have the life you saved, on your sleek
    flank, I swear,
Episcopalian rowel shall never ruffle hair !
Though sword to wield they've left me none—yet Wallace
    wight, I wis,
Good battle did, on Irvine side, wi' waur weapon than
    this.'—

" His fishing-rod with both his hands he griped it as he
    spoke,
And, where the butt and top were spliced, in pieces twain
    he broke ;
The limber top he cast away, with all its gear abroad,
But, grasping the tough hickory butt, with spike of iron
    shod,
He ground the sharp spear to a point ; then pulled his
    bonnet down,
And, meditating black revenge, set forth for Carrick
    town."

The only ballad equally racy is " The Croppy
Boy," by some anonymous but most promising
writer.

Griffin's "Gille Machree," is of another class—
is perfect—"striking on the heart," as Mr. Duffy
finely says, "like the cry of a woman ;" but his
" Orange and Green," and his " Bridal of Mala-
hide," belong to the same class, and suffer by
comparison with Mr. Ferguson's ballads.

Banim's greatest ballad, the " Soggarth Aroon,"
possesses even deeper tenderness and a more perfect Irish idiom than anything in the volume.

Among the collection are Colonel Blacker's
famous Orange ballad, " Oliver's Advice" ("Put
your trust in God, my boys, but keep your pow-

der dry,") and two versions of the "Boyne
Water." The latter and older one, given in the
appendix, is by far the finest, and contains two
unrivalled stanzas :—

"Both foot and horse they marched on, intending them
    to batter,
But the brave Duke Schomberg he was shot, as he crossed
    over the water.
When that King William he observed the brave Duke
    Schomberg falling,
He rein'd his horse, with a heavy heart, on the Ennis-
    killeners calling ;
' What will you do for me, brave boys, see yonder men
    retreating,
Our enemies encouraged are—and English drums are
    beating ;'
He says, ' my boys, feel no dismay at the losing of one
    commander,
For God shall be our King this day, and I'll be general
    under.' "

Nor less welcome is the comment :—

"Some of the Ulster ballads, of a restricted and provincial spirit, having less in common with Ireland than
with Scotland ; two or three Orange ballads, altogether
ferocious or foreign in their tendencies (preaching mur-
der, or deifying an alien), will be no less valuable to the
patriot or the poet on this account. They echo faith-
fully the sentiments of a strong, vehement, and indo-
mitable body of Irishmen, who may come to battle for
their country better than they ever battled for prejudices or their bigotries. At all events, to know what
they love and believe is a precious knowledge."

On the language of most of the ballads, Mr.
Duffy says :—

"Many of them, and generally the best, are just as
essentially Irish as if they were written in Gaelic. They
could have grown among no other people, perhaps under

o

no other sky or scenery. To an Englishman, to any
Irishman educated out of the country, or to a dreamer
asleep to impressions of scenery and character, they
would be achievements as impossible as the Swedish
Skalds or the *Arabian Nights*. They are as Irish as
Ossian or Carolan, and unconsciously reproduce the
spirit of those poets better than any translator can hope
to do. They revive and perpetuate the vehement native
songs that gladdened the halls of our princes in their
triumphs, and wailed over their ruined hopes or murdered bodies. In everything but language, and almost in
language, they are identical. That strange tenacity of
the Celtic race which makes a description of their habits
and propensities when Cæsar was still a Proconsul in
Gaul, true in essentials of the Irish people to this day,
has enabled them to infuse the ancient and hereditary
spirit of the country into all that is genuine of our modern poetry. And even the language grew almost Irish.
The soul of the country stammering its passionate grief
and hatred in a strange tongue, loved still to utter them
in its old familiar idioms and cadences. Uttering them,
perhaps, with more piercing earnestness, because of the
impediment; and winning out of the very difficulty a
grace and a triumph."

How often have we wished for such a companion as this volume. Worse than meeting un-
clean beds, or drenching mists, or Cockney
opinions, was it to have to take the mountains
with a book of Scottish ballads. They were
glorious to be sure, but they were not ours, they
had not the brown of the climate on their cheek,
they spoke of places far, and ways which are not
our country's ways, and hopes which were not
Ireland's, and their tongue was not that we first
made sport and love with. Yet how mountaineer
without ballads, any more than without a shille-
lagh? No; we took the Scots ballads, and felt
our souls rubbing away with envy and alienage

amid their attentions ; but now, Brighid be
praised ! we can have all Irish thoughts on Irish
hills, true to them as the music, or the wind, or
the sky.

Happy boys! who may grow up with such
ballads in your memories. Happy men! who
will find your hearts not only dutiful but joyous,
in serving and sacrificing for the country you
thus learned in childhood to love.*

A BALLAD HISTORY OF IRELAND.

OF course the first *object* of the work we project †
will be to make Irish History familiar to the
minds, pleasant to the ears, dear to the passions,
and powerful over the taste and conduct of the
Irish people in times to come. More *events* could
be put into a prose history. Exact dates, subtle
plots, minute connexions and motives, rarely
appear in Ballads, and for these ends the worst
prose history is superior to the best Ballad series;
but these are not the highest ends of history. To
hallow or accurse the scenes of glory and honor,
or of shame and sorrow ; to give to the imagination the arms, and homes, and senates, and battles
of other days; to rouse, and soften, and strengthen,

* A corresponding Essay on SONGS, written by Davis,
will be found prefixed to Mr. Barry's collection of " The
Songs of Ireland."—ED.

† It had been proposed in the *Nation*, by another contributor, to write ballads on the great events in our annals
and collect them into a " Ballad History of Ireland." ED.

and enlarge us with the passions of great periods; to lead us into love of self-denial, of justice, of beauty, of valour, of generous life and proud death; and to set up in our souls the memory of great men, who shall then be as models and judges of our actions—these are the highest duties of history, and these are best taught by a Ballad History.

A Ballad History is welcome to childhood, from its rhymes, its high colouring, and its aptness to memory. As we grow into boyhood, the violent passions, the vague hopes, the romantic sorrow of patriot ballads are in tune with our fitful and luxuriant feelings. In manhood we prize the condensed narrative, the grave firmness, the critical art, and the political sway of ballads. And in old age they are doubly dear; the companions and reminders of our life, the toys and teachers of our children and grandchildren. Every generation finds its account in them. They pass from mouth to mouth like salutations; and even the minds which lose their words are under their influence, as one can recall the starry heavens who cannot revive the form of a single constellation.

In olden times all ballads were made to music, and the minstrel sang them to his harp or screamed them in recitative. Thus they reached farther, were welcomer guests in feast and camp, and were better preserved. We shall have more to say on this in speaking of our proposed song collection. Printing so multiplies copies of ballads, and intercourse is so general, that there is less need of this adaptation to music now. Moreover, it may be disputed whether the dramatic effect in the more

solemn ballads is not injured by lyrical forms.
In such streaming exhortations and laments as
we find in the Greek choruses and in the adjura-
tions and caoines of the Irish, the breaks and
parallel repetitions of a song might lower the
passion.   Were we free to do so, we could point
out instances in the *Spirit of the Nation* in which
the rejection of song-forms seems to have been
essential to the awfulness of the occasion.

In pure narratives, and in the gayer and more
slendid, though less stern ballads, the song forms,
and adaptation to music are clear gains.

In the Scotch ballads this is usual, in the English
rare.   We look in vain through Southey's admirable ballads—" Mary the Maid of the Inn,"
" Jaspar," " Inchkape Rock," " Bishop Hatto,"
" King Henry V. and the Hermit of Dreux,"—
for either burden, chorus, or adaptation, to music.
In the " Battle of Blenheim " there is, however,
an occasional burden line ; and in the smashing
" March to Moscow " there is a great chorussing
about—

> " Morbleu ! Parbleu !
> What a pleasant excursion to Moscow."

Coleridge has some skilful repetitions, and exquisite versification, in his " Ancient Mariner,"
" Genevieve," " Alice du Clos," but no where a
systematic burden.   Campbell has no burdens in
his finest lyric ballads, though the subjects were
fitted for them.   The burden of the " Exile of
Erin " belongs very doubtfully to him.

Macaulay's best ballad, " The Battle of Ivry,"
is greatly aided by the even burden line ; but he
has not repeated the experiment, though he, too,

makes much use of repeating lines in his Roman
Lays and other ballads.

While, then, we counsel burdens in Historical
Ballads, we would recognise excepted cases where
they may be injurious, and treat them as in *no
case* essential to perfect ballad success.   In songs,
we would almost always insist either on a chorus
verse, or a burden of some sort.   A burden need
not be at the end of the verse ; but may, with
quite equal success, be at the beginning or in the
body of it, as may be seen in the Scotch Ballads,
and in some of these in the *Spirit of the Nation*.

The old Scotch and English ballads, and Lock-
hart's translations from the Spanish, are mostly
composed in one metre, though written down in
either of two ways.   Macaulay's Roman Lays and
"Ivry" are in this metre.   Take an example from
the last :—

" Press where ye see my white plume shine, amid the
        ranks of war,
And be your Oriflamme to-day the helmet of Navarre."

In the old ballads this would be printed in four
lines, of eight syllables and six alternately, and
rhyming only alternately—thus :—

        " Press where ye see my white plume shine,
            Amid the ranks of war,
          And be your Oriflamme to-day
            The helmet of Navarre."

So Macaulay himself prints this metre in some
of his Roman Lays.

But the student should rather avoid than seek
this metre.   The uniform old beat of eight and
six is apt to fall monotonously on the ear, and
some of the most startling effects are lost in it.

In the *Spirit of the Nation* the student will find many other ballad metres. Campbell's metres, though new and glorious things, are terrible traps to imitation, and should be warily used. The German ballads, and still more, Mr. Mangan's translations of them, contain great variety of new and safe, though difficult metres. Next in frequency to the fourteen syllable line is that in eleven syllables, such as "Mary Ambree," and "Lochinvar;" and for a rolling brave ballad 'tis a fine metre. The metre of fifteen syllables, with double rhymes (or accents) in the middle, and that of thirteen, with double rhymes at the end, is tolerably frequent, and the metre used by Father Prout, in his noble translation of "Duke d'Alencon" is admirable, and easier than it seems. By the way, what a grand burden runs through that ballad—

" Fools! to believe the sword could give to the children of the Rhine,
Our Gallic fields—the land that yields the Olive and the Vine!"

The syllables are as in the common metre, but it has thrice the rhymes.

We have seen great materials wasted in a struggle with a crotchetty metre; therefore, though we counsel the invention of metres, we would add, that unless a metre come out racily and appropriately in the first couple of verses, it should be abandoned, and some of these easily marked metres taken up.

A historical ballad will commonly be narrative in its form but not necessarily so. A hymn of exultation—a call to a council, an army, or a people—a prophecy—a lament--or a dramatic scene (as in Lochiel), may give as much of event, costume, character, and even scenery as a mere narration. The varieties of form are infinite, and it argues lack of force in a writer to keep always to mere narration, though when exact events are to be told, that may be the best mode.

One of the essential qualities of a good historical ballad is truth. To pervert history—to violate nature, in order to make a fine clatter, has been the aim in too many of the ballads sent us. He who goes to write a historical ballad should master the main facts of the time, and state them truly. It may be well for him perhaps either not to study or to half-forget minute circumstances until after his ballad is drafted out, lest he write a chronicle, not a ballad ; but he will do well, ere he suffers it to leave his study, to re-consider the facts of the time, or man, or act of which he writes, and see if he cannot add force to his statements, an antique grace to his phrases, and colour to his language.

Truth and appropriateness in ballads require great knowledge and taste.

To write an Irish historical ballad, one should know the events which he would describe, and know them not merely from an isolated study of his subject, but from old familiarity, which shall have associated them with his tastes and passions, and connected them with other parts of history. How miserable a thing is to put forward a piece of vehement declamation and vague description which might be uttered of any event, or by the man of any time, as a historical ballad. We have had battle ballads sent us that would be as characteristic of Marathon or Waterloo as of Clontarf—laments that might have been uttered by a German or a Hindu—and romances equally true to love all the world over.

Such historical study extends not merely to the events. A ballad writer should try to find the voice, colour, stature, passions, and peculiar faculties of his hero—the arms, furniture, and dress of the congress, or the champions, or the troops, he tells of—the rites wherewith the youth were married—the dead interred, and God worshipped; and the architecture—previous history and pursuits (and, therefore, probable ideas and phrases) of the men he describes.

Many of these things he will get in books. He should shun compilations, and take up original journals, letters, state papers, statutes, and cotemporary fictions, and narratives, as much as possible. Let him not much mind Leland or Curry (after he has run over them), but work like fury at the Archæological Society's books—at Harris's Hibernica, at Lodge's Desiderata Curiosa Hibernica, at Strafford's Pacata, Spencer's View, Giraldus's Narrative, Fynes Moryson's Itinerary, the Ormond Papers, the State Papers of Henry the Eighth, Strafford's and Cromwell's and Rinuncini's Letters, and the correspondence and journals, from Donald O'Neil's letter to the Pope down to Wolfe Tone's glorious memoirs.

In the songs, and even their names, many a fine hint can be got; and he is not likely to be a perfect Balladist of Ireland who has not felt to tears and laughter the deathless passions of Irish music.

We have condemned compilations; but the ballad student may well labour at Ware's Antiquities. He will find, in the History of British Costume published by the Useful Knowledge Society and in the illustrated work now in progress, called Old England, but, beyond all other books, in the historical works of Thierry, most valuable materials. Nothing—not even the Border Minstrelsy, Percy's Relics, the Jacobite Ballads, or the Archæological Tracts—can be of such service as a repeated study of The Norman Conquest, The Ten Years' Study, and The Merrovingian Times of Augustine Thierry.

We know he has rashly stated some events on insufficient authority, and drawn conclusions beyond the warrant of his premises; but there is more deep dramatic skill, more picturesque and coloured scenery, more distinct and characteristic grouping, and more lively faith to the look and spirit of the men and times and feelings of which he writes, in Thierry, than in any other historian that ever lived. He has almost an intuition in favor of liberty, and his vindication of the "men of '98" out of the slanderous pages of Musgrave is a miracle of historical skill and depth of judgment.

In the Irish Academy in Dublin there is a collection (now arranged and rapidly increasing) of ancient arms and utensils. Private collections exist in many provincial towns, especially in Ulster. Indeed, we know an Orange painter in

a northern village who has a finer collection of
Irish antiquities than all the Munster cities put
together.   Accurate observation of, and discussion
on, such collections, will be of vast service to a
writer of Historical Ballads.

Topography is also essential to a ballad, or to
any Historian.   This is not only necessary to
save a writer from such a gross blunder as we
met the other day in Wharton's Ballad, called
" The Grave of King Arthur," where he talks of
" the steeps of rough Kildare," but to give accuracy and force to both general references and
local description.

Ireland must be known to her Ballad Historians,
not by flat, but by shaded maps, and topographical and scenic descriptions ; not by maps of to-day
only, but by maps (such as Ortelius and the maps
in the State Papers) of Ireland in time past ; and
finally, it must be known by the *eye*.   A man
who has not raced on our hills, panted on our
mountains, waded our rivers in drought and flood,
pierced our passes, skirted our coast, noted our
old towns, and learned the shape and colour of
ground and tree, and sky, is not master of all a
Balladist's art.   Scott knew Scotland thus, and,
moreover, he seems never to have laid a scene in
a place that he had not studied closely and alone.

What we have heretofore advised relates to the
Structure, Truth, and Colouring of Ballads ; but
there is something more needed to raise a ballad
above the beautiful—it must have Force.   Strong
passions, daring invention, vivid sympathy for
great acts—these are the result of one's whole life
and nature.   Into the temper and training of

" A Poet," we do not now presume to speak. Few have spoken wisely of them. Emerson, in his recent essay, has spoken like an angel on the mission of "The Poet." Ambition for pure power (not applause); passionate sympathy with the good, and strong, and beautiful; insight into nature, and such loving mastery over its secrets as a husband hath over a wife's mind, are the surest tests of one "called" by destiny to tell to men the past, present, and future, in words so perfect that generations shall feel and remember.

We merely meant to give some " Hints on the Properties of Historical Ballads "—they will be idle save to him who has the mind of a Poet.

REPEAL READING ROOMS.

KNOWLEDGE and organisation must set Ireland free, and make her prosperous. If the People be not wise and manageable, they cannot gain liberty but by accident, nor use it to their service. An ignorant and turbulent race may break away from provincialism, but will soon relapse beneath a cunning, skilful, and unscrupulous neighbour. England is the one—Ireland must not be the other.

If she is to be self-freed—if she is not to be retaken slave, she must acquire all the faculties possessed by her enemy, without the vices of that foe. We have to defeat an old and compact government. We must acquire the perfect structure of a nation. We have to resist genius, skill, and immense resources; we must have wisdom, knowledge, and ceaseless industry.

We want the advisers of the People never for a day to forget these facts, that of persons above five years old, there are 829,000 females and 580,000 males who can only read, but cannot write; and that above the same age, there are 2,142,000 females and 1,623,000 males who can neither read nor write. Let them remember, too, that the arts of design do not exist here—that the leading economical difference between England and Ireland is the "industrial ignorance of the latter"—that we have little military or naval instruction—and that our literature is only beginning to bud.

We are not afraid for all these things, nor do we wish to muffle our eyes against them. We want a brave, modest, laborious, and instructed People. It is deep pleasure to serve, and glory to lead such a People. It is still deeper pleasure and honour to head a race full of virtue and industry, and a thirst for knowledge. But for a swaggering People, who shout for him who flatters them, and turn from those who would lead by plain, manful truth—who shall save them?

The Repeal Association has fronted the difficulty. You, it tells the People, are not educated nor organised as you should be. Your oppressor has millions, cunning in all arts and manufactures, for your thousands. Her literature is famous among men—your's still to be created. Her organisation embraces everything, from the machinery for moving an empire to that of governing a parish. You, too, must learn arts, and literature, and self-government, if you would repel and surpass her.

The generation that will cover Ireland in twenty years will have the instruction you want, but you must not surrender *your* claim to knowledge and liberty. You, too, must go to school and learn. You must learn to obey. You must learn from each other, and obey the highest wisdom that is among you all.

The Repeal Association has resolved that it is expedient to establish Reading-rooms in the Parishes of Ireland, and has appointed a Committee to carry out that resolution.

This is a great undertaking. A meeting, a gossip, or eloquent circular, will not accomplish it. It will take months of labour from strong minds, and large sums of money, to establish such a system; and only by corresponding zeal on the People's part can it be spread among them all.

The Repeal Association has now constituted itself Schoolmaster of the People of Ireland, and must be prepared to carry out its pretension. The People, knowing the attempt, must sustain it with increased funds and zeal.

A Reading-room Committee must not stop its preliminary labours till there is a Reading-room in every village; and then it will fill their hands and draw largely on their funds to make them Reading-rooms, and not idling rooms. Their first duty will be, of course, to ascertain what Reading-rooms exist—how each of them is supported—what books. maps, &c., it contains—at what hours it is open—and how it is attended. For each separate School—we beg pardon, Reading-room—the Committee should make separate arrangements. One will want increased space, another will want industrial books, another maps, another political and statistical tracts.

To the districts where the Irish language is spoken, they should send a purely Irish Grammar and an Anglo-Irish Grammar and Dictionary for each room, to be followed by other works containing general information, as well as peculiarly Irish knowledge, in Irish. Indeed, we doubt if the Association can carry out the plan—which they began by sending down Dr.

MacHale's translations—without establishing a newspaper, partly in English and partly in Irish, like the mixed papers of Switzerland, New Orleans, and Hungary.

To come back, however, to the working of such a Committee. Some of its members should attend from day to day to correspond with the Repeal Inspectors, and the Protestant and Catholic Clergy, who may consent to act as patrons of these Rooms. It will be most desirable that each Committee have an agent in Dublin, who will receive and forward *gratis* all books for it. The cost of postage would absorb the price of a library.

It seems to us to be almost necessary to have persons sent round the country from time to time to organize these Reading Committees—to fix, from inspection, the amount of help which the Association should give to the rent of each room, and to stimulate the People to fresh exertion. This, of course, could be united with a Repeal missionary system, on the same plan as the " Anti-Corn Law League" missions.

Help should be given by the Association in some proportion to the local subscriptions (say a third of them), or the Association might undertake to supply a certain amount of books upon proof of a local subscription large enough, and sufficiently secured, for the wants of the neighbourhood.

A catalogue of the books sent to each Room should be always accessible in the Corn Exchange.

Of course, in sending books a regular system

should be adopted. The Ordnance index map of the county, the townland map of the neighbourhood, a map of Ireland, and maps of the five great sections of the globe (Asia, America, Australia, Europe, and Africa), should be in every Room. Of course, the Reports of the Association will be there ; and they, we trust, will soon be a perfect manual of the industrial statistics, topography, history, and county, municipal, and general institutions of Ireland. Much has been done, and the Parliamentary Committee consists of men who are able and willing to carry out their work. What other works, fitted to cultivate the judgment or taste of the People, may be sent, must depend on the exertions of the parishes and the faithfulness of the Committee.

Were such a Room in every village, you would soon have a knot connected with it of young men who had abjured cards, tobacco, dissipation, and more fatal laziness, and were trying to learn each some science, or art, or accomplishment— anything that best pleased them, from mathematics to music. We shall feel unspeakable sorrow if, from the negligence of the Committee or the dulness or want of spirit in our country towns, this great opportunity pass away.

INFLUENCES OF EDUCATION.

" EDUCATE, that you may be free." We are most anxious to get the quiet, strong-minded People who are scattered through the country to see the force of this great truth; and we therefore ask them to listen soberly to us for a few minutes, and when they have done, to think and talk again and again over what we say.

If Ireland had all the elements of a nation, she might, and surely would, at once assume the forms of one, and proclaim her independence. Wherein does she now differ from Prussia? She has a strong and compact territory, girt by the sea; Prussia's lands are open and flat, and flung loosely through Europe, without mountain or river, breed, or tongue, to bound them. Ireland has a military population equal to the recruitment of, and a produce able to pay a first-rate army. Her harbours, her soil, and her fisheries, are not surpassed in Europe.

Wherein, we ask again, does Ireland now differ from Prussia? Why can Prussia wave her flag among the proudest in Europe, while Ireland is a farm?

It is not in the name of a kingdom, nor in the formalities of independence. We could assume them to-morrow—we could assume them with better warrants from history and nature than Prussia holds; but the result of such assumption would perchance be a miserable defeat.

The difference is in Knowledge. Were the offices of Prussia abolished to-morrow—her colleges and schools levelled—her troops disarmed and disbanded, she would within six months regain her whole civil and military institutions. Ireland has been struggling for years, and may have to struggle many more, to acquire liberty to form institutions.

Whence is the difference? Knowledge!

The Prussians could, at a week's notice, have their central offices at full work in any village in the kingdom, so exactly known are their statistics, and so general is official skill. Minds make administration—all the desks, and legers, and powers of Downing-street or the Castle would be handed in vain to the ignorants of——any untaught district in Ireland. The Prussians could open their collegiate classes and their professional and elementary schools as fast as the order therefor, from any authority recognized by the People, reached town after town—we can hardly in ten years get a few schools open for our people, craving for knowledge as they are. The Prussians could re-arm their glorious militia in a month, and re-organize it in three days; for the mechanical arts are very generally known, military science is familiar to most of the wealthier men, discipline and a soldier's skill are universal. If we had been offered arms to defend Ireland by Lord Heytesbury, as the Vo-

lunteers were by Lord Buckinghamshire, we
would have had to seek for officers and drill-
serjeants—though probably we could more rapidly advance in arms than anything else, from
the military taste and aptness for war of the
Irish People.

Would it not be better for us to be like the
Prussians than as we are—better to have religious squabbles unknown, education universal,
the People fed, and clad, and housed, and independent, as becomes men ; the army patriotic
and strong ; the public offices ably administered ;
the nation honoured and powerful ? Are not
these to be desired and sought by Protestant
and Catholic ? Are not these things *to be done*,
if we are good and brave men ? And is it not
plain, from what we have said, that the reason for our not being all that Prussia is, and
something more, is ignorance—want of civil and
military and general knowledge amongst all
classes ?

This ignorance has not been our fault, but our
misfortune. It was the interest of our ruler to
keep us ignorant, that we might be weak : and
she did so—first, by laws prohibiting education ;
then, by refusing any provision for it ; next, by
perverting it into an engine of bigotry ; and
now, by giving it in a stunted, partial, anti-
national way. Practice is the great teacher,
and the possession of independence is the natural and best way for a People to learn all
that pertains to freedom and happiness. Our
greatest voluntary efforts, aided by the amplest

provincial institutions, would teach us less in a century than we would learn in five years of Liberty.

In insisting on education, we do not argue against the value of *immediate independence. That would be our best teacher.* An Irish Government and a national ambition would be to our minds as soft rains and rich sun to a growing crop. But we insist on education for the People, whether they get it from the Government or give it to themselves, as a round-about, and, yet, the only means of getting strength enough to gain freedom.

Do our readers understand this? Is what we have said *clear* to *you*, reader!—whether you are a shopkeeper or a lawyer, a farmer or a doctor? If not, read it over again, for it is your own fault if it be not clear. If you now know our meaning, you must feel that it is your duty to your family and to yourself, to your country and to God, to *act* upon it, to go and remove some of that ignorance which makes you and your neighbours weak, and therefore makes Ireland a poor province.

All of us have much to learn, but some of us have much to teach.

To those, who, from superior energy and ability, can teach the People, we now address ourselves.

We have often before, and shall often again repeat, that the majority of our population can neither read nor write, and therefore that from the small minority must come those fitted to be

of any civil or military use beyond the lowest
rank. The People may be and are honest, brave,
and intelligent; but a man could as well dig with
his hands, as govern, or teach, or lead, without
the elements of Knowledge.

This, however, is a defect which time and
the National Schools must cure; and the duty
of the class to which we speak is to urge the
establishment of such Schools, the attendance of
the children at them, and occasionally to observe
and report, either directly or through the press,
whether the admirable rules of the Board are attended to. In most cases, too, the expenditure
of a pound note and a little time and advice
would give the children of a school that instruction in national history and in statistics so shame-
fully omitted by the Board. Reader! will you
do this?

Then, of the three hundred Repeal Reading-
rooms we know that some, and fear that many
are ill-managed, have few or no books, and are
mere gossiping-rooms. Such a room is useless;
such a room is a disgrace to its members and
their educated neighbours. The expense having
been gone to of getting a room, it only remains
for the members to establish fixed rules, and they
will be supplied with the Association Reports
(political reading enough for them), and it will
be the plain duty of the Repeal Wardens to bring
to such a room the newspapers supplied by the
Association. If such a body continue and give
proofs of being in earnest, the Repeal Association will aid it by gifts of books, maps, &c., and

thus a library, the centre of knowledge and nursery of useful and strong minds, will be made in
that district. So miserably off is the country for
books, that we have it before us, on some authority, that there are *ten counties in Ireland without a single bookseller in them.* We blush for
the fact; it is a disgrace to us; but we must
have no lying nor flinching. There is the hard
fact; let us face it like men who are able for a
difficulty—not as children putting their heads
under the clothes when there is danger. Reader!
cannot you do something to remedy this great,
this disabling misery of Ireland? Will not you
now try to get up a Repeal Reading-room, and,
when one is established, get for it good rules,
books from the Association, and make it a centre
of thought and power?

These are but some of the ways in which such
service can be done by the more, for the less,
educated. They have other duties, often pointed
out by us. They can sustain and advance the
different societies for promoting agriculture, manufactures, art, and literature, in Dublin and
the country. They can set on foot, and guide
the establishment of Temperance Bands and
Mechanics' Institutes, and Mutual Instruction
Societies. They can give advice and facilities
for improvement to young men of promise; and
they can make their circles studious, refined, and
ambitious, instead of being, like too many in
Ireland—ignorant, coarse, or lazy. The cheapness of books is now such, that even Irish po-

verty is no excuse for Irish ignorance—that ignorance which prostrates us before England We must help ourselves, and therefore we must educate ourselves.

THE END.

Stereotyped and Printed by T. Coldwell, 50, Capel-street.